OTHER OWNERSHIP RIGHTS

WATER RIGHTS

1. Riparian Doctrine: Water belongs to the owners of land bordering the watercourse.
   - **a.** Natural Flow: Riparian owner is entitled to water without diminution in its quantity.
   - **b.** Reasonable Use: Riparian owner must share with other riparian owners and is entitled only to reasonable use.
2. Prior Appropriation Doctrine: An individual may divert and use water whether or not she borders the watercourse; individual rights are established by actual use.

RIGHT TO LATERAL AND SUBJACENT SUPPORT

Strict liability for owner of land whose excavations cause a neighboring parcel to subside, or which damage buildings on adjacent land.

GIFTS

IN GENERAL

1. *Definition:* A gratuitous voluntary lifetime transfer of property from a donor to donee.
2. Requirements:
   - **a.** Present intent to make a gift;
   - **b.** Delivery by donor; and
   - **c.** Acceptance by donee
3. Classification:
   - **a.** *inter vivos:* Made during donor's lifetime; irrevocable unless donor retains right to revoke.
   - **b.** *gifts causa mortis:* Lifetime gift by donor in contemplation of impending death.
     - **i.** Contemplation of impending death;
     - **ii.** Automatic revocation if donor survives peril;
     - **iii.** Ambiguity of donor's intent; and
     - **iv.** Death from different peril.

INTEREST IN LAND: ESTATES

TYPE		
PRESENT POSSESSORY ESTATES *– Property interest in lanc*		*n*
FEE SIMPLE ABSOLUTE:	Right given by previous	E
FEE SIMPLE DETERMINABLE:	Right given by a grantor	E
FEE SIMPLE ON CONDITION SUBSEQUENT:	Right given by a grantor	E
FEE TAIL (FEE SIMPLE CONDITIONAL):	Right given by a grantor	E
LIFE ESTATE:	Right given by a grantor	E
CONCURRENT ESTATES *– Property interest in land currently possessed by several individuals at the same time,*		*p*
TENANCY IN COMMON:	Deed, will, or law of intestate succession	E c r
JOINT TENANCY:	Deed and will, but not by intestate succession; requires the following Four Unities: **1.** Time: Co-tenants acquire at same time **2.** Title: Interests acquired under same instrument **3.** Interest: Co-tenants have exactly same interest **4.** Possession: Co-tenants each have possession of entire estate	E c t s i c
TENANCY BY ENTIRETY:	Deed, will, or law of intestate succession	E c r
LEASEHOLDS (LANDLORD AND TENANT) *– Interest in land according to the terms of a lease agreement, in*		*tl*
PERIODIC TENANCY:	Created by lease; contractual agreement	F r
TENANCY FOR YEARS:	Created by lease; contractual agreement	F c
TENANCY AT WILL:	Created by lease; contractual agreement	F t
TENANCY AT SUFFERANCE:	Created by operation of law when tenant wrongfully remains in possession after end of lawful lease term	H e
FUTURE INTERESTS *– An interest in property that is not presently possessory, but will come into possession*		*sc*
REVERSION (IN GRANTOR):	Automatically at end of transferred estate or by express reservation by grantor after transferring title	E t
POSSIBILITY OF REVERTER (IN GRANTOR):	Occurrence of event terminating a fee simple determinable	E g
RIGHT OF ENTRY (IN GRANTOR):	Occurrence of condition terminating a fee simple on condition subsequent	E g
EXECUTORY INTEREST (IN GRANTEE):	Occurrence of condition as specified by grantor	E g
REMAINDERS (IN GRANTEE):	Occurrence of limitation (not a condition) terminating a prior possessory estate simultaneously created	A c s

INTEREST OWNED	UNIQUE FEATURES	HOW TERMINATED
tate in perpetuity, lasts forever	Highest estate recognized by law	Never terminated; perpetual
tate in perpetuity, lasts forever	Terminates automatically on occurrence of an event; otherwise lasts forever	Occurrence or nonoccurrence of condition sometime in future, as set out in governing instrument
tate in perpetuity, lasts forever	Doesn't terminate automatically; unless condition occurs, lasts forever	Grantor elects to terminate due to occurrence of condition
tate for duration of owner's life	Assures that lands stay within a family from generation to generation by passing to owner's heirs	Owner's death
tate with duration measured by life of another	Measuring life can be either land holder or another party	Measuring life ends
esent and future interests can be concurrent.		
ual right of possession of the whole by each -tenant, regardless of the actual share owned; ay be freely conveyed	Modern Law: Any conveyance to two or more people creates a presumption of a tenancy in common	Partitioned through mutual agreement of co-tenants or judicial decree
ual right of possession of the whole by each -tenant, regardless of the actual share owned; wever, cannot be freely conveyed (Right of rvivorship: once a co-tenant dies, remain- g co-tenants take property free and clear of ceased co-tenant's interest)	**1.** Common Law: Any conveyance to two or more people creates a presumption of a joint tenancy **2.** Conveyance: If any co-tenant conveys interest, transferee takes as a tenant-in-common, while remaining co-tenants continue to hold in joint tenancy	Partitioned through mutual agreement of co-tenants or judicial decree
ual right of possession of the whole by each -tenant, regardless of the actual share owned; ay be freely conveyed	Any conveyance to two or more people creates a presumption of a tenancy in common	Partitioned through mutual agreement of co-tenants or judicial decree
form of duties owed between a landlord and the renter of the land.		
ght to occupy tenancy for fixed period (year, onth, week, or day)	Automatically renews for a like period at the end of the preceding period	Notice must be given by either landlord or tenant a minimum of one whole period before last day of current period; death does not terminate
ght to occupy tenancy beginning on a fixed te and ending on a fixed date	Can also last for a period measured by the happening of an event or condition	Fixed end date arrives, or ending event takes place; no notice required
ght to occupy tenancy "at will" as long as both e landlord and tenant so desire	Law disfavors; some states have statutes requiring notice to terminate	May be terminated by either party without notice; death of either party can also terminate
oldover tenant is treated as trespasser and icted, or new periodic tenancy is imposed	Landlord has the right to elect either eviction or creation of new tenancy	If landlord chooses to evict, tenancy ends
netime in the future.		
lance of estate left after grantor transfers less an she has	May or may not become possessory in future; freely alienable, devisable, and descendible	Interest does not become possessory if prior estate given by grantor does not end
lance of estate in fee simple absolute, left after antor originally transfers less than she has	Landlord has the right to elect either eviction or creation of new tenancy	If landlord chooses to evict, prior tenancy ends
lance of estate in fee simple absolute, left after antor originally transfers less than she has	Does not go to grantor automatically; grantor must elect to enforce interest	If condition occurs and landlord chooses to enforce interest, prior tenancy ends
lance of estate in fee simple absolute, left after antor originally transfers less than she has	**1.** Springing interest: Becomes possessory upon occurrence of a condition, if no present possessory estate exists in another transferee **2.** Shifting interest: Becomes possessory after divesting a present possessory freehold	If condition occurs, prior tenancy ends unless property is currently possessed and interest is springing (and therefore cannot divest an existing possessor)
n interest limited by the existence of a rrently possessory estate created at the me time	**1.** Vested Remainders: Not subject to RAP, possessory right is certain **a.** Indefeasibly Vested: Born, ascertainable person **b.** Subject to Open/Partial Divestment: Class of persons, with at least one living member; interests divest in part as new class members are born; class closes when: **i.** Person who produces class members dies; or **ii.** Rule of Convenience: When any class member is entitled to demand possession of entitled shares; no outstanding present possessory estates/conditions precedent for any class member **2.** Contingent remainders: Subject to RAP, right to take is uncertain **a.** Subject to Condition Precedent: Words condition a person's right to take **b.** Unborn, unascertained persons	Remainder interest may never become possessory if outstanding, presently possessory estate continues to exist

ASPEN PUBLISHERS

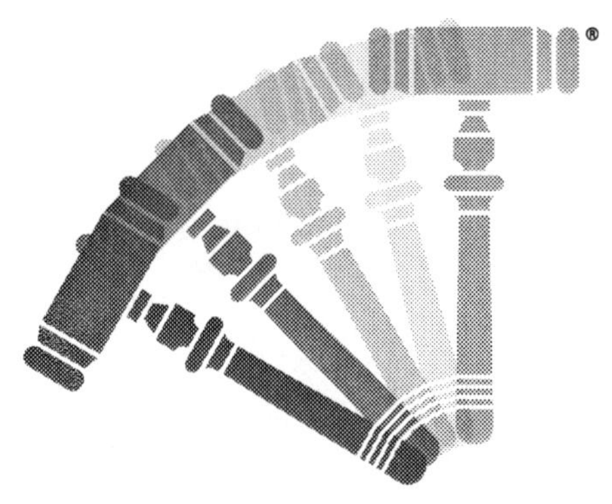

Casenote™ *Legal Briefs*

PROPERTY

Keyed to Courses Using

Dukeminier, Krier, Alexander, and Schill's
Property
Seventh Edition

Law & Business

AUSTIN BOSTON CHICAGO NEW YORK THE NETHERLANDS

Aspen Publishers
Attn: Permissions Dept.
76 Ninth Avenue, 7th Floor
New York, NY 10011-5201

To contact Customer Care, e-mail customer.care@aspenpublishers.com, call 1-800-234-1660, fax 1-800-901-9075, or mail correspondence to:

Aspen Publishers
Attn: Order Department
P.O. Box 990
Frederick, MD 21705

Printed in the United States of America.

2 3 4 5 6 7 8 9 0

ISBN 978-0-7355-9020-5

About Wolters Kluwer Law & Business

Wolters Kluwer Law & Business is a leading provider of research information and workflow solutions in key specialty areas. The strengths of the individual brands of Aspen Publishers, CCH, Kluwer Law International and Loislaw are aligned within Wolters Kluwer Law & Business to provide comprehensive, in-depth solutions and expert-authored content for the legal, professional and education markets.

CCH was founded in 1913 and has served more than four generations of business professionals and their clients. The CCH products in the Wolters Kluwer Law & Business group are highly regarded electronic and print resources for legal, securities, antitrust and trade regulation, government contracting, banking, pension, payroll, employment and labor, and health-care reimbursement and compliance professionals.

Aspen Publishers is a leading information provider for attorneys, business professionals and law students. Written by preeminent authorities, Aspen products offer analytical and practical information in a range of specialty practice areas from securities law and intellectual property to mergers and acquisitions and pension/benefits. Aspen's trusted legal education resources provide professors and students with high-quality, up-to-date and effective resources for successful instruction and study in all areas of the law.

Kluwer Law International supplies the global business community with comprehensive English-language international legal information. Legal practitioners, corporate counsel and business executives around the world rely on the Kluwer Law International journals, loose-leafs, books and electronic products for authoritative information in many areas of international legal practice.

Loislaw is a premier provider of digitized legal content to small law firm practitioners of various specializations. Loislaw provides attorneys with the ability to quickly and efficiently find the necessary legal information they need, when and where they need it, by facilitating access to primary law as well as state-specific law, records, forms and treatises.

Wolters Kluwer Law & Business, a unit of Wolters Kluwer, is headquartered in New York and Riverwoods, Illinois. Wolters Kluwer is a leading multinational publisher and information services company.

Format for the Casenote Legal Brief

Nature of Case: This section identifies the form of action (e.g., breach of contract, negligence, battery), the type of proceeding (e.g., demurrer, appeal from trial court's jury instructions), or the relief sought (e.g., damages, injunction, criminal sanctions).

Fact Summary: This is included to refresh your memory and can be used as a quick reminder of the facts.

Rule of Law: Summarizes the general principle of law that the case illustrates. It may be used for instant recall of the court's holding and for classroom discussion or home review.

Facts: This section contains all relevant facts of the case, including the contentions of the parties and the lower court holdings. It is written in a logical order to give the student a clear understanding of the case. The plaintiff and defendant are identified by their proper names throughout and are always labeled with a (P) or (D).

Party ID: Quick identification of the relationship between the parties.

Concurrence/Dissent: All concurrences and dissents are briefed whenever they are included by the casebook editor.

Analysis: This last paragraph gives you a broad understanding of where the case "fits in" with other cases in the section of the book and with the entire course. It is a hornbook-style discussion indicating whether the case is a majority or minority opinion and comparing the principal case with other cases in the casebook. It may also provide analysis from restatements, uniform codes, and law review articles. The analysis will prove to be invaluable to classroom discussion.

Palsgraf v. Long Island R.R. Co.

Injured bystander (P) v. Railroad company (D)

N.Y. Ct. App., 248 N.Y. 339, 162 N.E. 99 (1928).

NATURE OF CASE: Appeal from judgment affirming verdict for plaintiff seeking damages for personal injury.

FACT SUMMARY: Helen Palsgraf (P) was injured on R.R.'s (D) train platform when R.R.'s (D) guard helped a passenger aboard a moving train, causing his package to fall on the tracks. The package contained fireworks which exploded, creating a shock that tipped a scale onto Palsgraf (P).

RULE OF LAW

The risk reasonably to be perceived defines the duty to be obeyed.

FACTS: Helen Palsgraf (P) purchased a ticket to Rockaway Beach from R.R. (D) and was waiting on the train platform. As she waited, two men ran to catch a train that was pulling out from the platform. The first man jumped aboard, but the second man, who appeared as if he might fall, was helped aboard by the guard on the train who had kept the door open so they could jump aboard. A guard on the platform also helped by pushing him onto the train. The man was carrying a package wrapped in newspaper. In the process, the man dropped his package, which fell on the tracks. The package contained fireworks and exploded. The shock of the explosion was apparently of great enough strength to tip over some scales at the other end of the platform, which fell on Palsgraf (P) and injured her. A jury awarded her damages, and R.R. (D) appealed.

ISSUE: Does the risk reasonably to be perceived define the duty to be obeyed?

HOLDING AND DECISION: (Cardozo, C.J.) Yes. The risk reasonably to be perceived defines the duty to be obeyed. If there is no foreseeable hazard to the injured party as the result of a seemingly innocent act, the act does not become a tort because it happened to be a wrong as to another. If the wrong was not willful, the plaintiff must show that the act as to her had such great and apparent possibilities of danger as to entitle her to protection. Negligence in the abstract is not enough upon which to base liability. Negligence is a relative concept, evolving out of the common law doctrine of trespass on the case. To establish liability, the defendant must owe a legal duty of reasonable care to the injured party. A cause of action in tort will lie where harm, though unintended, could have been averted or avoided by observance of such a duty. The scope of the duty is limited by the range of danger that a reasonable person could foresee. In this case, there was nothing to suggest from the appearance of the parcel or otherwise that the parcel contained fireworks. The guard could not reasonably have had any warning of a threat to Palsgraf (P), and R.R. (D) therefore cannot be held liable. Judgment is reversed in favor of R.R. (D).

DISSENT: (Andrews, J.) The concept that there is no negligence unless R.R. (D) owes a legal duty to take care as to Palsgraf (P) herself is too narrow. Everyone owes to the world at large the duty of refraining from those acts that may unreasonably threaten the safety of others. If the guard's action was negligent as to those nearby, it was also negligent as to those outside what might be termed the "danger zone." For Palsgraf (P) to recover, R.R.'s (D) negligence must have been the proximate cause of her injury, a question of fact for the jury.

ANALYSIS

The majority defined the limit of the defendant's liability in terms of the danger that a reasonable person in defendant's situation would have perceived. The dissent argued that the limitation should not be placed on liability, but rather on damages. Judge Andrews suggested that only injuries that would not have happened but for R.R.'s (D) negligence should be compensable. Both the majority and dissent recognized the policy-driven need to limit liability for negligent acts, seeking, in the words of Judge Andrews, to define a framework "that will be practical and in keeping with the general understanding of mankind." The Restatement (Second) of Torts has accepted Judge Cardozo's view.

Quicknotes

FORESEEABILITY A reasonable expectation that change is the probable result of certain acts or omissions.

NEGLIGENCE Conduct falling below the standard of care that a reasonable person would demonstrate under similar conditions.

PROXIMATE CAUSE The natural sequence of events without which an injury would not have been sustained.

Issue: The issue is a concise question that brings out the essence of the opinion as it relates to the section of the casebook in which the case appears. Both substantive and procedural issues are included if relevant to the decision.

Holding and Decision: This section offers a clear and in-depth discussion of the rule of the case and the court's rationale. It is written in easy-to-understand language and answers the issue presented by applying the law to the facts of the case. When relevant, it includes a thorough discussion of the exceptions to the case as listed by the court, any major cites to the other cases on point, and the names of the judges who wrote the decisions.

Quicknotes: Conveniently defines legal terms found in the case and summarizes the nature of any statutes, codes, or rules referred to in the text.

Note to Students

Aspen Publishers is proud to offer *Casenote Legal Briefs*—continuing thirty years of publishing America's best-selling legal briefs.

Casenote Legal Briefs are designed to help you save time when briefing assigned cases. Organized under convenient headings, they show you how to abstract the basic facts and holdings from the text of the actual opinions handed down by the courts. Used as part of a rigorous study regimen, they can help you spend more time analyzing and critiquing points of law than on copying bits and pieces of judicial opinions into your notebook or outline.

Casenote Legal Briefs should never be used as a substitute for assigned casebook readings. They work best when read as a follow-up to reviewing the underlying opinions themselves. Students who try to avoid reading and digesting the judicial opinions in their casebooks or online sources will end up shortchanging themselves in the long run. The ability to absorb, critique, and restate the dynamic and complex elements of case law decisions is crucial to your success in law school and beyond. It cannot be developed vicariously.

Casenote Legal Briefs represents but one of the many offerings in Aspen's Study Aid Timeline, which includes:

- *Casenote Legal Briefs*
- *Emanuel Law Outlines*
- *Examples & Explanations* Series
- *Introduction to Law* Series
- Emanuel *Law in a Flash* Flashcards
- Emanuel *CrunchTime* Series

Each of these series is designed to provide you with easy-to-understand explanations of complex points of law. Each volume offers guidance on the principles of legal analysis and, consulted regularly, will hone your ability to spot relevant issues. We have titles that will help you prepare for class, prepare for your exams, and enhance your general comprehension of the law along the way.

To find out more about Aspen Study Aid publications, visit us online at *www.AspenLaw.com* or email us at *legaledu@wolterskluwer.com.* We'll be happy to assist you.

Get this Casenote Legal Brief as an AspenLaw Studydesk eBook today!

By returning this form to Aspen Publishers, you will receive a complimentary eBook download of this Casenote Legal Brief in the AspenLaw Studydesk digital format.* Learn more about AspenLaw Studydesk today at *www.AspenLaw.com.*

Name	**Phone** ( )
Address	**Apt. No.**
City **State**	**ZIP Code**
Law School	**Year** (check one) ☐ **1st** ☐ **2nd** ☐ **3rd**

Cut out the UPC found on the lower left corner of the back cover of this book. Staple the UPC inside this box. Only the original UPC from the book cover will be accepted. (No photocopies or store stickers are allowed.)

Attach UPC inside this box.

Email (Print legibly or you may not get access!)
Title of this book (course subject)
ISBN of this book (10- or 13-digit number on the UPC)
Used with which casebook (provide author's name)

Mail the completed form to:

Aspen Publishers, Inc.
Legal Education Division
130 Turner Street, Bldg 3, 4th Floor
Waltham, MA 02453-8901

* Upon receipt of this completed form, you will be emailed a code for the digital download of this book in AspenLaw Studydesk format. The AspenLaw Studydesk application is available as a 60-day free trial at *www.AspenLaw.com.*

For a full list of print titles by Aspen Publishers, visit *www.AspenLaw.com.*
For a full list of digital eBook titles by Aspen Publishers, visit *www.AspenLaw.com.*

Make a photocopy of this form and your UPC for your records.

For detailed information on the use of the information you provide on this form, please see the PRIVACY POLICY at *www.AspenLaw.com.*

How to Brief a Case

A. Decide on a Format and Stick to It

Structure is essential to a good brief. It enables you to arrange systematically the related parts that are scattered throughout most cases, thus making manageable and understandable what might otherwise seem to be an endless and unfathomable sea of information. There are, of course, an unlimited number of formats that can be utilized. However, it is best to find one that suits your needs and stick to it. Consistency breeds both efficiency and the security that when called upon you will know where to look in your brief for the information you are asked to give.

Any format, as long as it presents the essential elements of a case in an organized fashion, can be used. Experience, however, has led *Casenotes* to develop and utilize the following format because of its logical flow and universal applicability.

NATURE OF CASE: This is a brief statement of the legal character and procedural status of the case (e.g., "Appeal of a burglary conviction").

There are many different alternatives open to a litigant dissatisfied with a court ruling. The key to determining which one has been used is to discover *who is asking this court for what.*

This first entry in the brief should be kept as *short as possible.* Use the court's terminology if you understand it. But since jurisdictions vary as to the titles of pleadings, the best entry is the one that addresses who wants what in this proceeding, not the one that sounds most like the court's language.

RULE OF LAW: A statement of the general principle of law that the case illustrates (e.g., "An acceptance that varies any term of the offer is considered a rejection and counteroffer").

Determining the rule of law of a case is a procedure similar to determining the issue of the case. Avoid being fooled by red herrings; there may be a few rules of law mentioned in the case excerpt, but usually only one is *the* rule with which the casebook editor is concerned. The techniques used to locate the issue, described below, may also be utilized to find the rule of law. Generally, your best guide is simply the chapter heading. It is a clue to the point the casebook editor seeks to make and should be kept in mind when reading every case in the respective section.

FACTS: A synopsis of only the essential facts of the case, i.e., those bearing upon or leading up to the issue.

The facts entry should be a short statement of the events and transactions that led one party to initiate legal proceedings against another in the first place. While some cases conveniently state the salient facts at the beginning of the decision, in other instances they will have to be culled from hiding places throughout the text, even from concurring and dissenting opinions. Some of the "facts" will often be in dispute and should be so noted. Conflicting evidence may be briefly pointed up. "Hard" facts must be included. Both must be *relevant* in order to be listed in the facts entry. It is impossible to tell what is relevant until the entire case is read, as the ultimate determination of the rights and liabilities of the parties may turn on something buried deep in the opinion.

Generally, the facts entry should not be longer than three to five *short* sentences.

It is often helpful to identify the role played by a party in a given context. For example, in a construction contract case the identification of a party as the "contractor" or "builder" alleviates the need to tell that that party was the one who was supposed to have built the house.

It is always helpful, and a good general practice, to identify the "plaintiff" and the "defendant." This may seem elementary and uncomplicated, but, especially in view of the creative editing practiced by some casebook editors, it is sometimes a difficult or even impossible task. Bear in mind that the *party presently* seeking something from this court may not be the plaintiff, and that sometimes only the cross-claim of a defendant is treated in the excerpt. Confusing or misaligning the parties can ruin your analysis and understanding of the case.

ISSUE: A statement of the general legal question answered by or illustrated in the case. For clarity, the issue is best put in the form of a question capable of a "yes" or "no" answer. In reality, the issue is simply the Rule of Law put in the form of a question (e.g., "May an offer be accepted by performance?").

The major problem presented in discerning what is *the* issue in the case is that an opinion usually purports to raise and answer several questions. However, except for rare cases, only one such question is really the issue in the case. Collateral issues not necessary to the resolution of the matter in controversy are handled by the court by language known as *"obiter dictum"* or merely *"dictum."* While dicta may be included later in the brief, they have no place under the issue heading.

To find the issue, ask *who wants what* and then go on to ask *why did that party succeed or fail in getting it.* Once this is determined, the "why" should be turned into a question.

The complexity of the issues in the cases will vary, but in all cases a single-sentence question should sum up the issue. *In a few cases,* there will be two, or even more rarely, three issues of equal importance to the resolution of the case. Each should be expressed in a single-sentence question.

Since many issues are resolved by a court in coming to a final disposition of a case, the casebook editor will reproduce the portion of the opinion containing the issue or issues most relevant to the area of law under scrutiny. A noted law professor gave this advice: "Close the book; look at the title on the cover." Chances are, if it is Property, you need not concern yourself with whether, for example, the federal government's treatment of the plaintiff's land really raises a federal question sufficient to support jurisdiction on this ground in federal court.

The same rule applies to chapter headings designating sub-areas within the subjects. They tip you off as to what the text is designed to teach. The cases are arranged in a casebook to show a progression or development of the law, so that the preceding cases may also help.

It is also most important to remember to *read the notes and questions* at the end of a case to determine what the editors wanted you to have gleaned from it.

HOLDING AND DECISION: This section should succinctly explain the rationale of the court in arriving at its decision. In capsulizing the "reasoning" of the court, it should always include an application of the general rule or rules of law to the specific facts of the case. Hidden justifications come to light in this entry: the reasons for the state of the law, the public policies, the biases and prejudices, those considerations that influence the justices' thinking and, ultimately, the outcome of the case. At the end, there should be a short indication of the disposition or procedural resolution of the case (e.g., "Decision of the trial court for Mr. Smith (P) reversed").

The foregoing format is designed to help you "digest" the reams of case material with which you will be faced in your law school career. Once mastered by practice, it will place at your fingertips the information the authors of your casebooks have sought to impart to you in case-by-case illustration and analysis.

B. Be as Economical as Possible in Briefing Cases

Once armed with a format that encourages succinctness, it is as important to be economical with regard to the time spent on the actual reading of the case as it is to be economical in the writing of the brief itself. This does not mean "skimming" a case. Rather, it means reading the case with an "eye" trained to recognize into which "section" of your brief a particular passage or line fits and having a system for quickly and precisely marking the case so that the passages fitting any one particular part of the brief can be easily identified and brought together in a concise and accurate manner when the brief is actually written.

It is of no use to simply repeat everything in the opinion of the court; record only enough information to trigger your recollection of what the court said. Nevertheless, an accurate statement of the "law of the case," i.e., the legal principle applied to the facts, is absolutely essential to class preparation and to learning the law under the case method.

To that end, it is important to develop a "shorthand" that you can use to make marginal notations. These notations will tell you at a glance in which section of the brief you will be placing that particular passage or portion of the opinion.

Some students prefer to underline all the salient portions of the opinion (with a pencil or colored underliner marker), making marginal notations as they go along. Others prefer the color-coded method of underlining, utilizing different colors of markers to underline the salient portions of the case, each separate color being used to represent a different section of the brief. For example, blue underlining could be used for passages relating to the rule of law, yellow for those relating to the issue, and green for those relating to the holding and decision, etc. While it has its advocates, the color-coded method can be confusing and time-consuming (all that time spent on changing colored markers). Furthermore, it can interfere with the continuity and concentration many students deem essential to the reading of a case for maximum comprehension. In the end, however, it is a matter of personal preference and style. Just remember, whatever method you use, underlining must be used sparingly or its value is lost.

If you take the marginal notation route, an efficient and easy method is to go along underlining the key portions of the case and placing in the margin alongside them the following "markers" to indicate where a particular passage or line "belongs" in the brief you will write:

N (NATURE OF CASE)
RL (RULE OF LAW)
I (ISSUE)
HL (HOLDING AND DECISION, relates to the RULE OF LAW behind the decision)
HR (HOLDING AND DECISION, gives the RATIONALE or reasoning behind the decision)
HA (HOLDING AND DECISION, APPLIES the general principle(s) of law to the facts of the case to arrive at the decision)

Remember that a particular passage may well contain information necessary to more than one part of your brief, in which case you simply note that in the margin. If you are using the color-coded underlining method instead of marginal notation, simply make asterisks or checks in the margin next to the passage in question in the colors that indicate the additional sections of the brief where it might be utilized.

The economy of utilizing "shorthand" in marking cases for briefing can be maintained in the actual brief writing process itself by utilizing "law student shorthand" within the brief. There are many commonly used words and phrases for which abbreviations can be substituted in your briefs (and in your class notes also). You can develop abbreviations that are personal to you and which will save you a lot of time. A reference list of briefing abbreviations can be found on page xii of this book.

C. Use Both the Briefing Process and the Brief as a Learning Tool

Now that you have a format and the tools for briefing cases efficiently, the most important thing is to make the time spent in briefing profitable to you and to make the most advantageous use of the briefs you create. Of course, the briefs are invaluable for classroom reference when you are called upon to explain or analyze a particular case. However, they are also useful in reviewing for exams. A quick glance at the fact summary should bring the case to mind, and a rereading of the rule of law should enable you to go over the underlying legal concept in your mind, how it was applied in that particular case, and how it might apply in other factual settings.

As to the value to be derived from engaging in the briefing process itself, there is an immediate benefit that arises from being forced to sift through the essential facts and reasoning from the court's opinion and to succinctly express them in your own words in your brief. The process ensures that you understand the case and the point that it illustrates, and that means you will be ready to absorb further analysis and information brought forth in class. It also ensures you will have something to say when called upon in class. The briefing process helps develop a mental agility for getting to the *gist* of a case and for identifying, expounding on, and applying the legal concepts and issues found there. The briefing process is the mental process on which you must rely in taking law school examinations; it is also the mental process upon which a lawyer relies in serving his clients and in making his living.

Abbreviations for Briefs

acceptance .... acp
affirmed .... aff
answer .... ans
assumption of risk .... a/r
attorney .... atty
beyond a reasonable doubt .... b/r/d
bona fide purchaser .... BFP
breach of contract .... br/k
cause of action .... c/a
common law .... c/l
Constitution .... Con
constitutional .... con
contract .... K
contributory negligence .... c/n
cross x
cross-complaint .... x/c
cross-examination .... x/ex
cruel and unusual punishment .... c/u/p
defendant .... D
dismissed .... dis
double jeopardy .... d/j
due process .... d/p
equal protection .... e/p
equity .... eq
evidence .... ev
exclude .... exc
exclusionary rule .... exc/r
felony .... f/n
freedom of speech .... f/s
good faith .... g/f
habeas corpus .... h/c
hearsay .... hr
husband .... H
injunction .... inj
in loco parentis .... ILP
inter vivos .... I/v
joint tenancy .... j/t
judgment .... judgt
jurisdiction .... jur
last clear chance LCC
long-arm statute .... LAS
majority view .... maj
meeting of minds .... MOM
minority view .... min
Miranda rule .... Mir/r
Miranda warnings .... Mir/w
negligence .... neg
notice .... ntc
nuisance .... nus
obligation .... ob
obscene .... obs
offer .... O
offeree .... OE
offeror .... OR
ordinance .... ord
pain and suffering .... p/s
parol evidence .... p/e
plaintiff .... P
prima facie .... p/f
probable cause .... p/c
proximate cause .... px/c
real property .... r/p
reasonable doubt .... r/d
reasonable man .... r/m
rebuttable presumption .... rb/p
remanded .... rem
res ipsa loquitur .... RIL
respondeat superior .... r/s
Restatement .... RS
reversed .... rev
Rule Against Perpetuities .... RAP
search and seizure .... s/s
search warrant .... s/w
self-defense .... s/d
specific performance .... s/p
statute .... S
statute of frauds .... S/F
statute of limitations .... S/L
summary judgment .... s/j
tenancy at will .... t/w
tenancy in common .... t/c
tenant .... t
third party .... TP
third party beneficiary .... TPB
transferred intent .... TI
unconscionable .... uncon
unconstitutional .... unconst
undue influence .... u/e
Uniform Commercial Code .... UCC
unilateral .... uni
vendee .... VE
vendor .... VR
versus v
void for vagueness .... VFV
weight of authority .... w/a
weight of the evidence .... w/e
wife .... W
with .... w/
within .... w/i
without .... w/o
without prejudice .... w/o/p
wrongful death .... wr/d

Table of Cases

40 West 67th Street Corp. v. Pullman 118

A
Anderson v. City of Issaquah 124
Armory v. Delamirie 12

B
Baker v. Weedon 23
Bean v. Walker 76
Berg v. Wiley 50
Board of Education of Minneapolis v. Hughes 81
Boomer v. Atlantic Cement Co. 94
Broadway National Bank v. Adams 30
Brown v. Lober 67
Brown v. Voss 106

C
Cheney Brothers v. Doris Silk Corp. 7
Chicago Board of Realtors, Inc. v. City of Chicago 54
City of Edmonds, v. Oxford House, Inc. 130
City of Ladue v. Gilleo 125
Commonwealth v. Fremont Investment & Loan 74

D
Daniels v. Anderson 83
Delfino v. Vealencis 36
Dolan v. City of Tigard 146

E
Elkus v. Elkus 42
Ernst v. Conditt 48
Estancias Dallas Corp. v. Schultz 93

F
Fisher v. Giuliani 127
Frimberger v. Anzellotti 68

G
Garner v. Gerrish 46
Ghen v. Rich 4
Gruen v. Gruen 20
Guillette v. Daly Dry Wall, Inc. 82
Guru Nanak Sikh Society of Yuba City v. County of Sutter 126

H
Hadacheck v. Sebastian 137
Hannah v. Peel 13
Hannan v. Dusch 47
Harms v. Sprague 35
Harper v. Paradise 85
Hickey v. Green 58
Hilder v. St. Peter 53
Holbrook v. Taylor 100
Howard v. Kunto 17

I
Ink v. City of Canton 27
International News Service v. Associated Press 6

J
Johnson v. Davis 61
Johnson v. M'Intosh 2
Jones v. Lee 63

K
Keeble v. Hickeringill 5
Kelo v. City of New London 134
Kendall v. Ernest Pestana, Inc. 49
Kutzin v. Pirnie 65

L
Lempke v. Dagenais 62
Lewis v. Superior Court 84
Licari v. Blackwelder 57
Lick Mill Creek Apartments v. Chicago Title Insurance Co. 89
Lohmeyer v. Bower 59
Loretto v. Teleprompter Manhattan CATV Corp. 136
Lucas v. South Carolina Coastal Council 140
Luthi v. Evans 78

M
Mahrenholz v. County Board of School Trustees 25
Mannillo v. Gorski 16
Marriage of Graham, In re 41
McAvoy v. Medina 14
Messersmith v. Smith 80
Miller v. Lutheran Conference & Camp Association 105
Moore v. Regents of the University of California 9
Morgan v. High Penn Oil Co. 92
Mountain Brow Lodge No. 82, Independent Order of Odd Fellows v. Toscano 26
Murphy v. Fin. Dev. Corp. 73

N
Nahrstedt v. Lakeside Village Condominium Association, Inc. 116
Neponsit Property Owners' Association, Inc. v. Emigrant Industrial Savings Bank 110
Newman v. Bost 19
Nollan v. California Coastal Commission 145

O
O'Keeffe v. Snyder 18
Orr v. Byers 79
Othen v. Rosier 103

P
PA Northwestern Distributors, Inc. v. Zoning Hearing Board 122
Palazzolo v. Rhode Island 142
Penn Central Transportation Company v. City of New York 139
Pennsylvania Coal Co. v. Mahon 138
Pierson v. Post 3
Pocono Springs Civic Association, Inc. v. MacKenzie 115
Preseault v. United States 107

R
Raleigh Avenue Beach Assn. v. Atlantis Beach Club 104
Reste Realty Corp. v. Cooper 52

Rick v. West 114
Riddle v. Harmon 34
Rockafellor v. Gray.................................. 70
Rosengrant v. Rosengrant.......................... 72

S

Sanborn v. McLean................................ 109
Sawada v. Endo...................................... 40
Shelley v. Kraemer................................ 112
Sommer v. Kridel 51
Southern Burlington County NAACP v.
Township of Mount Laurel 131
Spiller v. Mackereth 37
Spur Industries, Inc. v. Del E. Webb
Development Co. 95
Stambovsky v. Ackley................................ 60
State ex rel. Stoyanoff v. Berkeley................ 123
Swartzbaugh v. Sampson............................ 38
Sweeney v. Sweeney 71
Symphony Space, Inc., The v. Pergola
Properties, Inc. 31

T

Tahoe-Sierra Preservation Council, Inc. v.
Tahoe Regional Planning Agency 143
Tulk v. Moxhay 108

V

Van Sandt v. Royster 101
Van Valkenburgh v. Lutz............................ 15
Varnum v. Brien...................................... 43
Village of Belle Terre v. Boraas................... 129
Village of Euclid v. Amber Realty Co. 120

W

Waldorff Insurance and Bonding, Inc. v.
Eglin National Bank.............................. 86
Walker Rogge, Inc. v.
Chelsea Title & Guaranty Co. 87
Western Land Co. v. Truskolaski 113
White v. Brown 22
White v. Samsung Electronics America, Inc. 8
Willard v. First Church of Christ,
Scientist.. 99
Woodrick v. Wood.................................. 24

CHAPTER 1

First Possession

Quick Reference Rules of Law

PAGE

1. **Acquisition by Discovery.** The discovery of the Native American-occupied lands of this nation vested absolute title in the discoverers, and rendered the Native American inhabitants themselves incapable of transferring absolute title to others. (Johnson v. M'Intosh) *2*

2. **Acquisition by Capture.** Property in wild animals is only acquired by occupancy, and pursuit alone does not constitute occupancy or vest any right in the pursuer. (Pierson v. Post) *3*

3. **Acquisition by Capture.** When all that is practicable in order to secure a wild animal is done, it becomes the property of the securer who has thus exercised sufficient personal control over the wild animal. (Ghen v. Rich) *4*

4. **Acquisition by Capture.** Damages may be recovered for the intentional frightening of game off another's land. (Keeble v. Hickeringill) *5*

5. **Acquisition by Creation.** Publication for profit of news obtained from other news-gathering enterprises is a misappropriation of a property right. (International News Service v. Associated Press) *6*

6. **Acquisition by Creation.** If a person cannot obtain a patent or copyright on its product, it cannot recover for the copying of it by others. (Cheney Brothers v. Doris Silk Corp.) *7*

7. **Property in One's Persona.** The right of publicity extends beyond the use of one's name and likeness to include any appropriation of one's identity. (White v. Samsung Electronics America, Inc.) *8*

8. **Property in One's Person.** A person whose tissue is used for profitable research and development without his knowledge may not maintain a conversion action therefor. (Moore v. Regents of the University of California) *9*

Johnson v. M'Intosh

Successor to Indian title (P) v. Subsequent purchaser (D)

21 U.S. (8 Wheat.) 543 (1823).

NATURE OF CASE: Appeal in an action to determine title to land.

FACT SUMMARY: Johnson (P) claimed valid title to land granted him by the chiefs of certain Native American tribes.

RULE OF LAW

The discovery of the Native American-occupied lands of this nation vested absolute title in the discoverers, and rendered the Native American inhabitants themselves incapable of transferring absolute title to others.

FACTS: Johnson (P) claimed valid title to land by reason of two grants, purportedly made, in 1773 and 1775 respectively, by the chiefs of certain Native American tribes. The proofs showed that the chiefs executing the conveyances had the authority to do so, and that the tribes were in rightful possession of the lands they sold. Nevertheless, the trial court denied the power of the Native American to convey such lands since, although they had retained title to the land's occupancy, they nevertheless remained incapable of transferring absolute title to others. Johnson (P) appealed.

ISSUE: Do the Native American tribes have the power of conveying absolute title of their lands to others?

HOLDING AND DECISION: (Marshall, C.J.) No. The discovery of the Native American-occupied lands of this nation vested absolute title in the discoverers; and while the Native American inhabitants retained title of occupancy, they were nevertheless incapable of transferring absolute title to others. As the result, this title claimed by Johnson (P) cannot be recognized by the U.S. courts. The very history of America, from its discovery to the present, demonstrates this principle. For example, when the English discoverers first acquired territory on this continent, they assumed title to the lands despite their admitted possession by the natives. While still under Native American occupation, these lands and waters were conveyed to others by the English monarch. These extensive grants cannot be regarded as nullities. That this principle has been ever recognized is seen in the history of wars, negotiations, and treaties. In fact, all the nations of Europe who have acquired territory on this continent have recognized the principle. The validity of these titles has never been questioned by the courts. Finally, an absolute title cannot exist at the same time in different governments over the same land. It would be incompatible to vest absolute title in the Indians as a distinct nation and country. Therefore, they are regarded as merely occupants, to be protected while at peace but to be deemed incapable of transferring absolute title to others. Affirmed.

ANALYSIS

As reflected in the case of *Tee-Hit-Ton Indians v. United States*, 348 U.S. 272 (1955), the courts have generally followed the principal case and denied Native American land titles. However, Congress has followed a fairly consistent policy of making voluntary payments to the Native Americans. See Cohen, "Original Indian Title," 32 *Minn. L. Rev.* 28 (1947). In his conclusion, Mr. Cohen said that: "The notion that America was stolen from the Indians is one of the myths by which we Americans are prone to hide our real virtues and make our idealism look as hard-boiled as possible." The story, nevertheless, is not pleasant.

Quicknotes

ABSOLUTE TITLE Exclusive title to land.

RIGHT OF DOMINION Possessing both title and ownership of property and having total power over its distribution.

Pierson v. Post

Fox killer (D) v. Fox hunter (P)

N.Y. Sup. Ct., 3 Cai. R. 175, 2 Am. Dec. 264 (1805).

NATURE OF CASE: Action of trespass on the case.

FACT SUMMARY: Post (P) was hunting a fox. Pierson (D), knowing this, killed the fox and carried it off.

RULE OF LAW

Property in wild animals is only acquired by occupancy, and pursuit alone does not constitute occupancy or vest any right in the pursuer.

FACTS: Post (P) found a fox upon certain wild, uninhabited, unpossessed waste land. He and his dogs began hunting and pursuing the fox. Knowing that the fox was being hunted by Post (P) and within Post's (P) view, Pierson (D) killed the fox and carried it off.

ISSUE: Has a person in pursuit of a wild animal acquired such a right to or property in the wild animal as to sustain an action against a person who kills and carries away the animal, knowing of the former's pursuit?

HOLDING AND DECISION: (Tompkins, J.) No. Property in wild animals is acquired by occupancy only. Mere pursuit vests no right in the pursuer. One authority holds that actual bodily seizure is not always necessary to constitute possession of wild animals. The mortal wounding of an animal or the trapping or intercepting of animals so as to deprive them of their natural liberty will constitute occupancy. However, here, Post (P) only shows pursuit. Hence there was no occupancy or legal right vested in Post (P) and the fox became Pierson's (D) property when he killed and carried it off. The purpose of this rule is that if the pursuit of animals without wounding them or restricting their liberty were held to constitute a basis for an action against others for intercepting and killing the animals, "it would prove a fertile source of quarrels and litigation." Reversed.

DISSENT: (Livingston, J.) A new rule should be adopted: that property in wild animals may be acquired without bodily touch, provided the pursuer be in reach or have a reasonable prospect of taking the animals.

ANALYSIS

The ownership of wild animals is in the state for the benefit of all her people. A private person cannot acquire exclusive rights to a wild animal except by taking and reducing it to actual possession in a lawful manner or by a grant from the government. After the animal has been lawfully subjected to control, the ownership becomes absolute as long as the restraint lasts. Mere ownership of the land that an animal happens to be on does not constitute such a reduction of possession as to give the landowner a property right in the animal, except as against a mere trespasser who goes on such land for the purpose of taking the animal.

Quicknotes

SEIZURE The removal of property from one's possession due to unlawful activity or in satisfaction of a judgment entered by the court.

TRESPASS ON THE CASE Action at common law in early England granting a remedy to a person who sustains injury to his person or property as a result of the defendant's conduct.

Ghen v. Rich

Whaling ship owner (P) v. Whale purchaser (D)

8 F. 159 (D. Mass. 1881).

NATURE OF CASE: Admiralty action to recover the value of a whale.

FACT SUMMARY: Rich (D) purchased a whale at auction from a man who found it washed up on the beach. The whale had been killed at sea by the crew of Ghen's (P) whaling ship which left Ghen's (P) identifying bomb-lance in the animal.

RULE OF LAW

When all that is practicable in order to secure a wild animal is done, it becomes the property of the securer who has thus exercised sufficient personal control over the wild animal.

FACTS: Because of the problems involved in capturing whales for commercial use in nineteenth-century New England, a trade usage arose as follows: when the crew of a whaling ship killed a whale using its identifying bomb-lance, the ship's owner by custom was considered to be the owner of that whale. When the whale washed ashore, the finder could identify the owner by the bomb-lance and would send notice of the find to the whaling center, Provincetown, Massachusetts. The finder would be paid a reasonable salvage fee. In this case, Ellis, the finder, did not notify Provincetown, but sold the whale at auction where Rich (D) purchased it. Rich (D) removed the blubber which he had processed into oil. Ghen (P) claimed to be the owner of the whale under the trade usage and sued Rich (D) for the value of the whale.

ISSUE: By the trade usage, was the whale placed under sufficient control by the capturing whaler so that it became his property?

HOLDING AND DECISION: (Nelson, J.) Yes. Ghen (P), through the use of the identifying bomb-lance, did all that was practicable in order to secure the whale. While local trade usages should not set aside maritime law, the custom can be enforced when it is embraced by an entire industry and has been utilized for a long time by everyone engaged in the trade. This particular trade usage was necessary to the survival of the whaling industry, for no one would engage in whaling if he could not be guaranteed the fruits of his labor. Decree for libellant.

ANALYSIS

Under the common law rule, for a wild animal to be reduced to a possession, it must be placed under the control of the one making the capture. Here, two major considerations modified the application of the rule to the situation. First, all that was practicable to secure the whale was done. Second, the trade usage was industry-wide, necessary to the survival of the industry, and fair to all parties (including the whale's finder, who received a reasonable salvage fee). Note also that the rule here was not being applied to a sport such as hunting or fishing, but, instead, to an industry. Economic interests were certainly important in the holding of this case.

Quicknotes

BOMB-LANCE Device used by whaling ships in the nineteenth century to identify themselves as the owner of a captured whale.

MARITIME LAW That area of law pertaining to navigable waters.

SALVAGE FEE Charge incurred in the salvage of property.

TRADE USAGE A course of dealing or practice commonly used in a particular trade.

Keeble v. Hickeringill

Duck pond owner (P) v. Duck frightener (D)

Queen's Bench, 11 East 574, 103 Eng. Rep. 1127 (1707).

NATURE OF CASE: Action for interference with lawful use of land.

FACT SUMMARY: Keeble (P) contended Hickeringill (D) scared ducks away from his pond resulting in damage.

RULE OF LAW

Damages may be recovered for the intentional frightening of game off another's land.

FACTS: Keeble (P) owned land containing a duck pond. He loaded the pond with decoys to seduce game to come to the pond so that he could hunt them. Hickeringill (D) discharged a shotgun near the pond which induced the game to stay away. Keeble (P) sued and was granted recovery. Hickeringill (D) appealed, contending Keeble (P) had no title to the game, and thus no cause of action existed.

ISSUE: May recovery of damages be had for the frightening of wild game off one's property?

HOLDING AND DECISION: (Holt, C.J.) Yes. Damages may be recovered for the intentional frightening of wild game off another's land. Although no title to the game existed, Keeble (P) was using his land in a lawful manner. Thus Hickeringill (D) interfered with this lawful use and is liable in damages.

ANALYSIS

Capture or control, in conjunction with being first in time, guides legal analysis of the ownership of wild animals. The present case represents somewhat of a departure from these rules, yet it is viewed as a natural and logical extension of them.

Quicknotes

INTERFERENCE WITH USE OF LAND An action to recover damages resulting from the wrongful interference with a party's property; otherwise, this is referred to as a trespass.

VIVARY A place where wild animals are kept.

International News Service v. Associated Press

Wire service (D) v. Wire service (P)

248 U.S. 215 (1918).

NATURE OF CASE: Appeal from denial of injunctive relief.

FACT SUMMARY: Associated Press (AP) (P) sued to enjoin International News Service (INS) (D) from publishing as its own news stories obtained from early editions of AP (P) publications.

RULE OF LAW

Publication for profit of news obtained from other news-gathering enterprises is a misappropriation of a property right.

FACTS: AP (P) sued INS (D) for the latter's admitted use of AP (P) news stories in INS (D) publications. INS (D) would obtain advance publication of AP (P) news and would then use such in its newspapers. AP (P) contended it had a proprietary right to all news it gathered through the efforts of its contributors. INS (D) contended any such right terminated upon its first publication. The court of appeals issued AP (P) an injunction, and the Supreme Court granted a hearing.

ISSUE: Is the publication for profit of news obtained from other news-gathering enterprises a misappropriation of a property right?

HOLDING AND DECISION: (Pitney, J.) Yes. Publication for profit of news obtained from other news-gathering enterprises is a misappropriation of a property right. News itself is a collection of observable facts which obviously cannot be owned vis-á-vis by the public at large. The nonprofit communication of news, regardless of source, is endemic in a free society and involves no property right. However, when two competing news organizations are involved, each gaining their livelihood from beating the other's deadline, the use of such news, for profit, is a misappropriation of the other's product. As a result, injunctive relief is properly issued. Affirmed.

ANALYSIS

Some commentators suggest this case as a prime example of the first in time–first in right principle of ownership. Some go so far as to argue it provides authority for the proposition that all things created, tangible or intangible, belong to the creator. This expands the reach of this case beyond news-gathering and into any area wherein exclusivity of design or idea is important. This would include everything from clothing design to computer programming.

Quicknotes

COPYRIGHT Refers to the exclusive rights granted to an artist pursuant to Article I, Section 8, Clause 8 of the United States Constitution over the reproduction, display, performance, distribution, and adaptation of his work for a period prescribed by statute.

MISAPPROPRIATION The unlawful use of another's property or funds.

Cheney Brothers v. Doris Silk Corp.

Silk manufacturer (P) v. Copycat designer (D)

35 F.2d 279 (2d Cir. 1929), *cert. denied*, 281 U.S. 728 (1930).

NATURE OF CASE: Appeal from order dismissing action seeking damages and equitable relief for unfair competition.

FACT SUMMARY: Cheney Brothers (P), unable to patent or copyright a garment pattern, sought damages for the copying thereof.

RULE OF LAW

If a person cannot obtain a patent or copyright on its product, it cannot recover for the copying of it by others.

FACTS: Cheney Brothers (P) designed and marketed silk garments. At one point Doris Silk Corp. (D) copied a design and successfully marketed it. Cheney Brothers (P), which could neither patent nor copyright the design, sued for damages and equitable relief under general property law. The trial court dismissed, and Cheney Brothers (P) appealed.

ISSUE: If a person cannot obtain a patent or copyright on its product, can it recover for the copying of it by others?

HOLDING AND DECISION: (Hand, J.) No. If a person cannot obtain a patent or copyright on its product, it cannot recover for the copying of it by others. In the absence of the statutory protection given a man's creations by patent or copyright law, a man's property is limited to the tangible objects which embody his invention. When another creates a chattel through imitation, the imitated person has no remedy. Here, it is conceded that the creations of Cheney Brothers (P) were neither patentable nor copyrightable, and therefore it has no remedy. Affirmed.

ANALYSIS

Probably the latest developing area of property law, intellectual property has become a hot topic in the information age. There has been considerable development in the field since the present decision. Nonetheless, the general rule remains valid. However, the class of things which can be copyrighted has grown considerably since 1929.

Quicknotes

CHATTEL An article of personal property, as distinguished from real property; a thing personal and moveable.

COPYRIGHT Refers to the exclusive rights granted to an artist pursuant to Article I, Section 8, clause 8 of the United States Constitution over the reproduction, display, performance, distribution, and adaptation of his work for a period prescribed by statute.

EQUITABLE RELIEF A remedy that is based upon principles of fairness as opposed to rules of law.

PATENT A limited monopoly conferred on the invention or discovery of any new or useful machine or process that is novel and nonobvious.

White v. Samsung Electronics America, Inc.

Celebrity (P) v. Corporation (D)

989 F.2d 1512 (9th Cir. 1992) (denying a rehearing), *cert. denied*, 508 U.S. 951 (1993).

NATURE OF CASE: Defendant's petition for rehearing of decision on appeal.

FACT SUMMARY: Samsung Electronics America, Inc., (Samsung) (D) parodied Vanna White (P) and the Wheel of Fortune game show in an advertisement in which a robot stood in front of the Wheel of Fortune game board.

RULE OF LAW

The right of publicity extends beyond the use of one's name and likeness to include any appropriation of one's identity.

FACTS: [The text briefly summarizes the following facts and procedural history of the case, but only includes the dissenting opinion of Judge Kozinski.] White (P) brought an action against Samsung (D) for violation of her common law right of publicity and a claim based on the Lanham Act for false advertising. The claims arose after Samsung (D) used an advertisement with a robot standing in front of the Wheel of Fortune game board. The trial court granted summary judgment in full to Samsung (D). The Ninth Circuit reversed on the grounds that material issues of fact precluded the granting of summary judgment. Samsung (D) filed a motion for a rehearing of the appeal, which the Ninth Circuit denied. Judge Kozinski then filed a dissenting opinion in support of Samsung's (D) position. The text only includes portions of his opinion.

ISSUE: Does the right of publicity extend beyond the use of one's name and likeness to include any appropriation of one's identity?

HOLDING AND DECISION: [Judge not listed in casebook excerpt.] Yes. The right of publicity extends beyond the use of one's name and likeness to include any appropriation of one's identity. [The text does not include the majority opinion. The Ninth Circuit reversed on the grounds factual issues precluded the granting of summary judgment to Samsung (D).] Reversed.

DISSENT: (Kozinski, J). The majority opinion is overly broad. The opinion essentially creates a tort when advertisers simply "remind" the public of a celebrity. Under California law, White (P) has an exclusive right to her name, likeness, signature, and voice. Here, Samsung (D) used none of those in its advertisement. The majority opinion pushes the balance between protection of copyrights and the right of the public too far in favor of the alleged copyright. Advertisers will now have to respond to unspecified claims of "appropriation of identity." In addition, federal copyright law allows such "fair use" parodies and the majority opinion contravenes the federal scheme by disallowing such parodies. Finally, the decision runs afoul of the First Amendment. Not allowing advertisers to remind the public of a person is a restriction on speech that is prohibited by the First Amendment.

ANALYSIS

Judge Kozinski's opinion has become well known as support for the position that courts should not unreasonably extend the common law right of publicity. Many courts in several jurisdictions have cited his opinion when denying similar claims by other celebrities and have declined to follow the majority opinion in the matter.

Quicknotes

COPYRIGHT LAW Refers to the exclusive rights granted to an artist pursuant to Article I, Section 8, clause 8 of the United States Constitution over the reproduction, display, performance, distribution, and adaptation of his work for a period prescribed by statute.

RIGHT OF PUBLICITY The right of a person to control the commercial exploitation of his name or likeness.

Moore v. Regents of the University of California

Leukemia patient (P) v. Medical center owners (D)

Cal. Sup. Ct., 51 Cal. 3d 120, 793 P.2d 479 (1990), *cert. denied,* 499 U.S. 936 (1991).

NATURE OF CASE: Review of order reversing dismissal of action seeking damages for conversion, fraud, and breach of fiduciary duty.

FACT SUMMARY: Researchers at the University of California, Los Angeles (UCLA), unbeknownst to Moore (D), used specimens of his tissue to produce a potentially lucrative cell line.

RULE OF LAW

A person whose tissue is used for profitable research and development without his knowledge may not maintain a conversion action therefor.

FACTS: In 1976 Moore (P) began treatment at UCLA for a life-threatening form of leukemia. Doctors there realized that his tissue had certain unique properties that showed promise of profitable development. While undergoing treatment, Moore (P) often had tissue removed, such as blood samples, as well as his spleen. While he consented to all these procedures, he was unaware of the nontreatment research being performed on his tissues. Eventually a cell line was developed, which showed promise of benefit in immunology. A patent on the cell line was issued. When he became aware of the use to which his tissue had been put, Moore (P) filed an action seeking damages for conversion, fraud, and breach of fiduciary duty. The trial court dismissed for failure to state a cause of action. The court of appeal reversed, holding that Moore (P) had stated a cause of action for conversion and breach of fiduciary duty. The California Supreme Court granted review.

ISSUE: May a person whose tissue is used for profitable research and development without his knowledge maintain a conversion action therefor?

HOLDING AND DECISION: (Panelli, J.) No. A person whose tissue is used for profitable research and development without his knowledge may not maintain a conversion action therefor. [The court first held that Moore (P) could maintain a breach of fiduciary duty cause of action based on nondisclosure, and then discussed the conversion cause of action.] This court is of the opinion that existing law would not permit such an action. To maintain such an action, a plaintiff must prove interference with ownership or right of possession. A plaintiff in a position such as Moore (P) clearly had no right of possession, so a conversion action would necessitate interference with a proprietary interest. It cannot be said, however, that a person's tissue is "property." Such a notion is at odds with common views on ethics. Beyond that, Health and Safety Code § 7054.4 severs the interest of a person and his removed body parts. Since existing law does not create a conversion action under the circumstances here, an extension of existing law would be required to allow Moore (P) to proceed. This court declines to do so. First, if so held would stifle beneficial research. Conversion is a strict liability tort, and the specter of a conversion suit might dissuade researchers from undertaking important investigations. Secondly, fiduciary duty principles protect a patient, so a conversion cause of action is not necessary. Finally, the present area is one better left to the legislature. For these reasons, this court concludes that Moore (P) has not stated a conversion cause of action. Affirmed in part; reversed in part.

CONCURRENCE: (Arabian, J.) Human tissue should never be viewed as property, even by the person whose tissue is at issue.

DISSENT: (Mosk, J.) Current conversion law should be applied to a person's tissue, as a person should have at the least the right to do with his own tissue what any other person can do with it. Assuming that current conversion law doesn't extend to body tissue, it should be extended. To allow a person to economically benefit from the nonconsensual use of another's tissue can be considered a modern version of slavery or indentured servitude.

ANALYSIS

Probably more than any other area of law, property law carries the weight of tradition in its classifications. Modern technology often creates situations that are difficult to apply to traditional legal categories. The present case represents a prime example. The tort of conversion was created in a time when what was and was not capable of being called "property" was pretty clear; things are not so simple today.

Quicknotes

CONVERSION The act of depriving an owner of his property without permission or justification.

FIDUCIARY DUTY A legal obligation to act for the benefit of another, including subordinating one's personal interests to that of the other person.

FRAUD A false representation of facts with the intent that another will rely on the misrepresentation to his detriment.

CHAPTER 2

Subsequent Possession

Quick Reference Rules of Law

PAGE

1. **Acquisition by Find.** A finder of chattel has title superior to all but the rightful owner upon which he may maintain an action at law or in equity. (Armory v. Delamirie) *12*

2. **Acquisition by Find.** The finder of a lost article is entitled to it as against all persons except the real owner. (Hannah v. Peel) *13*

3. **Acquisition by Find.** Misplaced goods (items intentionally placed by the owner where they were found and then forgotten or left there) are deemed to be in the bailment of the owner of the property on which they are found for the true owner. (McAvoy v. Medina) *14*

4. **The Theory and Elements of Adverse Possession.** Title to a parcel may vest in an adverse possessor who occupies the parcel under claim of right, protects the parcel by an enclosure, improves or cultivates the parcel, and maintains that state of affairs for the statutory period. (Van Valkenburgh v. Lutz) *15*

5. **The Theory and Elements of Adverse Possession.** To claim title by adverse possession, the possessor need not have been aware that the land in question was in fact owned by another. (Mannillo v. Gorski) *16*

6. **The Mechanics of Adverse Possession.** Where several successive purchasers received record title to tract *A* under the mistaken belief that they were acquiring tract *B*, immediately contiguous thereto, and where possession of tract *B* is transferred and occupied in a continuous manner for more than 10 years by successive occupants, there is sufficient privity of estate to permit tacking and thus establish adverse possession as a matter of law. (Howard v. Kunto) *17*

7. **Adverse Possession of Chattels.** The discovery rule controls in actions involving the adverse possession of chattels. (O'Keeffe v. Snyder) *18*

8. **Acquisition by Gift.** A constructive delivery of a gift *causa mortis* will be effective where it plainly appears that it was the intention of the donor to make the gift, and where the things intended to be given are not present, or, where present, are incapable of manual delivery from their size or weight. (Newman v. Bost) *19*

9. **Acquisition by Gift.** A valid *inter vivos* gift of chattel may be made where the donor reserves a life estate and the donee never has physical possession until the donor's death. (Gruen v. Gruen) *20*

Armory v. Delamirie

Jewel finder (P) v. Goldsmith (D)

King's Bench, 1 Strange 505 (1722).

NATURE OF CASE: Action in trover to recover the value of personal property.

FACT SUMMARY: Armory (P) found a jewel which he took to Delamirie (D), a goldsmith, for appraisal, but Delamirie's (D) apprentice removed the stones which Delamirie (D) refused to return.

RULE OF LAW

A finder of chattel has title superior to all but the rightful owner upon which he may maintain an action at law or in equity.

FACTS: Armory (P), a chimney sweeper's boy, found a jewel which he took to Delamirie's (D) goldsmith shop to learn what it was. Delamirie's (D) apprentice, under the pretense of weighing the jewel, removed the stones from the setting and told his master the value. Delamirie (D) offered Armory (P) three halfpence for the stones, but he refused. Delamirie (D) returned the setting without the stones.

ISSUE: Could Armory (P), who lacked legal title to the chattel, maintain an action to recover its value?

HOLDING AND DECISION: (Pratt, C.J.) Yes. The finder of lost property, although he does not acquire absolute ownership, does acquire title superior to everyone else except the rightful owner. Such title is a sufficient property interest in the finder upon which he may maintain an action against anyone (except the rightful owner) who violates that interest. Additionally, Delamirie (D) was liable as he was responsible for the actions of his apprentice. As for the measure of damages, if Delamirie (D) did not show the stones were not of the finest value, their value would be so determined.

ANALYSIS

As to ownership, the finder is in a position similar to that of a bailee. The finder does not obtain absolute ownership, but does have the right of ownership against everybody except the true owner. Here, the chattel, the jewel, was subsequently converted against the finder. Yet the finder, if he should subsequently lose the chattel, may reclaim it from a subsequent finder. The finder has a choice of remedies. He may recover the chattel in specie if it is still in the converter's possession, or he may recover full value from the wrongdoer. Notice that an action in trover, which is an action at law, is to recover the value of the chattel. If it is desired to have the item returned, an action in replevin must be brought in equity.

Quicknotes

BAILEE Person holding property in trust for another party.

Hannah v. Peel

Brooch finder (P) v. Homeowner (D)

King's Bench, K.B. 509 (1945).

NATURE OF CASE: Action to recover personal property.

FACT SUMMARY: Hannah (P) found a brooch at Peel's (D) home during World War II, and sought to recover it after police handed it over to Peel (D).

RULE OF LAW

The finder of a lost article is entitled to it as against all persons except the real owner.

FACTS: During the Second World War, Peel's (D) home was requisitioned for use by the military. In August 1940, lance corporal Hannah (P) found a brooch in a crevice in a bedroom of the house. Hannah (P) gave the brooch to his commanding officer a month later, and in August 1942, the police handed the brooch to Peel (D), who subsequently sold it. There was no evidence that Peel (D) had any knowledge of the existence of the brooch before it was found by Hannah (P). Hannah (P) refused a reward offer from Peel (D), and maintained his right to possession of the brooch as against all persons other than the owner, who was unknown. On October 21, 1943, Hannah (P) filed suit to recover the brooch or its value and damages for its detention.

ISSUE: Is the finder of a lost article entitled to it as against all persons except the real owner?

HOLDING AND DECISION: (Birkett, J.) Yes. The general rule is that the finder of a lost article is entitled to it as against all persons except the real owner. This is because an occupier of land does not in all cases possess an unattached thing on his land even though the true owner has lost possession. Although a man possesses everything which is attached to or under his land, a man does not necessarily possess a thing which is lying unattached on the surface of his land even though the thing is not possessed by someone else. Here, the brooch was lost in the ordinary meaning of that term, and it had been lost for a very considerable time. Peel (D) was never physically in possession of the premises at any time. It is clear that the brooch was never his, in the ordinary meaning of the term, in that he did not have the prior possession. Peel (D) had no knowledge of it, until it was brought to his attention by Hannah (P). Accordingly, judgment is rendered for Hannah (P).

ANALYSIS

The issue of finder's rights presented many problems for the English commentators. "The reason why these writers did not have better success in their efforts at definition was that they tried to state the essentials of all the possession cases in too simple a form; they tried, characteristically emphasizing human will, to reduce the essentials of possession to the form of a unilateral act. For them the type case was the act of taking-occupation." Shartel, "Meanings of Possession," 16 *Minn L. Rev.* 611, 615, 619 (1932).

Quicknotes

POSSESSION The holding of property with the right of disposition.

McAvoy v. Medina

Wallet finder (P) v. Barber shop owner (D)

Mass. Sup. Jud. Ct., 93 Mass. (11 Allen) 548 (1866).

NATURE OF CASE: Action to recover money.

FACT SUMMARY: A wallet was inadvertently left at a barber shop, a customer (P) found it, and the barber (D) asserted ownership.

RULE OF LAW

Misplaced goods (items intentionally placed by the owner where they were found and then forgotten or left there) are deemed to be in the bailment of the owner of the property on which they are found for the true owner.

FACTS: McAvoy (P) was a customer in Medina's (D) barber shop. McAvoy (P) found a wallet which was lying on a table. McAvoy (P) showed Medina (D) where he found the wallet and told Medina (D) to keep the wallet and the money in it and to give it to the real owner. Medina (D) promised to attempt to find the owner. McAvoy (P) later made three demands for return of the money, but Medina (D) refused. The wallet had been placed on the table by a transient customer of the barber shop, and had been accidentally left there. The true owner was never found.

ISSUE: Does the finder of misplaced goods on another's property obtain title to the goods?

HOLDING AND DECISION: (Dewey, J.) No. The owner of the premises on which misplaced goods are found is deemed to be the bailee of the goods for the true owner. This wallet was not lost. It had been voluntarily placed upon a table and then accidentally left there. This is different from lost property which had not been voluntarily placed by the owner where it was later found. When goods are misplaced, the finder acquires no original right to the property. Holding the owner of the premises as bailee of the goods is better adapted to secure the rights of the true owner. Exceptions overruled.

ANALYSIS

The focus of lost or misplaced property cases is to determine whether it is likely that the true owner can ever be found. Therefore, because the finder was the first in possession, he will have paramount rights. On the other hand, where goods have been voluntarily placed and then forgotten, the true owner is much more likely to be found. As the true owner would be more likely to return to where he remembered placing the article, the owner of the premises will be deemed a bailee for the true owner.

Quicknotes

BAILEE Person holding property in trust for another party.

BAILMENT The delivery of property to be held in trust and which is designated for a particular purpose, following the satisfaction of which the property is either to be returned or disposed of as specified.

Van Valkenburgh v. Lutz

Tract owner (P) v. Adverse possessor (D)

N.Y. Ct. App., 304 N.Y. 95, 106 N.E.2d 28 (1952).

NATURE OF CASE: Appeal from judgment establishing title by adverse possession.

FACT SUMMARY: Beginning around 1920, Lutz (D) traveled across a triangular tract to reach his home on a nearby parcel, and also built a shed and kept a garden on the tract, but in 1947 Van Valkenburgh (P) purchased the tract at a tax sale, and when Van Valkenburgh (P) demanded that Lutz (D) vacate the land, Lutz (D) obtained a judgment that granted him a right of way by prescription over the tract and then in a judicial proceeding established title to the tract by adverse possession.

RULE OF LAW

Title to a parcel may vest in an adverse possessor who occupies the parcel under claim of right, protects the parcel by an enclosure, improves or cultivates the parcel, and maintains that state of affairs for the statutory period.

FACTS: Lutz (D) and his family owned and occupied a parcel of land near a triangular tract in the City of Yonkers. Beginning around 1920, Lutz (D) used the tract to cross to his land. He then cleared part of the tract and built a shed thereon and maintained a garden, knowing that he had no title to the tract. In 1937, Van Valkenburgh (P) moved onto a parcel contiguous to the triangular tract and a small feud developed for unrelated reasons between the parties. In 1947, Van Valkenburgh (P) purchased the triangular tract at a tax sale and gave Lutz (D) notice to vacate the tract. At a meeting between the parties and counsel, Lutz (D) agreed to remove the shed and garden, but claimed a right of way by right of prescription across the tract. Though Van Valkenburgh (P) agreed, he erected a fence across the right of way path, whereupon Lutz (D) obtained a judgment awarding him a right of way, which was affirmed. Van Valkenburgh (P) then brought this suit to compel removal of encroachments and delivery of possession of the triangular tract. The trial court held for Lutz (D) granting title by adverse possession, and Van Valkenburgh (P) appealed.

ISSUE: May title to a parcel vest in an adverse possessor who occupies the parcel under claim of right, protects the parcel with an enclosure, improves or cultivates the parcel, and maintains that state of affairs for the statutory period?

HOLDING AND DECISION: (Dye, J.) Yes. In this case there was no proof offered of any protection of the parcel by enclosure by Lutz (D), and the proof shows that he did not cultivate the entire premises claimed. Furthermore there was no improvement of the land because the shed thereon, the only structure of any kind involved here, was built by Lutz (D) with the conceded knowledge that he did not own the land under it. Title to a parcel may vest in an adverse possessor who occupies the parcel under claim of right, protects the parcel with an enclosure, improves or cultivates the parcel, and maintains that state of affairs for the statutory period. In this case, the elements permitting taking title by adverse possession were not present. Reversed, judgment directed for Van Valkenburgh (P).

DISSENT: (Fuld, J.) The weight of the evidence establishes Lutz's (D) right to the property in question by adverse possession. There was a "traveled way" across the property. Lutz (D) operated a truck farm there of substantial size. The fact that Lutz (D) knew he had no title to the tract is irrelevant so long as he intended to acquire title in himself, as he did. Lutz (D) actually occupied the property and title vested in him.

ANALYSIS

The traditional requirements for adverse possession are that the possession be actual, open, notorious, exclusive, adverse or hostile, continuous, under a claim of right, and for the statutory period. These requirements are variously expressed in the statutes and in the cases.

Quicknotes

ADVERSE POSSESSION A means of acquiring title to real property by remaining in actual, open, continuous, exclusive possession of property for the statutory period.

CLAIM OF RIGHT Person claiming a right in property is in possession and intends to claim ownership of that property without regard to the record title owner.

EASEMENT The right to utilize a portion of another's real property for a specific use.

Mannillo v. Gorski

Lot owner (P) v. Encroacher (D)

N.J. Sup. Ct., 54 N.J. 378, 255 A.2d 258 (1969).

NATURE OF CASE: Review of judgment denying claimed title by adverse possession.

FACT SUMMARY: Since Gorski (D) had created a structure encroaching upon Mannillo's (P) property, not knowing that the structure so encroached, Mannillo (P) argued that Gorski (D) lacked the requisite hostile intent to obtain title by adverse possession.

RULE OF LAW
To claim title by adverse possession, the possessor need not have been aware that the land in question was in fact owned by another.

FACTS: Mannillo (P) and Gorski (D) owned adjoining lots. At one point Gorski (D) erected a set of steps and a concrete walk to her dwelling that, unbeknownst to her, encroached upon Mannillo's (P) property. Years later, upon discovering that the steps encroached, Mannillo (P) filed a complaint seeking an injunction against the tresspass. Gorski (D) counterclaimed for a declaratory jüdgment of title by adverse possession. The trial judge entered judgment for Mannillo (P), believing that an adverse possessor had to have been aware that her possession was hostile to be entitled to possession. The state supreme court granted review.

ISSUE: To claim title by adverse possession, must the possessor have been aware that the land in question was in fact owned by another?

HOLDING AND DECISION: (Haneman, J.) No. To claim title by adverse possession, the possessor need not have been aware that the land in question was in fact owned by another. To hold to the contrary, i.e., to require that the adverse possession claim must be accompanied by a knowing intentional hostility, is called the "Maine Rule" and has been the law of this state for many years, but is of questionable historical pedigree and leads to undesirable results. Specifically, it places a knowing wrongdoer in a better position than an innocent party, a result the law ought not to condone. *Stare decisis* is an important principle, but in cases where people do not frame their conduct in reliance thereon, it is of lesser vitality as a doctrine. With respect to adverse possession, it is unlikely that the state of the law in this regard will impact people's behavior in any manner, as adverse possession is more of an after-the-fact situation than one done through preplanning. Since the law here is bad law, and *stare decisis* does not mandate adherence thereto, this court concludes that knowledge of the adversity of one's possession is not an element of adverse possession. However, no presumption of knowledge on the part of the true owner arises from a minor encroachment along a common boundary. In such a case, only where the true owner has actual knowledge thereof may the possession be said to be open and notorious. Remanded.

ANALYSIS

The competing rules here are the "Maine Rule," discussed but rejected in the above case, and the "Connecticut Rule," which the court adopted. The Maine Rule at one time enjoyed widespread adherence, but it has increasingly been abandoned for the reasons explained in the opinion here. The problem with the "Connecticut Rule," however, is that the true owner may not be put on notice that someone is in possession of a very small strip of land. Hence, the court rejected the traditional presumption of knowledge as fallacious and unjustified.

Quicknotes

ADVERSE POSSESSION A means of acquiring title to real property by remaining in actual, open, continuous, exclusive possession of property for the statutory period.

ENCROACHMENT The unlawful intrusion onto another's property.

INJUNCTION A court order requiring a person to do or prohibiting that person from doing a specific act.

STARE DECISIS Doctrine whereby courts follow legal precedent unless there is good cause for departure.

TRESPASS Unlawful interference with, or damage to, the real or personal property of another.

Howard v. Kunto

Record title owner (P) v. Adverse-possessor (D)

Wash. Ct. App., 477 P.2d 210 (1970).

NATURE OF CASE: Action to quiet title.

FACT SUMMARY: The land occupied by Kunto (D) was not that to which he had record title, but he appealed a judgment quieting title in Howard (P) who did have record title.

RULE OF LAW

Where several successive purchasers received record title to tract *A* under the mistaken belief that they were acquiring tract *B*, immediately contiguous thereto, and where possession of tract *B* is transferred and occupied in a continuous manner for more than 10 years by successive occupants, there is sufficient privity of estate to permit tacking and thus establish adverse possession as a matter of law.

FACTS: The Kuntos (D) took possession of a summer home under a deed which unbeknownst to them described the adjoining property. After discovering the mistake, Howard (P) obtained a conveyance of the deed which described the property occupied by the Kuntos (D), then sought and obtained a judgment quieting title in himself. Several successive purchasers, over a period of over ten years, had taken possession of the disputed tract under the same mistaken deed. The Kuntos (D) appealed.

ISSUE: Where several successive purchasers received record title to tract *A* under the mistaken belief that they were acquiring tract *B*, immediately contiguous thereto, and where possession of tract *B* is transferred and occupied in a continuous manner for more than 10 years by successive occupants, is there sufficient privity of estate to permit tacking and thus establish adverse possession as a matter of law?

HOLDING AND DECISION: (Pearson, J.) Yes. Where several successive purchasers received record title to tract *A* under the mistaken belief that they were acquiring tract *B*, immediately contiguous thereto, and where possession of tract *B* is transferred and occupied in a continuous manner for more than ten years by successive occupants, there is sufficient privity of estate to permit tacking and thus establish adverse possession as a matter of law. The deed running between parties purporting to transfer land traditionally furnishes the privity of estate which connects the possession of successive occupants. The technical requirement of "privity" should not be used to upset the long periods of occupancy of those who in good faith received an erroneous deed description. The use of a summer cottage only in summer is uninterrupted possession sufficient to establish adverse possession. There is a public interest favoring early certainty as to the location of land ownership. Reversed with directions.

ANALYSIS

The *Howard* case provides a good example of how the sometimes seemingly unjust doctrine of adverse possession can produce a just result.

Quicknotes

PRIVITY OF ESTATE Common or successive relation to the same right in property.

QUIET TITLE Equitable action to resolve conflicting claims to an interest in real property.

RECORD TITLE Title to real property that is recorded in the public land records.

TAKING A governmental action that substantially deprives an owner of the use and enjoyment of his or her property, requiring compensation.

O'Keeffe v. Snyder

Artist (P) v. Adverse-possessor (D)

N.J. Sup. Ct., 83 N.J. 478, 416 A.2d 862 (1980).

NATURE OF CASE: Appeal from reversal of award of replevin.

FACT SUMMARY: Snyder (D) contended that he had acquired three of O'Keeffe's (P) paintings by adverse possession.

RULE OF LAW

The discovery rule controls in actions involving the adverse possession of chattels.

FACTS: The painter Georgia O'Keeffe (P) brought an action against Snyder (D) for replevin, or return of three small pictures painted by O'Keeffe (P). In her complaint, filed in March, 1976, O'Keeffe (P) alleged that she was the owner of the paintings, and that they had been stolen from a New York art gallery in 1946. Snyder (D) asserted that he was a purchaser for value of the paintings, that he had acquired title by adverse possession, and that O'Keeffe's (P) action was barred by the expiration of the six-year period of limitations pertaining to an action in replevin. The appellate court, in reversing the trial court, concluded that the paintings were stolen, the defenses of expiration of the statute of limitations and title by adverse possession were identical, and that Snyder (D) had not proved the elements of adverse possession.

ISSUE: Does the discovery rule control in actions involving the adverse possession of chattels?

HOLDING AND DECISION: (Pollock, J.) Yes. The discovery rule provides that, in an appropriate case, a cause of action will not accrue until the injured party discovers, or by exercise of reasonable diligence and intelligence should have discovered, facts which form the basis of a cause of action. Here, O'Keeffe's (P) cause of action accrued when she first knew, or reasonably should have known through the exercise of due diligence, of the cause of action, including the identity of the possessor of the paintings. The focus of the inquiry will no longer be whether the possessor has met the tests of adverse possession, but whether the owner has acted with due diligence in pursuing his or her personal property. Under the discovery rule, if an artist diligently seeks the recovery of a lost or stolen painting, but cannot find it or discover the identity of the possessor, the statute of limitations will not begin to run. Under the discovery rule, the burden is on the owner as the one seeking the benefit of the rule to establish facts that would justify deferring the beginning of the period of limitations. However, if the period of limitations does begin to run, the expiration of the six-year statutory limitation period should vest title as effectively under the discovery rule as under the doctrine of adverse possession. Reversed and remanded for further proceedings.

ANALYSIS

Prior to the ruling in this case, the discovery rule had been applied primarily in tort actions where the injuries allegedly suffered by the plaintiff were difficult to discover. The court in this case, after reviewing the difficulty of applying principles of adverse possession to cases involving artwork, ruled that the application of the discovery rule would mitigate the unjust results that would flow from strict adherence to the rules of adverse possession.

Quicknotes

ADVERSE POSSESSION A means of acquiring title to real property by remaining in actual, open, continuous, exclusive possession of property for the statutory period.

CHATTEL An article of personal property, as distinguished from real property; a thing personal and moveable.

DUE DILIGENCE The standard of care as would be taken by a reasonable person in accordance with the attendant facts and circumstances.

REPLEVIN An action to recover personal property wrongfully taken.

Newman v. Bost

Donee (P) v. Estate administrator (D)

N.C. Sup. Ct., 122 N.C. 524, 29 S.E. 848 (1898).

NATURE OF CASE: Appeal from a finding of a valid gift *causa mortis.*

FACT SUMMARY: **Newman (P) sought to recover the value of certain gifts *causa mortis* sold by the decedent's administrator (D) who did not believe any valid gifts were made to Newman (P).**

RULE OF LAW

A constructive delivery of a gift *causa mortis* will be effective where it plainly appears that it was the intention of the donor to make the gift, and where the things intended to be given are not present, or, where present, are incapable of manual delivery from their size or weight.

FACTS: The decedent was stricken with paralysis and died within a month. While so stricken, he directed his nurse, Houston, to call Newman (P), his housekeeper, into his bedroom. The decedent handed to Newman (P) his private keys and told her to take them and keep them, that he desired her to have them and everything in the house. He then pointed out certain articles of furniture, including a bureau, and repeated that everything was hers. One of the keys unlocked a bureau drawer in which was decedent's life insurance policy, payable to his estate, and a few notes. Newman (P) brought suit against Bost (D), the decedent's administrator, to recover $3,000, the proceeds of the life insurance policy; $300, the value of a piano which decedent allegedly gave Newman (P) and which was destroyed by fire; $200.94, the value of household property sold by Bost (D); and $45, the value of the bedroom furniture sold by Bost (D). The court found that decedent made a valid gift *causa mortis*, and Bost (D) appealed.

ISSUE: Will a constructive delivery of a gift *causa mortis* be effective where it plainly appears that it was the intention of the donor to make the gift, and where the things intended to be given are not present, or where present, are incapable of manual delivery from their size and weight?

HOLDING AND DECISION: (Furches, J.) Yes. A constructive delivery of a gift *causa mortis* will be effective where it plainly appears that it was the intention of the donor to make the gift, and where the things intended to be given are not present, or, where present, are incapable of manual delivery from their size or weight; but where the articles are present, and are capable of manual delivery, manual delivery must be made. Here, as for the life insurance policy, it could have been removed from the drawer and easily handed to Newman (P). The failure to do so prevented the policy from passing to her. However, the bureau and any other furniture which the keys would fit did pass to her because actual delivery would have been unreasonable because of their size and weight. The keys were thus an effective constructive delivery of those items. All other furniture, except that in Newman's own bedroom in the house, remained in the estate. The furniture in Newman's (P) bedroom passed to her, rather, as a gift *inter vivos* for she had use and control of it before decedent contemplated his death. As for the piano, it was not ever within her dominion and control and there was never any delivery, and so it did not pass to her. Remanded for a new trial.

ANALYSIS

The court above took a fairly restrictive view of the concept of delivery and believed that the concept of gifts *causa mortis* should be strictly construed. The court expressed the fear that to allow symbolic delivery would be to open the door to all sorts of fraud. Where one is holding the donor's property as a bailee, and the donor wishes to give to the bailee that property already in the possession of the bailee, it is not necessarily for the intended donee-bailee to return the property to the donor so that delivery of the gift can be made. To so require, it has been held, would be a senseless formality. *Matter of Mill's Estate*, 158 N.Y.S. 1100 (App. Div. 1916).

Quicknotes

CONSTRUCTIVE DELIVERY The transfer of title or possession of property by means other than actual delivery indicative of the parties' intent to effect a transfer.

GIFT *CAUSA MORTIS* A gift made contingent on the donor's anticipated death.

GIFT *INTER VIVOS* A gift that is made, and is to take effect, while the parties are living.

STATUTE OF WILLS An English law stating the requirements for a valid testamentary disposition.

SYMBOLIC DELIVERY A method of constructive delivery whereby the transfer of title or possession of property is effectuated by delivering an article symbolic of the property.

Gruen v. Gruen

Son/donee (P) v. Stepmother (D)

N.Y. Ct. App., 68 N.Y.2d 48, 496 N.E.2d 869 (1986).

NATURE OF CASE: Appeal from an enforcement of an *inter vivos* gift.

FACT SUMMARY: Mrs. Gruen (D) contended her husband could not make a valid *inter vivos* gift to his son (P) and still retain present exclusive possession of the property for his life.

RULE OF LAW

A valid *inter vivos* gift of chattel may be made where the donor reserves a life estate and the donee never has physical possession until the donor's death.

FACTS: Michael Gruen (P) received a letter from his father indicating the latter wished to make a gift of a painting, but that he wished to use it for his life. Gruen (P) never took possession of the painting. After his father's death, he requested the painting from his stepmother, Mrs. Gruen (D), who refused. Gruen (P) sued, contending a valid *inter vivos* gift had been made. His stepmother defended, contending no valid gift could be made if the donor retained a life estate and no physical delivery was made during life. The trial court held against Gruen (P), while the appellate court reversed. Mrs. Gruen (D) appealed.

ISSUE: May a valid *inter vivos* gift of chattel be made where the donor reserves a life estate and the donee does not take physical possession?

HOLDING AND DECISION: (Simons, J.) Yes. A valid *inter vivos* gift of chattel may be made where the donor reserves a life estate and the donee never takes physical possession until after the donor's death. In this case, donative intent was established constructively through the document of transfer, the letter. Acceptance is implied because the painting had value. Thus, a valid gift was made. Affirmed.

ANALYSIS

Various estates in chattel can be created just as various estates in land are. The property in this case happened to be personal rather than real, yet the creation of a remainder interest was valid. It is clear the elder Mr. Gruen intended to make a current transfer of such interest, while retaining a possessory interest.

Quicknotes

CHATTEL An article of personal property, as distinguished from real property; a thing personal and moveable.

DONATIVE INTENT Donor's intent to make a gift.

GIFT *INTER VIVOS* A gift that is made, and is to take effect, while the parties are living.

REMAINDER INTEREST An interest in land that remains after the termination of the immediately preceding estate.

CHAPTER 3

Possessory Estates

Quick Reference Rules of Law

PAGE

1. **The Life Estate.** Unless the words and context of a will clearly evidence an intention to convey only a life estate it will be interpreted as conveying a fee estate. (White v. Brown) *22*

2. **The Life Estate.** A court may order the sale of property which is held subject to a future interest, but only if a sale is necessary for the best interests of both the life tenant and the remainderman. (Baker v. Weedon) *23*

3. **The Life Estate.** For an act to constitute waste in Ohio, the act must diminish the value of the property. (Woodrick v. Wood) *24*

4. **Defeasible Estates.** Only where the grantor creates a possibility of reverter will he or his successors become possessory owners of the property immediately upon the breaking of the condition. (Mahrenholz v. County Board of School Trustees) *25*

5. **Defeasible Estates.** A limitation on the use of property, although it might serve to impede its transfer, will not be void as a restraint against alienation. (Mountain Brow Lodge No. 82, Independent Order of Odd Fellows v. Toscano) *26*

6. **Defeasible Estates.** Where land, restricted by a deed, is taken by eminent domain, a court shall divide the eminent domain damages award between the owner of the fee and the holder of the right of reverter. (Ink v. City of Canton) *27*

White v. Brown

Beneficiary (P) v. Heir at law (D)

Tenn. Sup. Ct., 559 S.W.2d 938 (1977).

NATURE OF CASE: Appeal from a will interpretation.

FACT SUMMARY: The trial court held that Lide's will created a life estate in White (P) based on the fact the will specified the property was not to be sold.

RULE OF LAW

Unless the words and context of a will clearly evidence an intention to convey only a life estate it will be interpreted as conveying a fee estate.

FACTS: Lide died leaving a will that provided, "I wish Evelyn White to have my home to live in and not be sold." Lide's niece, Brown (D), claimed the will created a life estate and she obtained a remainder interest. White (P) sued to quiet title, contending the will created a fee estate. The trial court found for Brown (D), and White (P) appealed.

ISSUE: Will a will be interpreted as conveying a fee estate unless the words and context clearly evidence an intention to convey a lesser estate?

HOLDING AND DECISION: (Brock, J.) Yes. Unless the words and context of a will clearly evidence an intention to convey only a life estate, it will be interpreted as conveying a fee estate. Interpreting the will language presented here as creating only a life estate would create a partial intestacy. There is a general policy against creating intestacy where a reasonable alternative interpretation exists. Taking these two policies together, the trial court should have construed the will as creating a fee estate in White (P). Reversed and remanded.

DISSENT: (Harbison, J.) The express language of the will indicated an insurmountable constraint on alienation, indicating a clear intent to create less than a fee estate.

ANALYSIS

This case illustrates two common rules of construction to which courts resort in interpreting conveyances. The intent of the testator is derived from the entire document, and extrinsic evidence is admissible only under limited circumstances. Because of this restraint on extrinsic evidence of intent, courts must resort to the rules of construction previously noted. Where the instrument is drafted by a layperson, such rules of construction are essential to provide uniformity in construction.

Quicknotes

ALIENATION Conveyance or transfer of property.

EXTRINSIC EVIDENCE Evidence that is not contained within the text of a document or contract but which is derived from the parties' statements or the circumstances under which the agreement was made.

HOLOGRAPHIC WILL A will that is handwritten by the testator or testatrix.

INTESTACY To die without leaving a valid testamentary instrument.

LIFE ESTATE An interest in land measured by the life of the tenant or a third party.

QUITCLAIM A deed whereby the grantor conveys whatever interest he or she may have in the property without any warranties or covenants as to title.

TESTATRIX A woman who dies having drafted and executed a will or testament.

Baker v. Weedon

Life tenant (P) v. Remaindermen (D)

Miss. Sup. Ct., 262 So. 2d 641 (1972).

NATURE OF CASE: Sale of property bequeathed by will.

FACT SUMMARY: Weedon's will gave his property to his wife (P) for life, remainder to his grandchildren (D). The court was asked to permit sale of certain real property.

RULE OF LAW

A court may order the sale of property which is held subject to a future interest, but only if a sale is necessary for the best interests of both the life tenant and the remainderman.

FACTS: Weedon's will bequeathed all his property, both real and personal, to his third wife, Anna (P), for life. The remainder interest was willed to Anna's (P) children, if any, with Weedon's grandchildren (D) designated as beneficiaries in the event that Anna (P) died without issue. Weedon expressly failed to provide for his own children by a previous marriage, none of whom had enjoyed a happy relationship with him. Weedon died in 1932, and Anna (P) continued to live on a farm which he had bequeathed to her. Anna (P) remarried, but this second union, although it lasted for 20 years, resulted in no children. In 1964, the Mississippi State Highway Department (the Department) sought a right-of-way through the farm occupied by Anna (P). The Department contacted Weedon's surviving grandchildren (D), who thus became aware, for the first time, of their interests as remaindermen. Anna (P) was by now aged and destitute, and the grandchildren (D) willingly agreed to let Anna (P) receive a substantial proportion of the amount paid by the Department for the right-of-way. Anna (P) then sought an order permitting her to sell all of part of the farm property, contending that such a sale was necessary for her support. Since the property, although of negligible value for agricultural purposes, was of substantial and rapidly increasing worth as a commercial site, Weedon's grandchildren (D) opposed its sale. The chancellor, noting Anna's (P) age and that the property was of little value as agricultural property, approved its sale. The grandchildren (D) then appealed, challenging the right of the court to order the sale of property in which they held a future interest.

ISSUE: May a court order the sale of property which is encumbered by a future interest?

HOLDING AND DECISION: (Patterson, J.) Yes. A court may order the sale of property which is held subject to a future interest, but only if a sale is necessary for the best interests of both the life tenant and the remainderman. In this case, the farm property is increasing in value and a significant financial loss to the remaindermen would result from the premature sale of the entire tract of land. This action should, therefore, be remanded so that the chancery court may entertain a motion by Anna Weedon (P) to sell only enough of the property to provide adequate support for her, unless a satisfactory compromise can be reached by all the interested parties. Reversed and remanded.

ANALYSIS

When property which is subject to a future interest is constantly diminishing in worth, most courts will consider permitting its sale according to the doctrine of ameliorative (or ameliorating) waste. The concept of ameliorative waste presumes that a decline in the value of a property will eventually prove detrimental to the best interests of the remaindermen as well as the life tenants. However, before the doctrine will be applied, most courts require that the property be demonstrated to be worthless, or at least of only negligible value, for any purpose.

Quicknotes

AMELIORATIVE WASTE An unauthorized change in a physical structure which, though technically "waste," in fact increases the value of the land.

CONTINGENT REMAINDERMAN One who has an interest in property to commence upon the termination of a present possessory interest and subject to a condition precedent.

DECREE PRO CONFESSO A decree founded upon a bill in equity to which the defendant fails to answer.

ECONOMIC WASTE An act done by someone in lawful possession of an interest in land, causing injury to other estate holders in the same property, that diminishes the value of the mineral resources that may be produced from the property.

FUTURE INTEREST An interest in property the right to possession or enjoyment of which is to take place at sometime in the future.

Woodrick v. Wood

Daughter (P) v. Mother (D)

1994 WL 236287 (Ohio App. 1994).

NATURE OF CASE: Appeal from decision denying plaintiff's motion for injunction.

FACT SUMMARY: Wood (D) was the life tenant of a piece of property in which Woodrick (P) held a 25 percent remainder interest. Wood (D) sought to raze a barn on the property and Woodrick (P) moved to enjoin her.

RULE OF LAW

For an act to constitute waste in Ohio, the act must diminish the value of the property.

FACTS: A barn sits atop two contiguous parcels of land, lots 105 and 106. Wood (D) has a life estate and 75 percent remainder in lot 105. Woodrick (P) has a 25 percent remainder in lot 105. Wood (D) and Woodrick's (P) brother own lot 106. Woodrick (P) has no interest in lot 106. Wood (D) sought to raze a decaying barn on the two parcels. Woodrick (P) moved to enjoin the action on the grounds the act would constitute waste under the common law. Wood (D) opposed the motion because the removal of the barn would actually increase the property value of the land. The trial court denied Woodrick's (P) motion, but ordered Wood (D) to pay Woodrick (P) $3,200, the value of the barn. Woodrick (P) appealed.

ISSUE: For an act to constitute waste in Ohio, must the act diminish the value of the property?

HOLDING AND DECISION: (Blackmon, J.) Yes. For an act to constitute waste in Ohio, the act must diminish the value of the property. Waste is the abuse or harm to property by one in possession. At common law, any act that altered the leased premises constituted waste, whether or not the act was beneficial or detrimental to the remainder interests in the property. Ohio never fully adopted the common law rule. Rather, for an act to constitute actionable waste, "substantial pecuniary damage to the reversion should be required." In this matter, there was valid evidence the removal of the barn would increase the value of the property. Therefore, there can be no action for waste. The lower court's decision to grant Woodrick (P) $3,200 for the value of the barn is a fair resolution of the matter. Affirmed.

ANALYSIS

This case is a good example of the modern concept of waste. Only those actions that harm or decrease the value of the land will provide grounds for an action of waste against the life tenant in possession. At common law, any alteration of the land by the life tenant would satisfy the definition of waste.

Quicknotes

REMAINDER BENEFICIARY A person who is to receive property that is held in trust after the termination of a preceding income interest.

REMAINDER INTEREST An interest in land that remains after the termination of the immediately preceding estate.

WASTE The mistreatment of another's property by someone in lawful possession.

Mahrenholz v. County Board of School Trustees

Possibility-of-reverter holder (P) v. Grantee (D)

Ill. Ct. App., 93 Ill. App. 3d 366, 417 N.E.2d 138 (1981).

NATURE OF CASE: Appeal from dismissal of action to quiet title.

FACT SUMMARY: Mahrenholz (P) contended he obtained a possessory interest in land when the School District (D) ceased using the property for classes, allegedly breaching a deed restriction.

RULE OF LAW

Only where the grantor creates a possibility of reverter will he or his successors become possessory owners of the property immediately upon the breaking of the condition.

FACTS: Mahrenholz (P) sued to quiet title to land deeded to the School District (D) "for school purposes." The land grant specifically stated that "this land to be used for school purpose only; otherwise to revert to Grantors herein." The heir of the grantors subsequently conveyed his interest in the land to Mahrenholz's (P) predecessor in interest. Mahrenholz (P) contended that the original conveyance created a fee simple determinable which gave rise to a possibility of reverter. This allowed him to become the possessory owner of the property by operation of law when the site ceased being used to hold classes. The trial court held that the conveyance created a fee simple subject to a condition subsequent and because the heir had not affirmatively enforced his right of re-entry, he had no possessory interest to convey. Mahrenholz (P) appealed.

ISSUE: Will a grantor automatically obtain possessory ownership of the estate only where the grant created a possibility of reverter?

HOLDING AND DECISION: (Jones, J.) Yes. Only where the grantor creates a possibility of reverter will he or his successors become possessory owners immediately upon the breach of the deed restriction. A grant of use for an exclusive purpose followed by an express provision for reverter creates a fee simple determinable and a possibility of reverter. The deed in this case created such use and therefore the heir held a possibility of reverter. His conveyance to Mahrenholz's (P) predecessor conveyed this interest which became possessory, if at all, when the land was no longer used for classes. Therefore, the trial court erred in dismissing the action. Reversed and remanded.

ANALYSIS

This case illustrates the difference in theory between the possibility of reverter created by a fee simple determinable and the right of re-entry created by a fee simple subject to a condition subsequent. In the former, the breach of condition precedent automatically terminates the possessory estate. In the latter, termination is merely a right which must be exercised by the holder. This is purely an academic distinction as any possessory interest will have to be formally terminated before the estate holder will abandon the estate.

Quicknotes

DETERMINABLE FEE An interest in property that may last forever or until the happening of a specified event.

FEE SIMPLE DEFEASIBLE ESTATE A fee simple interest in land that is subject to being terminated upon the happening of a future event.

FEE SIMPLE SUBJECT TO A CONDITION SUBSEQUENT An estate in land that represents total ownership, except that it is capable of being defeated upon the occurrence or nonoccurrence of a specified condition.

QUIET TITLE Equitable action to resolve conflicting claims to an interest in real property.

REVERSIONARY INTEREST An interest retained by a grantor of property in the land transferred, which is created when the owner conveys less of an interest than he or she owns and which returns to the grantor upon the termination of the conveyed estate.

RIGHT OF REENTRY An interest in property reserved in the conveyance of a fee that gives the holder the right to resume possession of property upon the happening of a condition subsequent.

Mountain Brow Lodge No. 82, Independent Order of Odd Fellows v. Toscano

Grantee (P) v. Possibility-of-reverter holders (D)

Cal. Ct. App., Fifth District, 64 Cal. Rptr. 816 (1967).

NATURE OF CASE: Appeal from denial of order to quiet title.

FACT SUMMARY: Mountain Brow Lodge (P) sought to have a clause in a gift deed declared void as a restraint on alienation, thereby quieting its title in the property.

RULE OF LAW

A limitation on the use of property, although it might serve to impede its transfer, will not be void as a restraint against alienation.

FACTS: Mountain Brow Lodge (Lodge) (P) acquired real property by a gift deed from Toscano. Included in the deed was a clause which purportedly restricted the use and ownership of the property to the Lodge (P). Upon violation of the restriction, the property was to revert to Toscano's estate (D). The Lodge (P) sought a court ruling that the restrictive condition was void as a restraint against alienation and that the Lodge (P) therefore owned the property outright. The trial court held that the conditions were not void and refused to quiet title. The Lodge (P) appealed.

ISSUE: Is a limitation on the use of property which also has the effect of restricting its transfer void as a restraint against alienation?

HOLDING AND DECISION: (Gargano, J.) No. Courts in this jurisdiction and many others have long recognized that limitations on the use of property, although they might also serve to impede its transfer, will not be void as a restraint against alienation. Thus, the part of the clause which limits the use of the property to Lodge (P) purposes is valid. However, the language which expressly restricts the sale or transfer of the property at issue will be stricken as an impermissible restraint against alienation. Affirmed as modified.

DISSENT: (Stone, J.) The restriction on use which appears in the deed is for all practical purposes a restraint against alienation and should be voided. Therefore the Lodge's (P) title should be quieted.

ANALYSIS

Other jurisdictions have found that a use restriction which effectively serves to limit the alienation of the property to a small group of people is void as an impermissible indirect restriction on alienation. See, e.g., *Falls City v. Missouri Pacific Railway So.,* 453 F.2d. 771 (8th Cir. 1971). In *Falls City,* the court framed the test as whether the imposed condition materially and adversely affected the marketability of the property. If it did, then it was an invalid limitation and the fee simple determinable was transmuted into a fee simple absolute.

Quicknotes

ALIENATION Conveyance or transfer of property.

HABENDUM CLAUSE A clause contained in a deed that specifies the parties to the transaction and defines the interest in land to be conveyed.

QUIET TITLE Equitable action to resolve conflicting claims to an interest in real property.

RESTRAINT AGAINST ALIENATION A provision restricting the transferee's ability to convey interests in the conveyed property.

RESTRICTIVE CONDITION A promise contained in a deed to limit the uses to which the property will be made.

USE RESTRICTION A restriction on the right to utilize one's personal or real property.

Ink v. City of Canton

Individuals (P) v. City (D)

212 N.E.2d 574 (Ohio 1965).

NATURE OF CASE: Plaintiff's appeal of lower court decisions in favor of defendant.

FACT SUMMARY: Harry Ink granted the City of Canton (the City) (D) 33 acres of land to be used only as a public park, with his heirs holding a right of reverter. The state of Ohio took a large portion of the land by eminent domain and a lower court granted all of the damages to Canton (D).

RULE OF LAW

Where land, restricted by a deed, is taken by eminent domain, a court shall divide the eminent domain damages award between the owner of the fee and the holder of the right of reverter.

FACTS: Harry Ink granted the City (D) 33 acres of land. The deed stated that the City (D) could only use the land for a public park. If the city used the land otherwise, the land would revert to Mr. Ink's heirs (P). The state of Ohio then took all but six acres of the land for a highway project. The courts below awarded all of the eminent domain damages, $130,822, to the City (D). The heirs (P) appeal.

ISSUE: When land, restricted by a deed, is taken by eminent domain, must a court divide the eminent domain damages award between the owner of the fee and the holder of the right of reverter?

HOLDING AND DECISION: (Taft, C.J.) Yes. When land, restricted by a deed, is taken by eminent domain, a court shall divide the eminent domain damages award between the owner of the fee and the holder of the right of reverter. The common law rule was that all eminent domain damages would go to the grantee of the deed, here, the City (D). The holder of the reverter would receive nothing. Many jurisdictions have refused to apply this harsh rule. Instead, Ohio has previously recognized that such a scenario would result in a significant windfall to the grantee of the restricted deed, who paid nothing for the land. In this matter, we hold that the eminent domain action does not force a reversion of the remaining property back to Mr. Ink's heirs (P). However, the City (D) must use the damages award solely for maintenance of the remaining six acres of the park. In the event that the $130,822 exceeds the city's maintenance costs, the city should turn that excess over to the holders of the right of reverter. Reversed.

ANALYSIS

Most jurisdictions respond to this scenario in similar fashions, eschewing the common law rule in favor of a more equitable result. One other factor the court relied upon was the fiduciary duty the City (D) owed the plaintiffs to maintain the park. Accordingly, the City (D) had to use the damages award for the park's benefit.

Quicknotes

EMINENT DOMAIN The governmental power to take private property for public use so long as just compensation is paid therefor.

REVERTER A reversionary interest referring to an interest in land that remains in the grantor until the happening of a condition precedent.

CHAPTER 4

Future Interests

Quick Reference Rules of Law

PAGE

1. **The Trust.** A founder of a trust may lawfully restrict the grantee's power of anticipatory alienation of the trust benefits and bar creditors from reaching the trust funds. (Broadway National Bank v. Adams) *30*

2. **The Rule Against Perpetuities–The Common Law Rule.** Commercial option agreements are not exempted from the Rule Against Perpetuities. (The Symphony Space, Inc. v. Pergola Properties, Inc.) *31*

Broadway National Bank v. Adams

Creditor (P) v. Debtor (D)

133 Mass. 170 (1882).

NATURE OF CASE: Appellate court's consideration of plaintiff's bill in equity.

FACT SUMMARY: Adams (D) owed Broadway National Bank (Broadway) (P) money. Broadway (P) sought to reach and apply a portion of a trust that Adams's (D) brother created for Adams's (D) benefit.

RULE OF LAW

A founder of a trust may lawfully restrict the grantee's power of anticipatory alienation of the trust benefits and bar creditors from reaching the trust funds.

FACTS: Adams (D) owed Broadway (P) money. Adams's (D) brother created a lifetime trust for Adams, with the provision that such funds may not be alienated to satisfy a debt. Adams would receive semi-annual payments from the trust only. Broadway (P) filed this bill in equity to reach the trust funds to satisfy the debt.

ISSUE: May a founder of a trust lawfully restrict the grantee's power of anticipatory alienation of the trust benefits and bar creditors from reaching the trust funds?

HOLDING AND DECISION: (Morton, C.J.) Yes. A founder of a trust may lawfully restrict the grantee's power of anticipatory alienation of the trust benefits and bar creditors from reaching the trust funds. The common law rule was that one could not attach to a grant or transfer of property a restriction that the property not be alienated. Some courts in England and in our own country have applied this rule to similar circumstances. However, we hold the rule does not apply for a lifetime trust created by one for the benefit of another where the grantor restricts the grantee's ability to alienate the trust funds. In this matter, Adams's (D) brother, as the owner of the property in question, has the right to dispose of the property in any manner he sees fit. His clear intention was not to give Adams (D) complete control of the trust funds, but only semi-annual payments. The court should give effect to his intention unless those intentions run afoul of public policy. Broadway (P) argues the provision may defraud creditors and induce them to give credit to Adams (D) based on his apparent wealth. However, the creditors, by their due diligence, may ascertain the precise nature of his estate prior to giving credit. Whether a man may transfer funds into a trust for his own benefit, simply to place funds beyond the reach of creditors, is a different question that we do not answer today. Broadway's (P) bill in equity is dismissed.

ANALYSIS

This case is still good law and is a seminal case regarding the creation of spendthrift trusts. A spendthrift trust is created with limitations on the grantee's access to the trust funds. The grantee's creditors may not reach the trust funds until the funds are distributed from the trust to the grantee. The trust document requires a specific provision denoting such limitations.

Quicknotes

BILL IN EQUITY First pleading in a lawsuit in which a plaintiff seeks equitable remedies.

SPENDTHRIFT PROVISION A provision in a trust providing for the beneficiary's support, but with restrictions imposed so as to safeguard against the beneficiary's alienation of his interest therein.

SPENDTHRIFT TRUST A trust formed for the beneficiary's support, but with restrictions imposed so as to safeguard against the beneficiary's alienation of his interest therein.

The Symphony Space, Inc. v. Pergola Properties, Inc.

Buyer (P) v. Seller (D)

N.Y. Ct. App., 88 N.Y.2d 466, 669 N.E.2d 799, 646 N.Y.S.2d 641 (1996).

NATURE OF CASE: Suit for declaratory judgment.

FACT SUMMARY: Symphony Space, Inc. (Symphony) (P) sought a declaratory judgment that an option clause in its agreement to purchase property from Broadwest Realty Corp. (Broadway) was unenforceable in violation of the Rule Against Perpetuities.

RULE OF LAW

Commercial option agreements are not exempted from the Rule Against Perpetuities.

FACTS: Symphony (P), a nonprofit organization dedicated to the arts, leased a theatre from Broadwest. Broadwest sold the building to Symphony (P) and leased back the income producing property, minus the theatre, for one year. The purpose of the agreement was to provide Symphony (P) with a tax exemption. The agreement also contained an option clause allowing Broadwest to purchase the property during specified periods. Pergola Properties, Inc. (Pergola) (D), a nominee of Broadwest, notified Symphony (P) of its intent to exercise the option, and Symphony (P) brought suit seeking a declaratory judgment that the option violated New York's Rule Against Perpetuities. The Appellate Division held the clause unenforceable.

ISSUE: Are commercial option agreements exempted from the Rule Against Perpetuities?

HOLDING AND DECISION: (Kaye, C.J.) No. Commercial option agreements are not exempted from the Rule Against Perpetuities. Options to purchase are to be treated differently than preemptive rights, which impede transferability only minimally in contrast to purchase options, which vest substantial control over the alienability of the property upon the option holder. Only where the preemptive right arises in a governmental or commercial agreement is the minor restraint offset by the holder's incentive to improve the property. The option agreement here creates the type of control over the transferability over property that the rule against remote vesting has sought to prevent. An option "appurtenant" to purchase land that originates in a lease provision that is not exercisable after the expiration of the lease, and is incapable of separation from the lease agreement, is still generally valid even though the holder's interest may vest beyond the perpetuities period. Here the option does not qualify as an option appurtenant, since it significantly deters the development of the property. Affirmed.

ANALYSIS

The exception to the Rule Against Perpetuities for preemptive rights was developed in order to provide an incentive for the development of property. At common law, options to purchase land were subject to the rule, since they worked as a disincentive to such development. Although such options are typically found in commercial contracts, they are still subject to the rule against remote vesting.

Quicknotes

FREE ALIENABILITY Unrestricted transferability.

OPTION A contract pursuant to which a seller agrees that property will be available for the buyer to purchase at a specified price and within a certain time period.

RULE AGAINST PERPETUITIES The doctrine that a future interest that is incapable of vesting within twenty-one years of lives in being at the time it is created is immediately void.

VESTING The attaining of the right to pension or other employer-contribution benefits when the employee satisfies the minimum requirements necessary in order to be entitled to the receipt of such benefits in the future.

CHAPTER 5

Co-ownership and Marital Interests

Quick Reference Rules of Law

PAGE

1. **Severance of Joint Tenancies.** A joint tenancy may be terminated by the conveyance by one joint tenant of his interest in the joint tenancy property to himself. (Riddle v. Harmon) *34*
2. **Severance of Joint Tenancies.** A mortgage on a joint tenant's interest does not survive the mortgagor. (Harms v. Sprague) *35*
3. **Relations among Concurrent Owners–Partition.** Partition sales are employed only where partition in kind is unworkable. (Delfino v. Vealencis) *36*
4. **Sharing the Benefits and Burdens of Co-ownership.** Absent an owner physically barring a cotenant from entry upon the owned premises, that owner is not liable to the cotenant for rent. (Spiller v. Mackereth) *37*
5. **Sharing the Benefits and Burdens of Co-ownership.** The act of one joint tenant without express or implied authority from, or consent of, his cotenant cannot bind or prejudicially affect the rights of that cotenant; but, a lease to all of the joint property by one joint tenant is not a nullity but rather is valid to the extent of his interest in the joint property. (Swartzbaugh v. Sampson) *38*
6. **During Marriage.** Tenancy-by-the-entirety property may not be reached by the separate creditors of either spouse. (Sawada v. Endo) *40*
7. **Termination of Marriage by Divorce.** An educational degree cannot be marital property subject to division upon divorce. (In re Marriage of Graham) *41*
8. **Termination of Marriage by Divorce.** Celebrity status with the accompanying economic opportunities may be a marital asset subject to equitable dissolution. (Elkus v. Elkus) *42*
9. **Rights of Domestic Partners.** Iowa's marriage statute, defining marriage as between one man and one woman, violates the equal protection clause of the Iowa constitution. (Varnum v. Brien) *43*

Riddle v. Harmon

Joint tenant (P) v. Estate executrix (D)

Cal. App., First District, 162 Cal. Rptr. 530 (1980).

NATURE OF CASE: Appeal from summary judgment upholding joint tenancy and quieting title.

FACT SUMMARY: **Riddle (P) sought to enforce a joint tenancy right of survivorship against Harmon (D), the executrix of his wife's estate, after the wife had deeded her one-half joint tenancy interest in the Riddle property to herself in order to sever and terminate Riddle's (P) right to succeed to the whole.**

RULE OF LAW

A joint tenancy may be terminated by the conveyance by one joint tenant of his interest in the joint tenancy property to himself.

FACTS: Riddle's (P) wife, the decedent, owned certain real property in joint tenancy with Riddle (P). When she was planning her estate, she did not want her interest in the parcel to pass to Riddle (P). Her attorney advised her to terminate the joint tenancy by granting herself an undivided one-half interest in the property, making her a tenant in common. A grant deed was drawn up to that effect, and a will devising her tenancy in common to a third party was executed. Riddle (P), upon his wife's death, challenged her estate plan, and the trial court quieted title in him. Harmon (D), the wife's executrix, appealed.

ISSUE: May a joint tenancy be terminated by the conveyance by one joint tenant of his interest in the joint tenancy property to himself?

HOLDING AND DECISION: (Poche, J.) Yes. A joint tenancy may be terminated by the conveyance by one joint tenant of his interest in the joint tenancy property to himself. At common law, the creation of joint tenancy required the "four unities": interest, time, title, and possession. This required that both tenants acquire their interest at the same moment, which in turn required that one party holding the whole had to convey his interest to a third person ("straw man") who would convey to the joint tenants in order for such party to create a joint tenancy between himself and another. Modern law has abandoned this obsolete requirement as to creation. There is little virtue in adhering to cumbersome feudal law requirements. One joint tenant may unilaterally sever the joint tenancy without the use of an intermediary device. A "straw man" is not necessary. Reversed.

ANALYSIS

The purchaser of an interest in property from a joint tenant becomes a tenant in common with the other joint tenants, who remain joint tenants as to each other only. A minority of jurisdictions not requiring reconveyance to a straw man for severance permit termination of a joint tenancy by the filing of a declaration of an intention to do so, eliminating even the fiction of having to convey to sever.

Quicknotes

FOUR UNITIES The four unities that must be present in order for a joint tenancy to be formed, including unity of interest, possession, time, and title.

GRANT DEED A deed conveying an interest in real or personal property.

JOINT TENANCY An interest in property whereby a single interest is owned by two or more persons and created by a single instrument; joint tenants possess equal interests in the use of the entire property, and the last survivor is entitled to absolute ownership.

LIVERY OF SEISIN A ceremony in which an interest in land is formally delivered usually by delivering a piece of earth.

QUIET TITLE Equitable action to resolve conflicting claims to an interest in real property.

SEVERANCE Dividing or separating.

STRAW MAN A third party to whom a transfer of property is made in order to effectuate a transaction that may not otherwise be allowed.

TENANCY IN COMMON An interest in property held by two or more people, each with equal right to its use and possession; interests may be partitioned, sold, conveyed, or devised.

Harms v. Sprague

Joint tenant (P) v. Mortgage assignee (D)

Ill. Sup. Ct., 105 Ill. 2d 215, 473 N.E.2d 930 (1984).

NATURE OF CASE: Appeal of reversal of court order quieting title.

FACT SUMMARY: John Harms, deceased former joint tenant in property with William Harms (P) had executed a mortgage in favor of the predecessor in interest of Sprague (D) who claimed the mortgage survived John.

RULE OF LAW

A mortgage on a joint tenant's interest does not survive the mortgagor.

FACTS: William (P) and John Harms owned property in joint tenancy. John executed a mortgage favoring Simmons, who later assigned his interest to Sprague (D). After John died, William (P) contended that the mortgage had died with John and brought an action to quiet title. The trial court held that Sprague's (D) mortgage survived John's death and entered judgment in favor of Sprague (D). The appellate court reversed. Sprague (D) appealed.

ISSUE: Does a mortgage on a joint tenant's interest survive the mortgagor?

HOLDING AND DECISION: (Moran, J.) No. A mortgage on a joint tenant's interest does not survive the mortgagor. One requirement for joint tenancy is a unity of title. If a mortgage constituted a change in title, it would destroy this unity. However, this state recognizes that a mortgage will not constitute a change of title until foreclosure plus the running of any redemption period. Since a mortgage does not sever a joint tenancy, the entire estate of the decedent joint tenant passes to the survivor. This effects a nullification of any liens thereon. For this reason, Sprague's (D) interest was extinguished upon John's death. Affirmed.

ANALYSIS

An issue regarding both real property law and secured transaction law is the "lien" vs. "title" theories. As discussed in the case, mortgages have been seen as both transfers of title and mere encumbrances. It seems that most jurisdictions adhere to the lien theory.

Quicknotes

JOINT TENANCY An interest in property whereby a single interest is owned by two or more persons and created by a single instrument; joint tenants possess equal interests in the use of the entire property, and the last survivor is entitled to absolute ownership.

LIEN A claim against the property of another in order to secure the payment of a debt.

MORTGAGE An interest in land created by a written instrument providing security for the payment of a debt or the performance of a duty.

QUIET TITLE Equitable action to resolve conflicting claims to an interest in real property.

REDEMPTION PERIOD The period during which a mortgagor has the right to reclaim forfeited property, following a default on mortgage payments, by the payment of the mortgage debt and any other interest, fees, and costs.

UNITY OF TITLE Requirement that cotenants in a joint tenancy or tenancy by the entirety obtain their interest in the property under the same legal title.

Delfino v. Vealencis

Tenant in common (P) v. Cotenant (D)

Conn. Sup. Ct., 181 Conn. 533, 436 A.2d 27 (1980).

NATURE OF CASE: Appeal from judicially ordered partition sale.

FACT SUMMARY: The trial court held the rights of the parties would be best protected by a partition sale rather than a partition in kind.

RULE OF LAW

Partition sales are employed only where partition in kind is unworkable.

FACTS: The Delfinos (P) owned an undivided 99/144 interest in land, in which Vealencis (D) owned an undivided 45/144 interest. The property was held as a tenancy in common. Delfino (P) wanted to develop residential housing on the tract and sought a partition sale. Vealencis (D) defended, contending partition in kind. She used her portion of the property for the operation of a rubbish removal business. The court held the partition in kind was unavailable and a partition sale was necessary. Vealencis (D) appealed, contending the property, rectangular in shape and having only three cotenants, could easily be subjected to partition in kind.

ISSUE: Are partition sales employed only where partition in kind is unworkable?

HOLDING AND DECISION: (Healey, J.) Yes. Partition sales are employed only where partition in kind is unavailable. Partition sales should be employed only in extraordinary circumstances, as the forced sale of a party's interest should be avoided. In this case, the limited number of competing interests, and the relative ease of division makes partition in kind very workable. Reversed and remanded.

ANALYSIS

The court rejected the proposition that the property could not be used jointly. The trial court had found that the use for residential property was mutually exclusive with use as rubbish removal business. The shape of the property allowed for easy partition.

Quicknotes

PARTITION IN KIND A separation of undivided interests in land so that the parties may possess their interests separately.

PARTITION SALE A court-ordered sale of property held in joint tenancy, as a cotenant or in tenancy by the entirety, if the property is incapable of being divided; the income is distributed in proportion to the parties' interests in the sold property.

Spiller v. Mackereth

Cotenant in possession (D) v. Tenant in common (P)

Ala. Sup. Ct., 334 So. 2d 859 (1976).

NATURE OF CASE: Appeal from judgment awarding damages for back rent.

FACT SUMMARY: Spiller (D), cotenant of a warehouse with Mackereth (D), ignored her demand that he cease using the whole premises or pay her rent.

RULE OF LAW

Absent an owner physically barring a cotenant from entry upon the owned premises, that owner is not liable to the cotenant for rent.

FACTS: Spiller (D) and Mackereth (P) were tenants in common of a warehouse. When their tenant vacated, Spiller (D) began using the entire warehouse as a storage facility. Mackereth (P) demanded that he either vacate half the premises or pay rent. He ignored the demand. Mackereth (P) sued for rent. A trial court awarded $2,100 back rent. Spiller (D) appealed.

ISSUE: Absent an owner physically barring a cotenant from entry upon the owned premises, is that owner liable to the cotenant for rent?

HOLDING AND DECISION: (Jones, J.) No. Absent an owner physically barring a cotenant from entry upon the owned premises, the owner is not liable to the cotenant for rent. As a general rule, a cotenant has the full right to use the premises and cannot be liable to cotenants for rent. The only exception to this occurs when there is an "ouster." For there to be an ouster, a cotenant must physically bar the other cotenant from entry. Merely ignoring an order to partially vacate does not constitute ouster. Here, there is no evidence that Spiller (D) physically barred Mackereth (P) from entry, so there was no ouster. Reversed.

ANALYSIS

Ouster can exist in different degrees. When it is not done under a claim of absolute ownership, it can support an action for back rent. When done under a claim of such ownership, it can give rise to adverse possession, if the other elements required therefor are present.

Quicknotes

ABSOLUTE OWNERSHIP Ownership of property that exists exclusively to one party.

ADVERSE POSSESSION A means of acquiring title to real property by remaining in actual, open, continuous, exclusive possession of property for the statutory period.

OUSTER The unlawful dispossession of a party lawfully entitled to possession of real property.

PER MY ET PER TOUT By half and by whole; refers to the holding of interests in a joint tenancy whereby a joint tenant is entitled to the whole property for purposes of survivorship and to his or her share for purposes of alienation.

Swartzbaugh v. Sampson

Joint tenant (P) v. Cotenant/lessor (D) and lessee (D)

Cal. App., Fourth District, 11 Cal. App. 2d 451, 54 P.2d 73 (1936).

NATURE OF CASE: Action to cancel a lease made by a co-joint tenant with a third party.

FACT SUMMARY: Mrs. Swartzbaugh (P) refused to agree to a lease between Sampson (D) and Mr. Swartzbaugh (D), her husband, for land held by the Swartzbaughs in joint tenancy.

RULE OF LAW

The act of one joint tenant without express or implied authority from, or consent of, his cotenant cannot bind or prejudicially affect the rights of that cotenant; but, a lease to all of the joint property by one joint tenant is not a nullity but rather is valid to the extent of his interest in the joint property.

FACTS: Mrs. Swartzbaugh (P) and Mr. Swartzbaugh (D) had acquired title to certain real property as joint tenants. (They are husband and wife.) Subsequently, Mr. Swartzbaugh (D) and Sampson (D) executed two leases for parcels of this property. At all times however, Mrs. Swartzbaugh (P) objected to the lease, refused to participate in it, and made these facts well known to both Mr. Swartzbaugh (D) and Sampson (D). At no time has she received any rent from this lease. She sued to cancel the lease, claiming it was a total nullity without her participation as a joint tenant. From a nonsuit decision, she appealed.

ISSUE: Can one joint tenant who has not joined in leases executed by her cotenant and a third party maintain an action to cancel the leases where the third party is in exclusive possession of the leased property?

HOLDING AND DECISION: (Marks, J.) No. The act of one joint tenant without express or implied authority from, or consent of, his cotenant cannot bind or prejudicially affect the rights of that cotenant; but, a lease of all of the joint property by one joint tenant is not a nullity but rather is valid to the extent of his interest in the joint property. Each joint tenant has an equal right to possession of the fee involved. As such, a joint tenant is free to convey his interest in the property by lease or other transfer free of any challenge by his cotenant. While it is true that he may owe an accounting to his cotenant for any rents received from third parties from such a lease, and that such cotenant may bring an action in ejectment to be allowed to re-enter and jointly occupy the fee, the lease or transfer itself is not challengeable. Here, there is no evidence that either Sampson (D) or Mr. Swartzbaugh (D) ever attempted to interfere with Mrs. Swartzbaugh's (P) enjoyment of her interest. While she may be entitled to an accounting for rents received, she has no right to challenge the lease itself. The nonsuit was properly granted. Affirmed.

ANALYSIS

This case points up the general rule that a joint tenancy cannot be severed by the unilateral transfer of one joint tenant's interest to a third party. An estate in joint tenancy may be destroyed by voluntary or involuntary acts of all joint tenants which destroy one of the necessary unities of joint tenancy (interest, time, title, and possession) but only in extraordinary cases (adverse possession) may it be done unilaterally. Note further that even when a unilateral act results in a transfer of a joint tenant's interest (as here), it will not result in any partition of property which the other cotenant must recognize. Here, therefore, the leasing of certain parts of property does not in any way divide or affect the cotenants' undivided cotenant interest in the property.

Quicknotes

ACCOUNTING The evaluation of assets for the purpose of assigning relative interests.

CO-JOINT TENANT Two or more persons who own a single interest in property which is created by a single instrument; joint tenants possess equal interests in the use of the entire property and the last survivor is entitled to absolute ownership.

EJECTMENT An action to oust someone in unlawful possession of real property and to restore possession to the party lawfully entitled to it.

EXPRESS AUTHORITY Authority that is delegated pursuant to expressly stated words.

FOUR UNITIES The four unities that must be present in order for a joint tenancy to be formed, including unity of interest, possession, time, and title.

IMPLIED AUTHORITY Inferred power granted to an agent to act on behalf of the principal in order to effectuate the principal's objective.

JOINT TENANCY An interest in property whereby a single interest is owned by two or more persons and created by a single instrument; joint tenants possess equal interests in the use of the entire property, and the last survivor is entitled to absolute ownership.

MOIETY A one-half interest.

Continued on next page.

NONSUIT Judgment against a party who fails to make out a case.

NULLITY An act having no legal effect.

PRESCRIPTION The acquisition of an easement in or on another's property as a result of continuous use for the statutory period.

Sawada v. Endo

Judgment creditors (P) v. Judgment debtor (D)

Haw. Sup. Ct., 57 Hawaii 608, 561 P.2d 1291 (1977).

NATURE OF CASE: Action to set aside conveyance of real property.

FACT SUMMARY: Endo (D) and his wife conveyed tenancy-by-the-entirety property to their son after Endo (D) had been sued.

RULE OF LAW

Tenancy-by-the-entirety property may not be reached by the separate creditors of either spouse.

FACTS: Endo (D), who had no liability insurance, severely injured Helen (P) and Masako Sawada (P). Suits for personal injuries were filed against Endo (D). Endo's (D) only real asset was real property held as a tenant by the entirety with his wife. This was conveyed to their son, for no consideration, shortly after the Sawadas (P) had filed suit. Endo (D) and his wife continued to live on the land even though they had not reserved an estate in it. The Sawadas (P) each recovered a judgment against Endo (D) but they were unable to satisfy it. The Sawadas (P) subsequently brought an action to set aside the conveyance of Endo's (D) property to the son, alleging that it was fraudulent. Endo's (D) wife had died prior to the action. Endo (D) alleged that the conveyance could not be deemed fraudulent because the separate creditor of either spouse may not reach property held as tenants by the entirety.

ISSUE: May the separate creditor of either spouse reach property held in tenancy by the entirety?

HOLDING AND DECISION: (Menor, J.) No. While this is a question of first impression, and there are four separate views, we hold that the separate creditors of either spouse cannot reach property held as a tenancy by the entirety. The other views are that: (1) the creditor may reach the entire property subject to the wife's contingent right of survivorship if the husband is the debtor; (2) the creditor may reach the property subject only to the other spouse's right of survivorship; and (3) the right of survivorship may be levied upon. Tenancy-by-the-entirety property is generally the family residence and public policy considerations of promoting family solidarity, as well as *stare decisis*, favor the result reached herein. Since the Sawadas (P) could not have reached the property, the conveyance to the son was not fraudulent. Affirmed.

DISSENT: (Kidwell, J.) Under the Married Women's Act there is equality between the spouses. On this basis, the court should choose to allow creditors of either spouse to reach their right of survivorship.

ANALYSIS

In *Hurd v. Hughes*, 12 Del. Ch. at 193, the court stated in support of its decision not to allow creditors of one spouse to reach tenancy-by-the-entirety property, "But creditors are not entitled to special consideration. If the debt arose prior to the creation of the estate, the property was not a basis of credit, and if the debt arose subsequently, the creditor presumably had notice of the characteristics of the estate which limited his right to reach the property."

Quicknotes

FRAUDULENT CONVEYANCE Conveyances made within one year of filing the bankruptcy petition with intent to defraud creditors and which may be voidable.

MARRIED WOMEN'S PROPERTY ACT Legislation which secured to women the separate and independent control of their property.

STARE DECISIS Doctrine whereby courts follow legal precedent unless there is good cause for departure.

TENANCY BY THE ENTIRETY The ownership of property by a husband and wife whereby they hold undivided interests in the property with right of survivorship.

In re Marriage of Graham

Wife (P) v. Husband with an educational degree (D)

Colo. Sup. Ct., 574 P.2d 75 (1978).

NATURE OF CASE: Appeal of ruling dividing property in marital dissolution.

FACT SUMMARY: Anne Graham (P) provided substantial support for Dennis Graham (D), her husband, while he attained an education leading to B.S. and M.B.A. degrees.

RULE OF LAW
An educational degree cannot be marital property subject to division upon divorce.

FACTS: During most of the marriage of Anne and Dennis Graham, Anne (P) provided financial support while Dennis (D) pursued an education that led to B.S. and M.B.A. degrees with lucrative earning potential. Not long after Dennis (D) had completed his education, the spouses separated and the marriage ended. In dividing marital assets, the trial court ruled that Anne (P) was entitled to an interest in Dennis' (D) degrees, and awarded her installment payments based on the estimated increased earning capacity of Dennis (D), who appealed. The court of appeals reversed, and Anne appealed.

ISSUE: Can an educational degree be marital property subject to division upon divorce?

HOLDING AND DECISION: (Lee, J.) No. An educational degree cannot be marital property subject to division upon divorce. There are limits on what can be considered "property." Property may be defined as "everything that has an exchangeable value or which goes to make up wealth or estate." A degree is not exchangeable and has no value on an open market and cannot be willed. It is simply an intellectual achievement that can assist in property acquisition, but is not property itself. While it can be taken into account in awarding support, it cannot be considered property. Affirmed.

DISSENT: (Carrigan, J.) It is not the degree itself, but the increased earning capacity upon which focus should be given. Since damages for lost earning capacity can be awarded, there is no reason that increased earning capacity cannot be divided.

ANALYSIS

Several other jurisdictions have considered this issue. The great majority have agreed with the court here. Some have seen fit to award the supporting spouse reimbursement under a variety of theories, such as return on investment.

Quicknotes

EQUITABLE Just; fair.

GOODWILL An intangible asset reflecting a corporation's favorability with the public and expectation of continued patronage.

MAINTENANCE The upkeep or preservation of property.

MARITAL DISSOLUTION Legal termination of the marital relationship.

MARITAL PROPERTY Property accumulated by a married couple during the term of their marriage.

Elkus v. Elkus

Opera star/wife (P) v. Manager/husband (D)

N.Y. App. Div., 169 A.D.2d 134, 572 N.Y.S.2d 901 (1991).

NATURE OF CASE: Appeal from order dividing marital property.

FACT SUMMARY: Elkus (P), an opera diva, contended that her artistic career was not a marital asset.

RULE OF LAW
Celebrity status with the accompanying economic opportunities may be a marital asset subject to equitable dissolution.

FACTS: Frederica Elkus (P) was a major opera star with the New York Metropolitan Opera Company. She had married in 1973, when her career was just beginning. Her husband, a voice coach, gave up his career to concentrate on coaching her, as well as taking the primary role in child-rearing. In 1989, Mrs. Elkus (P) sued for divorce. The trial court rejected Mr. Elkus's (D) contention that Mrs. Elkus's (P) celebrity status and career were marital assets and incorporated that holding into its property division award. Mr. Elkus (D) appealed.

ISSUE: May celebrity status with the accompanying economic opportunities, be a marital asset subject to equitable distribution?

HOLDING AND DECISION: (Rosenberger, J.) Yes. Celebrity status with the accompanying economic opportunities may be a marital asset subject to equitable dissolution. Section 236 of the New York Domestic Relations law broadly defines marital property acquired during a marriage, regardless of the form it takes. The law was intended to give effect to the notion that marriage is a joint economic enterprise and that both partners thereto are entitled to enjoy, upon dissolution, the fruits of their endeavor. Marital property may be any thing of value, even if it falls outside of traditional concepts of property. The New York Court of Appeals has already held that a medical license and practice acquired during a marriage may be a marital asset; the same analysis applies to a show business career. Here, Mrs. Elkus (P) rose to fame in some part due to the sacrifices made by Mr. Elkus (D), and her career may properly be considered a marital asset. Reversed and remanded.

ANALYSIS

Here, Mr. Elkus (D) took an active role in helping his wife's career, and his having a stake in that career comports with common notions of fairness. The decision does not seem to limit itself to such a situation, however. Its language would seem to make it applicable even when the claiming spouse did not actively contribute to the other spouse's career.

Quicknotes

CELEBRITY STATUS Any person who is generally known in the community.

EQUITABLE DISTRIBUTION The means by which a court distributes all assets acquired during a marriage by the spouses equitably upon dissolution.

MARITAL PROPERTY Property accumulated by a married couple during the term of their marriage.

Varnum v. Brien

Same-sex couples (P) v. State county (D)

763 N.W.2d 862 (Iowa 2009).

NATURE OF CASE: Appeal of lower court decision in favor of plaintiffs.

FACT SUMMARY: Polk County (D) in the state of Iowa denied marriage licenses to six same-sex couples.

RULE OF LAW

Iowa's marriage statute, defining marriage as between one man and one woman, violates the equal protection clause of the Iowa constitution.

FACTS: Six same-sex couples (P) applied for marriage licenses in Polk County, Iowa (the County) (D). The County (D) denied their requests. Varnum (P), the lead plaintiff representing the couples, brought suit, alleging the state's marriage statute violated their right to equal protection and denied them the fundamental right to marry. The federal district court granted summary judgment to the plaintiffs. The County (D) appealed.

ISSUE: Does Iowa's marriage statute, defining marriage as between one man and one woman, violate the equal protection clause of the Iowa constitution?

HOLDING AND DECISION: (Cady, J.) Yes. Iowa's marriage statute, defining marriage as between one man and one woman, violates the equal protection clause of the Iowa constitution. The equal protection clause of the Iowa constitution requires that similarly situated people be treated equally under the law. First, as a threshold matter, we hold that same-sex couples are similarly situated to heterosexual couples. The plaintiffs here are in long term relationships and are raising families just like heterosexual couples. Second, we hold that intermediate scrutiny shall apply. There is no question the gay and lesbian community has been the subject of past discrimination. Moreover, it is clear the legislature's refusal to grant same-sex couples the right to marry is because of their sexual orientation. Therefore, to uphold the statute, the County (D) must prove that the marriage statute is substantially related to an important governmental interest. Third, the County (D) has failed to advance any important governmental interests to survive intermediate scrutiny. Maintaining the traditional definition of marriage, without anything more, is not an important governmental interest. Also, the plaintiffs have adequately shown by scientific studies that the interests of children are "served equally by same-sex parents and opposite-sex parents." The marriage statute itself does not prevent same-sex couples from having, adopting and/or raising children. Using the "over and under" inclusive type of analysis, denying marriage to same-sex couples simply because they cannot procreate is under-inclusive. There are many reasons heterosexual couples may not procreate, such as age, disability, or choice. The legislature has not moved to deny those couples marriage rights. Also, there is no evidence granting marriage licenses to same-sex couples would put a strain on state resources. Lastly, while many may oppose same-sex marriages on religious grounds, civil marriage is judged under our state constitution, and not on any religious belief. Accordingly, we hold that Iowa's marriage statute violates our constitution's equal protection clause. Affirmed.

ANALYSIS

Iowa became the third state to grant marriage rights to same-sex couples. Currently, 35 states have statutes or constitutional amendments that define marriage as between one man and one woman. There have been attempts in Iowa since this decision to pass a constitutional amendment limiting marriage to one man and one woman. Recently, California has been the epicenter of the national debate on same-sex marriages. After the state's highest court granted same-sex couples the right to marry, California's residents passed Proposition 8, which added a constitutional amendment defining marriage as between one man and one woman. As of February 2010, a court challenge to Proposition 8 was under way in federal court in San Francisco. An appeal of the trial court's decision, either way, may rise to the U.S. Supreme Court.

Quicknotes

EQUAL PROTECTION CLAUSE A constitutional provision that each person be guaranteed the same protection of the laws enjoyed by other persons in like circumstances.

INTERMEDIATE SCRUTINY A standard of reviewing the propriety of classifications pertaining to gender or legitimacy under the Equal Protection Clause of the United States Constitution which requires a court to ascertain whether the classification furthers an important state interest and is substantially related to the attainment of that interest.

CHAPTER 6

Tradition, Tension, and Change in Landlord-Tenant Law

Quick Reference Rules of Law

PAGE

1. **The Tenancy at Will.** A lease may provide for termination at the will of the tenant only. (Garner v. Gerrish) *46*
2. **Delivery of Possession.** A landlord is obligated only to place a tenant in legal possession of rented real property. (Hannan v. Dusch) *47*
3. **Subleases and Assignments.** An assignment arises when a lessee transfers his entire interest under a lease. (Ernst v. Conditt) *48*
4. **Subleases and Assignments.** Absent contractual language to the contrary, a lessor may not arbitrarily withhold consent to an assignment. (Kendall v. Ernest Pestana, Inc.) *49*
5. **The Tenant Who Defaults–The Tenant in Possession.** A landlord may not remove a breaching or defaulting tenant's possessions or bar such tenant's access to the leasehold without resorting to judicial remedies. (Berg v. Wiley) *50*
6. **The Tenant Who Defaults–The Tenant Who Has Abandoned Possession.** A landlord has a duty to mitigate damages when he seeks to recover rents due from a defaulting tenant. (Sommer v. Kridel) *51*
7. **Quiet Enjoyment and Constructive Eviction.** When a landlord causes a substantial interference with the enjoyment and use of the leased premises, the tenant may claim constructive eviction. (Reste Realty Corp. v. Cooper) *52*
8. **The Implied Warranty of Habitability.** An implied warranty of habitability exists in residential leases. (Hilder v. St. Peter) *53*
9. **The Problem of Affordable Housing.** [Not included in casebook excerpt.] (Chicago Board of Realtors, Inc. v. City of Chicago) *54*

Garner v. Gerrish

Estate administrator (P) v. Lessee (D)

N.Y. Ct. App., 473 N.E.2d 223 (1984).

NATURE OF CASE: Appeal of eviction proceeding.

FACT SUMMARY: A dispute arose as to whether Gerrish's (D) tenancy was terminable at the will of the lessor.

RULE OF LAW

A lease may provide for termination at the will of the tenant only.

FACTS: Donovan granted a lease of a house to Gerrish (D). The lease contained a clause granting Gerrish (D) the ability to terminate the lease at the date of his choice. No such right was reserved for the lessor. Upon Donovan's death, the administrator (P) attempted to evict Gerrish (D), claiming that the will was indefinite as to time, and, therefore, a tenancy at will had been created. The trial court held for the administrator (P), and Gerrish (D) appealed.

ISSUE: May a lease provide for its termination at the will of the tenant only?

HOLDING AND DECISION: (Wachtler, J.) Yes. A lease may provide for termination at the will of the tenant only. Ancient authority held to the contrary. However, this rule grew out of medieval rituals involving livery of seisin, a symbolic act no longer followed. Since livery of seisin has long been abandoned, it is appropriate to interpret leases based on the will of the parties as expressed by the terms of the lease. Here, the language unequivocally reserves the right of termination to Gerrish (D), so he may not be evicted. Reversed.

ANALYSIS

Livery of seisin was a ritual necessary in ancient times for conveying land. The grantor had to present a clod of earth or other symbol to the grantee. A tenancy which could last a tenant's lifetime was considered legally equivalent to a life estate, so the old rule maintained that such a tenancy could not be created without livery of seisin.

Quicknotes

EVICTION The removal of a person from possession of property.

LEASE An agreement or contract which creates a relationship between a landlord and tenant (real property) or lessor and lessee (real or personal property).

LIVERY OF SEISIN A ceremony in which an interest in land is formally delivered usually by delivering a piece of earth.

TENANCY AT WILL Someone who is in possession of property with the consent of the owner or landlord for an unfixed period of time.

Hannan v. Dusch

Tenant (P) v. Lessor (D)

Va. Sup. Ct. App., 154 Va. 356, 153 S.E. 824 (1930).

NATURE OF CASE: Appeal from decision denying action for damages for breach of contract and deed.

FACT SUMMARY: Hannan (P), the lessee, alleged that Dusch (D), the lessor, failed to deliver possession of rented property by allowing a former tenant to remain in possession.

RULE OF LAW

A landlord is obligated only to place a tenant in legal possession of rented real property.

FACTS: On August 31, 1927, Dusch (D) leased certain real estate to Hannan (P), for a period of 15 years, the term to begin on January 1, 1928. Hannan (P) alleged that Dusch (D) had allowed the prior tenants to remain in possession of the premises after January 1, 1928, and had refused to take any legal or other actions to remove them. There was no express covenant in the rental agreement regarding either delivery of the premises or quiet enjoyment of the premises. Dusch (D) demurred to the complaint on the grounds that he was under no duty to deliver actual possession to Hannan (P).

ISSUE: Is a landlord obligated only to place a tenant in legal possession of rented real property?

HOLDING AND DECISION: (Prentis, C.J.) Yes. Under the American rule, a landlord does not impliedly covenant against the wrongful acts of others, and is not responsible for the tortious acts of third parties unless he expressly contracts so. Where a new tenant fails to obtain possession of rented premises solely because a former tenant wrongfully holds over, his remedy is against the former tenant and not against the landlord. Under the English rule, in the absence of express provisions to the contrary, there is in every lease an implied covenant by the landlord that the premises will be open to entry by the tenant at the time fixed by the lease for the beginning of the term. Here, Hannan (P) should have brought an action for unlawful entry or unlawful detainer against the former tenant, rather than seeking relief from Dusch (D). Affirmed.

ANALYSIS

There still exists a split of authority over application of the American or English rule for delivery of possession. The American rule provides that a tenant may sue to recover possession and damages from the person wrongfully in possession. The English remedy allows the tenant to terminate the lease, and sue the landlord for damages, or, if the third party is in possession of only part of the premises, to take possession of the remainder with a proportionate abatement in rent and damages.

Quicknotes

DEMURRER The assertion that the opposing party's pleadings are insufficient and that the demurring party should not be made to answer.

EXPRESS COVENANT A promise created by the express words of a document.

HOLDOVER TENANT A tenancy that arises upon the expiration of a lawful tenancy and the tenant remains in possession of the property.

IMPLIED COVENANT A promise inferred by law from a document as a whole and the circumstances surrounding its implementation.

LEGAL POSSESSION Party having possession of property that it is legally entitled to.

TORTIOUS ACTS Acts that constitute legal wrongs, resulting in breach of a duty.

UNLAWFUL DETAINER The unlawful withholding of real or personal property from an individual who is lawfully entitled to it.

Ernst v. Conditt

Lessor (P) v. Sublessees (D)

Tenn. Ct. App., 54 Tenn. App. 328, 390 S.W.2d 703 (1964).

NATURE OF CASE: Appeal from award of damages for past due rent and removal of improvements constructed on leased real property.

FACT SUMMARY: After Ernst (P) leased property to Rogers, who assigned his lease to Conditt (D), Ernst (P) sought damages from Conditt (D) for past due rent and removal of improvements.

RULE OF LAW

An assignment arises when a lessee transfers his entire interest under a lease.

FACTS: On June 18, 1960, Ernst (P) leased a tract of land to Frank D. Rogers for a term of one year and seven days, beginning on June 23, 1960. On August 4, 1960, Rogers, having sold his business to Conditt (D), executed a document which extended the term of the lease to two years, and "sublet" the premises to Conditt (D). The document, which stated that Rogers remained personally liable under the terms of the amended lease, was signed by Rogers, Ernst (P) and Conditt (D). At the end of the lease term, Ernst (P) filed suit against Conditt (D), seeking past due rent and removal of improvements constructed on the property. The trial court, holding that the document constituted an assignment, rather than a sublease, held that Conditt (D), and not Rogers, was directly liable for the monies owed.

ISSUE: Does an assignment arise when a lessee transfers his entire interest under a lease?

HOLDING AND DECISION: (Chattin, J.) Yes. Under the common-law rule, if an instrument purports to transfer the lessee's interest for the entire remainder of the lease term, an assignment has occurred. However, if the instrument purports to transfer the lessee's interest for any length of time less than the remainder of the lease term, a sublease has been established. Under the modern rule, the intention of the parties governs in construing deeds, leases, and other written transfers of property interests. Here, under both the common law and modern rule, the agreement between Rogers and Conditt (D) is an assignment, rather than a sublease. Rogers did not retain any interest in the lease, and he also did not reserve a right of re-entry in the event of a breach of any of the conditions or covenants of the lease by Conditt (D). The use of the word "sublet" is not conclusive, because it appears from all of the facts and circumstances and the instrument itself that all of the parties intended an assignment rather than a sublease. Affirmed.

ANALYSIS

This case illustrates the two methods used to distinguish an assignment from a sublease. Under the common law test, an assignment arises when a lessee transfers his right to possession for the entire term of the lease. Under the less commonly used modern rule, the intention of the parties governs, although the actual words used are often persuasive in the final determination.

Quicknotes

ASSIGNMENT A transaction in which a party conveys his or her entire interest in property to another.

RIGHT OF REENTRY An interest in property reserved in the conveyance of a fee that gives the holder the right to resume possession of property upon the happening of a condition subsequent.

SUBLEASE A transaction in which a tenant or lessee conveys an interest in the leased premises that is less than his own or retains a reversionary interest.

Kendall v. Ernest Pestana, Inc.

Tenant (P) v. Lessor (D)

Cal. Sup. Ct., 40 Cal. 3d 488, 709 P.2d 837 (1985).

NATURE OF CASE: Appeal of denial of injunctive relief and damages.

FACT SUMMARY: Ernest Pestana, Inc. (D) arbitrarily withheld permission from Kendall (P), its tenant, to sublet its leasehold.

RULE OF LAW

Absent contractual language to the contrary, a lessor may not arbitrarily withhold consent to an assignment.

FACTS: Through a series of leases and assignments, Ernest Pestana, Inc. (D) became lessor of certain hangar space at a municipal airport, with Kendall (P) and other lessees. The lease contained a consent clause regarding subleases. At one point, Kendall (P) and other lessees approached management of Ernest Pestana, Inc. (D), requesting permission to sublet. Permission was denied for no apparent commercially reasonable reason. Kendall (P) and the others sued Ernest Pestana, Inc. (D) for injunctive and declaratory relief, as well as damages. The trial court sustained Ernest Pestana, Inc.'s (D) demurrer, and the appellate court affirmed. The state supreme court granted review.

ISSUE: Absent contractual language to the contrary, may a lessor arbitrarily withhold consent to an assignment?

HOLDING AND DECISION: (Broussard, J.) No. Absent contractual language to the contrary, a lessor may not arbitrarily withhold consent to an assignment. The basic social policy in this area is that interests in property, including those of a leasehold nature, should be freely alienable. Restrictions on alienability are to be strictly construed against the lessor. The lessor does have a reversionary interest in the property, and therefore is entitled to assurance that a lessee will not sublet to an irresponsible individual who may commit waste. This is a commercially reasonable rationale for denying permission to sublet. There are no doubt others. Absent some sort of reasonable basis for denial of permission, however, it seems that public policy favoring free alienability should override whatever minor interest a lessor might have in arbitrarily denying permission to sublet. The major arguments in favor of retaining the right are unpersuasive. The lessor's common law right to look to no one but the lessee for rent has been curtailed. The argument that the lessee could have bargained for free subletting rights does not stand up to scrutiny. What the parties contemplated is not always clear, and doubts should be resolved in favor of alienability. Finally, the argument based on *stare decisis* is also to be found wanting. When changed conditions warrant overruling precedent, a court may do so. Here, since the complaint alleged that Ernest Pestana, Inc. (D) had unreasonably withheld approval, a cause of action was stated. Reversed.

ANALYSIS

The rule of the present case could well prove to have a more limited application than one might gather at first glance. The opinion does give a lessor the option of contracting in the power to arbitrarily veto a sublease. Also, it only applies to commercial leases. How the court would rule in residential leases is a matter of speculation.

Quicknotes

ASSIGNMENT A transaction in which a party conveys his or her entire interest in property to another.

DEMURRER The assertion that the opposing party's pleadings are insufficient and that the demurring party should not be made to answer.

FREE ALIENABILITY Unrestricted transferability.

INJUNCTIVE RELIEF A court order issued as a remedy, requiring a person to do, or prohibiting that person from doing, a specific act.

STARE DECISIS Doctrine whereby courts follow legal precedent unless there is good cause for departure.

Berg v. Wiley

Locked-out tenant (P) v. Landlord (D)

Minn. Sup. Ct., 264 N.W.2d 145 (1978).

NATURE OF CASE: Appeal from award of damages for wrongful eviction.

FACT SUMMARY: Wiley (D), lessor of commercial property to Berg (P) for the purpose of operating a restaurant thereon, locked Berg (P) out of the premises when Berg (P) delayed making certain remodeling changes to meet health code requirements.

RULE OF LAW

A landlord may not remove a breaching or defaulting tenant's possessions or bar such tenant's access to the leasehold without resorting to judicial remedies.

FACTS: Wiley (D) leased commercial property to Berg (P) for the purpose of operating an establishment called "A Family Affair Restaurant." Wiley (D) made demand that Berg (P) make certain remodeling changes to alleviate alleged health code violations and notified Berg (P) of his intention to retake possession if the changes were not made within a two-week period. At the end of the period, Berg (P) closed the restaurant and put up a sign that said "Closed for Remodeling." Wiley (D) then entered the premises in Berg's (P) absence and changed the locks. Berg (P) brought this action to recover lost profits, damage to chattels and emotional distress due to the wrongful eviction. The trial court awarded Berg (P) $31,000 for lost profits and $3,540 for loss of chattels, and the jury specially found that Berg (P) neither abandoned nor surrendered the premises. Wiley (D) appealed.

ISSUE: May a landlord remove a breaching or defaulting tenant's possessions or bar such tenant's access to the leasehold without resorting to judicial remedies?

HOLDING AND DECISION: (Rogosheske, J.) No. The evidence amply supports the jury's finding that Berg (P) did not abandon or surrender the premises, and the lockout was thus not justified on the ground of abandonment and surrender. As to self-help procedures employed by landlords to remove defaulting tenants, the common-law rule was to permit such removal if accomplished peaceably. Wiley (D) contended that only actual or threatened violence constitutes a nonpeaceable entry. This is not correct. In response to a long-applied policy to discourage landlords from taking the law into their own hands, the modern trend in this area of the law has been to bar self-help to dispossess a breaching tenant, and this represents the rule that should be applied here. A landlord may not remove a breaching or defaulting tenant's possessions or bar the tenant's access to the leasehold without resorting to judicial remedies. Wiley's (D) failure to resort to judicial remedies rendered the lockout wrongful as a matter of law. Affirmed.

ANALYSIS

In this respect, the trend of the law on leaseholds is moving toward the property law concept that the covenant to pay rent and the right to quiet possession are not interdependent. The notion of the sanctity of one's home and the emphasis in recent legal history on the right of privacy have doubtless swayed legislators, commentators, and courts in this area.

Quicknotes

SELF-HELP Acting without recourse to the legal system.

TENANT IN POSSESSION A party in possession of property by title or right.

WRONGFUL EVICTION The unlawful dispossession of a person from property.

Sommer v. Kridel

Landlord (P) v. Repudiating-lessee (D)

N.J. Sup. Ct., 74 N.J. 446, 378 A.2d 767 (1977).

NATURE OF CASE: Appeal from award of damages for past due rent.

FACT SUMMARY: Kridel (D), the lessee, vacated the apartment, which he leased from Sommer (P), before the end of the lease term.

RULE OF LAW
A landlord has a duty to mitigate damages when he seeks to recover rents due from a defaulting tenant.

FACTS: On March 10, 1972, Kridel (D), the lessee, entered into a lease with Sommer (P), for the rental of an apartment. The term of the lease was from May 1, 1972 to April 30, 1974. One week after signing the agreement, Kridel (D) paid Sommer (P) a sum of money to satisfy the first month's rent and security deposit. On May 19, 1972, Kridel (D) repudiated the lease and acknowledged the forfeiture of the sum already paid to Sommer (P). Although a third party was subsequently interested in renting the same apartment, Sommer (P) did not re-let the apartment until September 1, 1973. Sommer (P) brought suit against Kridel (D) to recover the total amount due for the full two-year term of the lease. The trial court's ruling in favor of Kridel (D) was reversed at the appellate level, and Kridel (D) appealed.

ISSUE: Does a landlord have a duty to mitigate damages when he seeks to recover rents due from a defaulting tenant?

HOLDING AND DECISION: (Pashman, J.) Yes. A landlord does have an obligation to make a reasonable effort to mitigate damages when a tenant defaults on a lease. The landlord's duty to mitigate consists of making reasonable efforts to re-let the apartment. The burden of proof shall be upon the landlord to establish that he used reasonable diligence in attempting to re-let the premises. Among the factors to be considered in determining whether the landlord has exercised reasonable diligence are whether the landlord offered or showed the apartment to any prospective tenants, or whether the availability of the apartment was advertised in local newspapers. Here, despite the availability of a prospective tenant who was ready, willing, and able to rent the apartment, Sommer (P) allowed the apartment to lie empty in order to increase the amount of damages. Sommer (P) could have reasonably avoided the damages which accrued by virtue of the apartment lacking a tenant. Reversed.

ANALYSIS

This case illustrates the modern trend of analyzing landlord-tenant issues under contract, rather than real property law. Increasingly, the courts agree that the contract rule requiring mitigation of damages for residential leases best effectuates notions of basic fairness and equity. The contract rule also promotes efficiency considerations by giving landlords an incentive to make use of any available property.

Quicknotes

DEFAULT Failure to carry out a legal obligation.

MITIGATION Reduction in penalty.

Reste Realty Corp. v. Cooper

Lessor (P) v. Tenant (D)

N.J. Sup Ct., 53 N.J. 444, 251 A.2d 268 (1969).

NATURE OF CASE: Appeal from award of past rent due.

FACT SUMMARY: After being sued for back rent, Cooper (D) claimed the defense of constructive eviction.

RULE OF LAW
When a landlord causes a substantial interference with the enjoyment and use of the leased premises, the tenant may claim constructive eviction.

FACTS: Reste (P) sued Cooper (D) to recover rent allegedly due under a written commercial lease. Cooper (D) rented the basement floor of an office building in Hackensack, New Jersey, on May 13, 1958. Whenever it rained during the first year of Cooper's (D) occupancy, water ran off the driveway and into Cooper's (D) offices and meeting rooms, either through or under the exterior of the foundation wall. The resident manager, Donigian, repaired the premises once and was about to fix them again when he died. Subsequently, the flooding problem became increasingly severe, and Cooper's (D) complaints were ignored. After notifying the lessor of her intention to vacate, Cooper (D) left the premises on December 30, 1961. After Reste (P) acquired the lease, it brought suit to recover rent for the unexpired term of Cooper's (D) lease. The appellate court found no constructive eviction, and held for Reste (P).

ISSUE: Can a tenant claim constructive eviction when the landlord causes a substantial interference with the enjoyment and use of the leased premises?

HOLDING AND DECISION: (Francis, J.) Yes. Ordinarily a covenant of quiet enjoyment is implied in a lease. Where there is such a covenant, whether express or implied, and it is breached substantially by the landlord, the doctrine of constructive eviction is available as a remedy for the tenant. An act or omission by the landlord which renders the premises substantially unsuitable for the purpose for which they are leased, or which seriously interferes with the beneficial enjoyment of the premises, is a breach of the covenant of quiet enjoyment and constitutes a constructive eviction of the tenant. Here, there was sufficient interference with the use and enjoyment of the leased premises to justify Cooper's (D) departure, and to relieve her from the obligation to pay further rent. A tenant's right to claim a constructive eviction will be lost if he does not vacate the premises within a reasonable time after the right comes into existence. Here, Cooper's (D) cooperative building manager died nine months before Cooper (D) vacated, during which time Cooper (D) expected that repairs would be performed. Accordingly, under the circumstances, such vacation was within a reasonable time, and the delay was not sufficient to establish a waiver of the constructive eviction. Reversed.

ANALYSIS

The general rule is that constructive eviction requires a substantial breach, after which the tenant must vacate the premises within a reasonable time under the circumstances. The court in this case also held that Cooper (D) did not acquire notice of the defective condition prior to the execution of the lease.

Quicknotes

CONSTRUCTIVE EVICTION An action whereby the landlord renders the property unsuitable for occupancy either in whole or in part, so that the tenant is forced to leave the premises.

COVENANT OF QUIET ENJOYMENT A promise contained in a lease or a deed that the tenant or grantee will enjoy unimpaired use of the property.

DEMISED PREMISES Leased property.

Hilder v. St. Peter

Lessee (P) v. Lessor (D)

Vt. Sup. Ct., 144 Vt. 150, 478 A.2d 202 (1984).

NATURE OF CASE: Action by tenant to recover rent.

FACT SUMMARY: Hilder (P) leased a residential premise from St. Peter (D) which had serious deficiencies.

RULE OF LAW

An implied warranty of habitability exists in residential leases.

FACTS: Hilder (P) leased an apartment from St. Peter (D). During the course of the tenancy various problems with the apartment manifested themselves, including sewage leaks, nonfunctioning toilets, water leaks, falling plaster, and broken locks. These were brought to St. Peter's (D) attention, but nothing was done. Hilder (P) paid the agreed rent, but after 14 months of renting the premises, she brought an action seeking recovery of the rental monies. The trial court awarded damages to Hilder (P), and St. Peter (D) appealed.

ISSUE: Does an implied warranty of habitability exist in residential leases?

HOLDING AND DECISION: (Billings, C.J.) Yes. An implied warranty of habitability exists in residential leases. The old view of leases was that the lessee took the property as he found it. This view was proper in an agrarian society, but in a modern urban setting is improper. The modern tenant bargains for viable habitation, and if he receives less, he is not getting that for which he contracts in a lease. For this reason a rented dwelling which is not habitable amounts to a breach of contract by the lessor, and standard contract damages are available, as well as tort damages arising therefrom. Affirmed in part, reversed in part, and remanded.

ANALYSIS

The seminal case in this area was *Green v. Superior Ct.,* 10 Cal. 3d 616 (1974). The analysis of the court there was the same as the analysis here. Residential tenancies, the court determined, were no longer land conveyances but rather contracts with certain inherent expectations embodied in them.

Quicknotes

IMPLIED WARRANTY OF HABITABILITY A warranty implied by a landlord that the premises are suitable, and will remain suitable, for habitation.

Chicago Board of Realtors, Inc. v. City of Chicago

Property owner (P) v. Municipality (D)

819 F.2d 732 (7th Cir. 1987).

NATURE OF CASE: Appeal from denial of injunction against enforcement of a landlord-tenant ordinance.

FACT SUMMARY: Chicago Board of Realtors (Realtors) (P), a group of property owners, challenged the constitutionality of Chicago's Residential Landlord and Tenant Ordinance (D), contending that it violated various clauses of the Constitution.

RULE OF LAW

[Rule of law not included in casebook excerpt.]

FACTS: Realtors (P), a group of property owners, challenged the constitutionality of Chicago's Residential Landlord and Tenant Ordinance (D), arguing that it violated the Contracts Clause, procedural and substantive due process, void-for-vagueness doctrine, equal protection, the Takings Clause, and the Commerce Clause. The district court denied a motion for a preliminary injunction, concluding that Realtors (P) did not have a reasonable likelihood of prevailing on the merits. Realtors (P) appealed, contesting the district court's ruling with respect to all but the Takings and Commerce Clause issues. The court of appeals affirmed. Realtors (P) appealed.

ISSUE: [Issue not included in casebook excerpt.]

HOLDING AND DECISION: (Cudahy, J.) [The majority opinion, in which the lower court decisions were upheld on the basis that the ordinance was sufficiently reasonable in light of its stated purpose (to promote public safety, health, and welfare), was not included in the casebook excerpt. The policy analysis of J. Posner in his separate opinion was included and follows below.]

SEPARATE OPINION: (Posner, J.) The majority's opinion, although reaching the correct result, does not go far enough. It makes the rejection of the appeal seem easier than it is, by refusing to acknowledge the strong case that can be made for the unreasonableness of the ordinance. While the stated purpose of the ordinance is the promotion of public health, safety, and welfare and the quality of housing in Chicago, it is unlikely that this is the real purpose, and it is not the likely effect. Forbidding landlords to charge interest at market rates on late payment of rent could hardly be thought to be calculated to improve the health, safety, and welfare of Chicagoans, and it may have the opposite effect. The initial consequence of the rule will be to reduce the resources that landlords devote to improve the quality of housing by making the provision of rental housing more costly. Landlords will try to offset the higher cost by raising rents. The ordinance is not in the interest of poor people. The principal beneficiaries will be the middle class. Affirmed.

ANALYSIS

In the separate opinion by Judge Posner, which was joined by Judge Easterbrook (like Judge Posner, a former professor at the University of Chicago), the judge seemed more concerned with analyzing the economic impact of the ordinance than its constitutional impact. In addition, both judges seemed more concerned with making Judge Cudahy aware of the economic impact that the ordinance will have on the city than discussing his legal analysis. Judge Posner cited different literature to show that the Chicago (D) ordinance may not be unsound, but if economic theory holds true, the poorer and newer tenants will be hurt by the ordinance.

Quicknotes

COMMERCE CLAUSE Article 1, Section 8, clause 3 of the United States Constitution, granting Congress the power to regulate commerce with foreign countries and between the states.

PRELIMINARY INJUNCTION A judicial mandate issued to require or restrain a party from certain conduct; used to preserve a trial's subject matter or to prevent threatened injury.

TAKINGS CLAUSE Provision of the Fifth Amendment to the United States Constitution prohibiting the government from taking private property for public use without providing just compensation therefor.

CHAPTER 7

The Land Transaction

Quick Reference Rules of Law

PAGE

1. **Brokers.** Real estate brokers must fully, fairly, and promptly inform their clients of all known facts that might be material to the transaction for which the brokers were employed. (Licari v. Blackwelder) *57*

2. **The Statute of Frauds.** An oral contract for the transfer of interest in land may be specifically enforced despite the Statute of Frauds if the party seeking performance changed his position in reasonable reliance on the contract and injustice can be avoided only through specific performance. (Hickey v. Green) *58*

3. **Marketable Title.** A party cannot convey good merchantable title if violations of covenants or zoning ordinances exist on the subject property at the time it is to be sold. (Lohmeyer v. Bower) *59*

4. **The Duty to Disclose Defects.** Where a condition that has been created by the seller materially impairs the value of the contract and is peculiarly within the knowledge of the seller or unlikely to be discovered by a prudent purchaser exercising due care with respect to the subject transaction, nondisclosure constitutes a basis for rescission as a matter of equity. (Stambovsky v. Ackley) *60*

5. **The Duty to Disclose Defects.** Where the seller of a home knows the facts affecting the value of a home that are not readily observable, the seller is under a duty to disclose. (Johnson v. Davis) *61*

6. **The Implied Warranty of Quality.** A subsequent purchaser of property may recover from one performing defective contractor services for the prior owner if the work contained latent defects not apparent at the time of purchase. (Lempke v. Dagenais) *62*

7. **Remedies for Breach of the Sales Contract.** The non-defaulting party under a real estate contract is entitled to an award of damages following a breach of the contract. (Jones v. Lee) *63*

8. **Remedies for Breach of the Sales Contract.** A buyer who materially breaches a real estate purchase contract can recover in restitution for benefits he conferred on the seller through either part performance on the contract or reliance beyond the loss that his own breach caused. (Kutzin v. Pirnie) *65*

9. **Warranties of Title.** The mere existence of a superior title does not constitute a breach of the covenant of quiet enjoyment. (Brown v. Lober) *67*

10. **Warranties of Title.** Latent violations of state or municipal land use regulations (1) that do not appear on the land records, (2) that are unknown to the seller of the property, (3) as to which the agency charged with enforcement has taken no official action to compel compliance at the time the deed was executed, and (4) that have not ripened into an interest that can be recorded on the land records do not constitute an encumbrance for the purpose of the deed warranty. (Frimberger v. Anzellotti) *68*

11. **Warranties of Title.** The breach of the covenant of seisin creates a chose in action which passes by assignment to subsequent grantees of the deed. (Rockafellor v. Gray) *70*

12. **Delivery.** Where a deed has been formally executed and delivered, the presumption that the grantee assented to delivery can be overcome only by evidence that no delivery was in fact intended. (Sweeney v. Sweeney) *71*

13. **Delivery.** Grantors do not legally deliver a deed if they reserve the right to retrieve the deed, require that the delivery may become operative only when the grantors have died, and keep using the property as if it were still their own. (Rosengrant v. Rosengrant) *72*

14. **Mortgage Foreclosure.** Mere compliance with statutory requirements may not discharge a mortgagee's duty to exercise good faith and due diligence in selling the property at foreclosure. (Murphy v. Fin. Dev. Corp.) *73*

15. **The Subprime Mortgage Crisis.** Mortgage loans with the following four characteristics would likely be "unfair" under Massachusetts' Consumer Protection Act: (1) the loans were adjustable with a preliminary rate for three years; (2) the initial rate was typically three points lower than the usual mortgage rate on 30-year loans; (3) the debt to income ratio would exceed 50 percent after the introductory period expired; and (4) the loan-to-value ratio was 100 percent. (Commonwealth v. Fremont Investment & Loan) *74*

16. **Mortgage Substitutes: The Installment Land Contract.** The vendee under a land sale contract acquires an interest in the property of such a nature that it must be extinguished before the vendor may resume possession. (Bean v. Walker) *76*

Licari v. Blackwelder

Real estate sellers (P) v. Real estate brokers (D)

Conn. App. Ct., 539 A.2d 609 (1988).

NATURE OF CASE: Suit to recover damages for the defendants' breaches of their fiduciary duties as real estate brokers.

FACT SUMMARY: Six siblings enlisted a real estate broker to help them sell a home they had inherited, and the broker in turn enlisted another broker for further assistance. The second broker himself bought the home for less than market value and sold it six days later for $45,000 more than his purchase price.

RULE OF LAW

Real estate brokers must fully, fairly, and promptly inform their clients of all known facts that might be material to the transaction for which the brokers were employed.

FACTS: Six brothers and sisters, who were unsophisticated laypersons with little experience in real estate, inherited a home and related property from their parents. Wanting to sell the property, though they knew nothing of its potential value, they contacted a real estate broker, Schwartz, for help in finding a buyer. Schwartz in turn contacted another real estate broker, Blackwelder (D), who was knowledgeable about real estate values near the plaintiffs' property. Blackwelder (D) and Schwartz entered a "co-broke" agreement under which they would evenly divide the commissions from a sale to one of Blackwelder's (D) prospective buyers. During an exclusive 24-hour window to sell the property for $125,000, an agent of Schwartz showed the property to a prospective buyer generated by Blackwelder (D). Within that 24-hour period, Blackwelder (D) himself offered $115,000 for the property. The plaintiffs accepted the offer. At no time did Blackwelder (D) either negotiate on the plaintiffs' behalf with the prospective buyer Blackwelder (D) had arranged or disclose the true value that Blackwelder (D) himself had assigned the property. The plaintiffs accepted a cash payment of $11,500 and a purchase money mortgage for the $103,500 balance of Blackwelder's (D) $115,000 purchase price; at the time of the transaction, the plaintiffs thought that their property had sold at market value and that Blackwelder (D) himself would use the property. Blackwelder (D), however, immediately contracted to sell the property for $160,000 to a buyer the plaintiffs had forbidden Schwartz from considering as a potential buyer for the property. The plaintiffs sued Blackwelder (D) and an associate of his, alleging that the defendants had breached their duties by withholding information from them and by intentionally misrepresenting who would purchase the property. The trial court found for the plaintiffs, holding that Blackwelder (D) had breached obligations to the plaintiffs that arose in their initial relationship with Schwartz. Judgment was entered for the plaintiffs in the amount of $45,000, which the trial judge found to be Blackwelder's (D) unconscionable profit from the transaction. Blackwelder (D) appealed.

ISSUE: Must real estate brokers fully, fairly, and promptly inform their clients of all known facts that might be material to the transaction for which the brokers were employed?

HOLDING AND DECISION: (Bieluch, J.) Yes. Real estate brokers must fully, fairly, and promptly inform their clients of all known facts that might be material to the transaction for which the brokers were employed. Real estate brokers are fiduciaries, and accordingly they must act with the highest fidelity and good faith in promoting their clients', and not their own, interests. Those duties flow to a broker who acts as a subagent of another broker if the subagent has the primary broker's express permission to act on the clients' behalf. The broker—the subagent—therefore has an obligation to disclose to the client all known facts about a potentially more advantageous transaction before concluding a sale that is less advantageous for the client. This record contains evidence supporting the trial court's findings that Blackwelder (D) breached those duties here. There is no error.

ANALYSIS

Licari illustrates a fiduciary's constant obligation to know—and remember—where his loyalties lie. They won't lie with his self-interest. Giving Blackwelder (D) some benefit of the doubt in this case, it is at least conceivable that he saw some duty of loyalty to the prospective ultimate buyers. The duties of the primary broker (Schwartz), however, which ran to the plaintiffs, would have negated even that hypothetical defense for Blackwelder (D) here.

Quicknotes

BREACH OF FIDUCIARY DUTY The failure of a fiduciary to observe the standard of care exercised by professionals of similar education and experience.

BROKERAGE A business in which brokers or agents are paid for entering transactions on behalf of others.

FIDUCIARY DUTY A legal obligation to act for the benefit of another, including subordinating one's personal interests to that of the other person.

INTENIONAL MISREPRESENTATION A statement or conduct by one party to another that constitutes a false representation of fact.

Hickey v. Green

Would-be buyer (P) v. Breaching seller (D)

Mass. Ct. App., 14 Mass. App. Ct. 671, 442 N.E.2d 37 (1982), *rev. denied*, 445 N.E.2d 156 (1983).

NATURE OF CASE: Appeal from grant of specific performance of a real estate contract.

FACT SUMMARY: Green (D) contended that the real estate sales contract she orally entered into with Hickey (P) was unenforceable based on the Statute of Frauds.

RULE OF LAW

An oral contract for the transfer of interest in land may be specifically enforced despite the Statute of Frauds if the party seeking performance changed his position in reasonable reliance on the contract and injustice can be avoided only through specific performance.

FACTS: Green (D) orally agreed to sell a parcel to Hickey (P), and accepted a check as a deposit. In reliance on the contract, Hickey (P) accepted a deposit on his home from a purchaser, intending to build a new home on the land he purchased from Green (D). Subsequently, Green (D), knowing Hickey (P) sold his house in reliance on the contract, refused to sell the land to Hickey (P). Hickey (P) sued for specific performance. Green (D) defended, contending the contract was unenforceable under the Statute of Frauds. The trial court granted specific performance, and Green (D) appealed.

ISSUE: Can an oral contract for the sale of real estate be specifically enforced if the party seeking enforcement changed his position in reasonable reliance upon the contract?

HOLDING AND DECISION: (Cutter, J.) Yes. An oral contract for the transfer of an interest in land may be specifically enforced, despite the Statute of Frauds requirement of writing, if the party seeking enforcement changed his position in reasonable reliance on the contract and injustice can be avoided only through specific performance. In this case, Hickey (P) clearly changed his position in reliance on the contract by selling his house in anticipation of occupying another on Green's (D) land. The reliance was reasonable, and Green (D) was fully aware of this change in position when she refused to honor the contract. As a result, it would be manifestly unjust to refuse specific performance in this case. Therefore, it must be ordered. Remanded.

ANALYSIS

This case could have been decided on different grounds. Some commentators, spurred by dicta in the opinion, contend that the check which Hickey (P) gave Green (D) as a deposit on the land constituted an adequate memorandum to satisfy the requirements of the Statute of Frauds.

Quicknotes

RELIANCE Dependence on a fact that causes a party to act or refrain from acting.

SPECIFIC PERFORMANCE An equitable remedy whereby the court requires the parties to perform their obligations pursuant to a contract.

STATUTE OF FRAUDS A statute that requires specified types of contracts to be in writing in order to be binding.

Lohmeyer v. Bower

Property buyer (P) v. Seller (D)

Kan. Sup. Ct., 170 Kan. 442, 227 P.2d 102 (1951).

NATURE OF CASE: Specific performance of real estate contract.

FACT SUMMARY: Lohmeyer (P), claiming unmerchantable title, sued for rescission of real estate sales contract, which Bower (D) cross-complained for specific performance.

RULE OF LAW

A party cannot convey good merchantable title if violations of covenants or zoning ordinances exist on the subject property at the time it is to be sold.

FACTS: Lohmeyer (P) contracted to buy a specific parcel of property from Bower (D). The contract provided that Bower (D) would convey, by warranty deed good merchantable title, free and clear of encumbrances, but subject to all recorded restrictions and easements applying to the property. The contract further stated that Bower (D) would be allowed sufficient time to correct any defects in the title. Upon examination of the title, Lohmeyer (P) learned that the subject property was in violation of both a city zoning ordinance and a restrictive covenant previously imposed on the lot. He then sued for rescission of the contract and return of his money. Bower (D) contested Lohmeyer's (P) right to rescind and cross-complained for specific performance. The trial court held for Bower (D) and ordered specific performance of the contract. Lohmeyer (P) appealed.

ISSUE: May property which is in violation of restrictive covenants or city zoning ordinances be conveyed under good merchantable title?

HOLDING AND DECISION: (Parker, J.) No. In order for a title to be merchantable, it must be free from reasonable doubt and must not expose the prospective purchaser to the hazard of potential litigation. A title to property which is in violation of city zoning ordinances or restrictive covenants clearly does not meet the requirement of merchantability. It is obvious that Lohmeyer (P) would be exposed to potential litigation upon purchase of the property in question. It must be stressed that it is the existence of the violation of the ordinance and covenant which makes the title unmerchantable, not the presence of the ordinance or covenant, themselves. Furthermore, the contract provision allowing Bower (D) to correct any defect in title is immaterial in the present case, since any action Bower (D) might take to correct the title defects would materially alter the subject property and effect a breach of contract. Accordingly, the trial court is reversed and Lohmeyer's (P) plea for rescission is granted.

ANALYSIS

As stated in the principal case, the existence of zoning laws generally does not make a title unmarketable. There are several exceptions to this general principle. First, if violations of the laws exist, as in *Lohmeyer*, title may be deemed unmarketable. This is due, however, to the risk of litigation, rather than the presence of the ordinances in and of themselves. Also, where zoning regulations are imposed after the contract is entered into and where they would materially frustrate the buyer's intended use of the property, many courts will not enforce the contract. This again is done for reasons other than unmarketable title. Finally, where the seller knows of relevant zoning laws which would interfere with the buyer's intended use of the property but informs the buyer such use would be permitted, the courts will refuse to enforce the contract.

Quicknotes

EARNEST MONEY A payment made by a buyer to a seller to evidence the intent to fulfill the obligations of a contract to purchase property.

EASEMENT The right to utilize a portion of another's real property for a specific use.

MERCHANTABLE TITLE Title that, although not perfect, would be acceptable to a reasonably well-informed buyer exercising ordinary business prudence.

RESCISSION The canceling of an agreement and the return of the parties to their positions prior to the formation of the contract.

RESTRICTIVE COVENANT A promise contained in a deed to limit the uses to which the property will be made.

SPECIFIC PERFORMANCE An equitable remedy whereby the court requires the parties to perform their obligations pursuant to a contract.

Stambovsky v. Ackley

Repudiating homebuyer (P) v. Haunted house owner (D)

N.Y. App. Div., First Dept., 169 A.D.2d 254, 572 N.Y.S.2d 672 (1991).

NATURE OF CASE: Appeal from the dismissal action for rescission of contract of sale.

FACT SUMMARY: Stambovsky (P), purchaser, contended that he should be entitled to rescind the contract of sale and recover his down payment because Ackley (D), the owner of the house, did not disclose that the house was haunted.

RULE OF LAW

Where a condition that has been created by the seller materially impairs the value of the contract and is peculiarly within the knowledge of the seller or unlikely to be discovered by a prudent purchaser exercising due care with respect to the subject transaction, nondisclosure constitutes a basis for rescission as a matter of equity.

FACTS: Stambovsky (P) discovered that the house he had recently contracted to purchase was widely reputed to be possessed by poltergeists, reportedly seen by Ackley (D), the seller, and members of her family on numerous occasions over the previous nine years. Stambovsky (P) promptly sought rescission of the contract of sale. The New York Supreme Court dismissed the complaint, holding that Stambovsky (P) had no remedy at law within the jurisdiction. Stambovsky (P) appealed.

ISSUE: Does nondisclosure of a condition that has been created by the seller and is peculiarly within the knowledge of the seller or unlikely to be discovered by a prudent purchaser exercising due care with respect to the subject transaction constitute a basis for rescission as a matter of equity?

HOLDING AND DECISION: (Rubin, J.) Yes. Where a condition that has been created by the seller materially impairs the value of the contract and is peculiarly within the knowledge of the seller or unlikely to be discovered by a prudent purchaser exercising due care with respect to the subject transaction, nondisclosure constitutes a basis for rescission as a matter of equity. The unusual facts of this case clearly warrant a grant of equitable relief to Stambovsky (P), who did not have any familiarity with the folklore of the village of Nyack, where the house was located, and could not readily learn that the home he had contracted to buy was haunted. New York law fails to recognize any remedy for damages incurred as a result of the seller's mere silence, applying the doctrine of *caveat emptor.* However, Ackley (D) deliberately fostered the public belief that her home was possessed. Having undertaken to inform the public-at-large, to whom she has no legal relationship, about the supernatural occurrences on her property, she may be said to owe no less a duty to her contract vendee. Where, as here, Ackley (D) not only took unfair advantage of the buyer's (P) ignorance but created and perpetuated a condition about which he was unlikely even to inquire, enforcement of the contract would be offensive to the court's sense of equity. Application of the remedy of rescission, within the bounds of the narrow exception to the doctrine of *caveat emptor,* is entirely appropriate to relieve Stambovsky (P) from the consequences of a most unnatural bargain. Reversed.

DISSENT: (Smith, J.) This court should require something more substantial than a poltergeist before discarding the doctrine of *caveat emptor.*

ANALYSIS

The doctrine of *caveat emptor* requires that a buyer act prudently to assess the fitness and value of his purchase and operates to bar the purchaser who fails to exercise due care from seeking the equitable remedy of rescission. It was apparent from this case, however, that the most careful inspection would not reveal the presence of ghosts at the premises. Therefore, there was no sound policy reason to deny the buyer relief for failing to discover a state of affairs which the most prudent purchaser would not be expected even to contemplate.

Quicknotes

CAVEAT EMPTOR Let the buyer beware; doctrine that a buyer purchases something at his or her own risk.

EQUITY Fairness; justice; the determination of a matter consistent with principles of fairness and not in strict compliance with rules of law.

NONDISCLOSURE The failure to communicate certain facts to another person.

POLTERGEIST Noise; ghost responsible for making noises.

RESCISSION The canceling of an agreement and the return of the parties to their positions prior to the formation of the contract.

Johnson v. Davis

Nondisclosing seller (D) v. Repudiating buyer (P)

Fla. Sup. Ct., 480 So. 2d 625 (1985).

NATURE OF CASE: Appeal of order rescinding a land sale contract.

FACT SUMMARY: The Johnsons (D) failed to disclose to the Davises (P) certain roof defects prior to conveyance of the Johnson (D) residence.

RULE OF LAW

Where the seller of a home knows of facts affecting the value of a home that are not readily observable, the seller is under a duty to disclose.

FACTS: The Davises (P) negotiated with the Johnsons (D) for purchase of the Johnson (D) house. The parties inserted into the sale contract a clause making the Johnsons (D) liable for minor roof repairs. After signing but before conveyance, Ms. Davis (P) noticed certain water spots. Mr. Johnson (D) assured her that they evidenced minor problems already fixed. Not long after conveyance, a storm occurred and water leaked extensively. A roofer concluded that a new roof was necessary. The Davises (P) sued for rescission and return of their deposit, plus costs. The Johnsons (D) counter-claimed, seeking liquidated damages of $5,000. The trial court rescinded, ordered the deposit returned, and awarded liquidated damages. The appellate court reversed the liquidated damages award, and the Johnsons (D) appealed.

ISSUE: Where the seller of a home knows of facts affecting the value of a home that are not readily observable, is the seller under a duty to disclose?

HOLDING AND DECISION: (Adkins, J.) Yes. Where the seller of a home knows of facts affecting the value of a home that are not readily observable, the seller is under a duty to disclose. Common law tort doctrine recognized the difference between nonfeasance and malfeasance, often sanctioning the latter but not the former. However, as more and more courts are realizing, the two circumstances have more similarities than differences, having the same bad motivations and effects. The fact is that in certain situations, a land conveyance being one of them, the seller is in a far better position to be aware of relevant facts than the buyer and should not be permitted to exploit the buyer's poor position. For this reason, the court thinks it fundamentally fair for *caveat emptor* to be abandoned in land sale contracts, and the seller to be placed under a duty to disclose. Affirmed.

ANALYSIS

The court also briefly discussed fraud. The Johnsons (D) apparently fraudulently misrepresented the condition of the roof. They then argued that since the fraud occurred after contract execution it was irrelevant. The court hinted that any fraud prior to conveyance justified rescission, but the broader rule enunciated made a ruling on this issue superfluous.

Quicknotes

CAVEAT EMPTOR Let the buyer beware; doctrine that a buyer purchases something at his or her own risk.

DUTY TO DISCLOSE The duty owed by a fiduciary to reveal those facts that have a material effect on the interests of the party that must be informed.

FRAUDULENT MISREPRESENTATION A statement or conduct by one party to another that constitutes a false representation of fact.

LATENT DEFECTS A defect that cannot be discovered upon ordinary examination.

LIQUIDATED DAMAGES An amount of money specified in a contract representing the damages owed in the event of breach.

MALFEASANCE The commission of an unlawful act.

MISFEASANCE The commission of a lawful act in a wrongful manner.

NONFEASANCE The omission, or failure to perform, an obligation.

RESCISSION The canceling of an agreement and the return of the parties to their positions prior to the formation of the contract.

Lempke v. Dagenais

Subsequent purchaser (P) v. Contractor (D)

N.H. Sup. Ct., 130 N.H. 782, 547 A.2d 290 (1988).

NATURE OF CASE: Appeal of dismissal of action against a contractor for unworkmanlike performance.

FACT SUMMARY: Lempke (P) sought to recover from Dagenais (D) the cost of rebuilding a garage Dagenais (D) had built for the prior owner, which Lempke (P) claimed had been built in a substandard manner.

RULE OF LAW

A subsequent purchaser of property may recover from one performing defective contractor services for the prior owner if the work contained latent defects not apparent at the time of purchase.

FACTS: Lempke's (P) predecessor contracted with Dagenais (D) for the latter to build a garage, which he did. After Lempke (P) purchased the property, structural problems appeared which Lempke (P) claimed were due to substandard work by Dagenais (D). Lempke (P) sued Dagenais (D) for the cost of repair and/or replacement. The trial court dismissed the complaint, ruling that privity was a condition precedent to a cause of action against a builder for unworkmanlike performance. Lempke (P) appealed.

ISSUE: May a subsequent purchaser of property recover from one performing defective contractor services for the prior owner if the work contained latent defects not apparent at the time of purchase?

HOLDING AND DECISION: (Thayer, J.) Yes. A subsequent purchaser of property may recover from one performing defective contractor services for the prior owner if the work contained latent defects not apparent at the time of purchase. New Hampshire, like most states, recognizes in building construction work an implied warranty of workmanlike quality. Much debate has been generated as to whether this warranty is a creature of tort or contract, on the notion that the latter would require privity. However, in a final analysis, the implied warranty, be it tort or contract, arises by operation of law as a matter of public policy. Consequently, whether privity is required is determined by a reference to policy. In this respect, numerous policy reasons for not imposing a privity requirement exist. First, our society is increasingly mobile, and a builder/vendor should not be surprised by a change in ownership. Second, experience teaches us that latent defects often will not show up for years, so a sale to an unsuspecting purchaser is not unlikely. Third, a builder is in a better position to control the quality of the work than a subsequent buyer. Fourth, a contractor is already under an obligation to perform in a workmanlike manner, so the nature of his obligation is not changed by dispensing with privity. Finally, to impose a privity requirement would encourage sham first sales. These policy concerns lead this court to conclude that privity should not be required for a homeowner to sue a vendor/builder for latent defects resulting from substandard work. [The court went on to hold that the measure of damages would be the cost of repair or replacement, and also noted that a vendor/builder's duty did not go on indefinitely, but only for a reasonable time.] Reversed and remanded.

DISSENT: (Souter, J.) This issue was addressed by this court only two years ago, and the result was the opposite. Adequate justification for departure therefrom has not been shown.

ANALYSIS

All jurisdictions recognize some form of implied warranty such as that discussed here. Whether privity is required to assert it varies among the jurisdictions. The trend is generally toward disposing of the requirement. Some jurisdictions take the warranty out of contract and put it into tort. Others simply dispense with the requirement, as this court did.

Quicknotes

CONDITION PRECEDENT The happening of an uncertain occurrence, which is necessary before a particular right or interest may be obtained or an action performed.

IMPLIED WARRANTY An implied promise made by one party to a contract that the other party may rely on a fact, relieving that party from the obligation of determining whether the fact is true and indemnifying the other party from liability if that fact is shown to be false.

LATENT DEFECTS A defect that cannot be discovered upon ordinary examination.

PRIVITY OF CONTRACT A relationship between the parties to a contract that is required in order to bring an action for breach.

Jones v. Lee

Real estate sellers (P) v. Real estate buyers (D)

N.M. Ct. App., 971 P.2d 858 (1998).

NATURE OF CASE: Suit to recover damages for breach of a contract to purchase real estate.

FACT SUMMARY: The Lees (D) entered a written contract to buy real estate owned by the Joneses (P) for $610,000. Three months after the Lees (D) backed out of the deal, the Joneses (P) sold the property for $540,000.

RULE OF LAW
The non-defaulting party under a real estate contract is entitled to an award of damages following a breach of the contract.

FACTS: The parties entered a written agreement under which the Lees (D) would buy a home owned by the Joneses (P) for $610,000, with the Lees (D) paying $6,000 in earnest money to solidify the deal. Two months after entering the written contract, the Lees (D) informed the Joneses (P) that they could not go through with the purchase for financial reasons. The Joneses (P) rejected the Lees' (D) proposed termination agreement and sold the home three months after the breach for $540,000. The Joneses (P) sued the Lees (D) for breach of contract, requesting an award of damages. The trial court returned judgment for the Joneses (P) for the $70,000 difference between the contract price and the actual sale price, for special damages in the amount of $4,109, and for punitive damages, with a total judgment in the amount of $157,118.94. The Lees (D) appealed.

ISSUE: Is the non-defaulting party under a real estate contract entitled to an award of damages following a breach of the contract?

HOLDING AND DECISION: (Donnelly, J.) Yes. The non-defaulting party under a real estate contract is entitled to an award of damages following a breach of the contract. A seller generally can choose from three remedies when a buyer breaches an agreement to purchase real estate: (1) rescission of the contract, (2) specific performance, or (3) damages. In this case, by choosing to pursue damages, the Joneses (P) had the burden of proving the damages they sought. New Mexico analyzes such damages claims under the "loss of the bargain" rule, which requires a showing of the difference between the purchase price and the property's market value when the breach occurred. The parties here agreed that the market value was $610,000 when the breach occurred—which means that the Joneses (P) suffered no compensatory damages, the Lees (D) argued, because the market value and the contract price were identical when the breach occurred. Such an identity of value normally limits a seller's recovery to nominal damages or retention of the buyer's earnest money; the exception to this rule occurs when, as here, the sellers also have incurred special damages. The trial court in this case failed to enter the required findings of fact on the date of the breach and the property's market value on that date. The case therefore must be remanded on the issue of compensatory damages so that the trial court can enter the appropriate factual determinations. Further, the trial court correctly awarded the Joneses (P) special damages for $1,859 in expenses incurred because of the home's solar system and heating warranty. Such expenses are recoverable if they were reasonably foreseeable, and the purchase agreement rendered them reasonably foreseeable in this case. Special damages here also properly included $2,250 for half of the interest on mortgage payments made by the Joneses (P) after the breach. These damages, too, were reasonably foreseeable. Finally, the record also supports an award of punitive damages against the Lees (D). When they breached the contract, claiming "financial reasons" for terminating the transaction, their checking account held approximately $577,000, and their monthly income totaled more than $16,000. The record shows further that the Lees (D) intimidated the Joneses (P) to induce them to accept the termination agreement. Under the circumstances, the Lees (D) breached the contract in a wanton and utterly reckless manner, thereby justifying an award of punitive damages. Affirmed in part; vacated in part and remanded.

ANALYSIS

On remand, the trial judge in *Jones* must calculate compensatory damages by choosing between the parties' stipulated value for the property at the time of the breach—$610,000—and the eventual actual sale price of $540,000. Though the parties' purpose in stipulating to the property's value at the time of the breach was unclear, a stipulation on a fact-issue should receive special, deferential consideration when a trial court establishes a factual record. The Joneses' (P) compensatory damages on remand thus were very likely limited to retention of the Lees' (D) earnest money because the market value and contract price at the time of the breach would have been identical.

Quicknotes

EARNEST MONEY A payment made by a buyer to a seller to evidence the intent to fulfill the obligations of a contract to purchase property.

Continued on next page.

MEASURE OF DAMAGED Monetary compensation that may be awarded by the court to a party, who has sustained injury or loss to his person, property, or rights due to another party's unlawful act, omission, or negligence.

PUNITIVE DAMAGED Damages exceeding the actual injury suffered for the purposes of punishment of the defendant, deterrence of the wrongful behavior or comfort to the plaintiff.

SPECIAL DAMAGED Damages caused by a specific act that are not the usual consequence of that act and which must be specifically pled and proven.

Kutzin v. Pirnie

Real estate sellers (P) v. Real estate buyers (D)

N.J. Sup. Ct., 591 A.2d 932 (1991).

NATURE OF CASE: Suit by real estate sellers for damages sustained from the breach of a purchase contract.

FACT SUMMARY: The Pirnies (D) paid a $36,000 deposit toward the purchase of the Kutzins' (P) house. After the Pirnies (D) defaulted on the purchase, the trial court ordered the Kutzins (P) to return $18,675 of the Pirnies' (D) deposit.

RULE OF LAW

A buyer who materially breaches a real estate purchase contract can recover in restitution for benefits he conferred on the seller through either part performance on the contract or reliance beyond the loss that his own breach caused.

FACTS: The Pirnies (D) entered a written agreement to purchase the Kutzins' (P) house for $365,000. Under the contract, the Pirnies (D) agreed to pay a total deposit of $36,000 within seven days of signing the contract; the contract, however, contained no liquidated-damages clause governing the deposit's return if the sale did not occur. Although the Pirnies (D) performed on their obligation to pay the deposit, they later breached the contract. Six months after the original closing date, the Kutzins (P) sold their house for $352,500 after also incurring extra expenses for utilities, real estate taxes, insurance, and carpeting that they would not have incurred had the Pirnies (D) fulfilled the original purchase agreement. The Kutzins (P) sued, and the trial court awarded them various damages totaling $17,325: $12,500 for the difference between the contract price and the eventual sale price; $3,825 in utilities; and $1,000 for new carpet. The trial court also ordered the Kutzins (P) to return $18,675 to the Pirnies (D) as the difference between the deposit and the Kutzins' (P) actual damages. The Kutzins (P) appealed, claiming that the trial court should have awarded them the entire deposit; the Pirnies (D) cross-appealed, arguing that the contract had been rescinded and that they therefore were entitled to a return of their entire deposit. The appellate court affirmed the trial court's denial of recovery for taxes and insurance, reasoning that such expenses were too speculative, but the appellate court followed well-established law and reversed the trial court's order requiring a return of part of the deposit. The Kutzins (P), the appellate court held, were entitled to keep the entire deposit of $36,000. The Pirnies (D) requested further review in the Supreme Court of New Jersey.

ISSUE: Can a buyer who materially breaches a real estate purchase contract recover in restitution for benefits he conferred on the seller through either part performance on the contract or reliance beyond the loss that his own breach caused?

HOLDING AND DECISION: (Clifford, J.) Yes. A buyer who materially breaches a real estate purchase contract can recover in restitution for benefits he conferred on the seller through either part performance on the contract or reliance beyond the loss that his own breach caused. The majority rule is that a buyer who breaches his purchase contract may not recover his deposit. A definite recent trend in the law, however, sees an injustice in permitting a seller to retain a deposit in excess of his actual damages. In this respect, Professor Corbin has observed that a defaulting buyer should receive restitution for that portion of his deposit that the evidence shows to be a penalty rather than compensatory damages. Section 374(1) of the Restatement (Second) of Contracts now states this developing position: the party in breach may recover restitution for benefits he conferred through either part performance or reliance beyond the loss that his own breach caused. Any New Jersey cases to the contrary are hereby overruled, and this Court adopts the approach described in Section 374(1) of the Restatement. Accordingly, in this case the Pirnies (D) are entitled to a return of that portion of their deposit that exceeds the Kutzins' (P) actual damages: $18,675. The buyer has the burden of proving entitlement to such a recovery, and the Pirnies (D) have met that burden here. Also worth noting is that the contract in this case contained no liquidated-damages provision; such a provision would have required New Jersey courts to use Section 374(2) of the Restatement. The trial court's damages award should be reinstated. With that modification, the appellate court's judgment is affirmed.

ANALYSIS

Kutzin points up the tension in the law between fairness and administrative or evidentiary expedience. As the *Kutzin* court notes, courts are recognizing an injustice in permitting a non-defaulting seller to withhold a deposit that exceeds his actual damages. As always, though, balanced against the interests of fairness and accuracy are the evidentiary and administrative issues involved with ascertaining actual damages in such cases. According to the casebook, most courts permit retaining the deposit in these cases, partly because of the evidentiary difficulties of proving damages. The New Jersey Supreme Court goes some distance in *Kutzin* to resolve this difficulty by placing the burden of proof on the buyer who demands return of his deposit.

Continued on next page.

Quicknotes

FORFEITURE CLAUSE A clause providing for the loss of property or a right without compensation therefor.

LIQUIDATED DAMAGED An amount of money specified in a contract representing the damages owed in the event of breach.

PART PERFORMANCE Partial performance of a contract, promise, or obligation.

RELIANCE Dependence on a fact that causes a party to act or refrain from acting.

RESTITUTION The return or restoration to rightful owner to prevent unjust enrichment.

UNJUST ENRICHMENT Principle that one should not be unjustly enriched at the expense of another.

Brown v. Lober

Purchaser (P) v. Seller's executor (D)

Ill. Sup. Ct., 75 Ill. 2d 547, 389 N.E.2d 1188 (1979).

NATURE OF CASE: Appeal from award of damages for breach of the covenant of quiet enjoyment.

FACT SUMMARY: Brown (P) acquired the subject property under a general warranty deed despite the fact that a two-thirds interest in mineral rights had previously been reserved.

RULE OF LAW

The mere existence of a superior title does not constitute a breach of the covenant of quiet enjoyment.

FACTS: Brown (P) acquired a parcel of property from Bost under a general warranty deed containing no exceptions. Unknown to Brown (P), the property contained a reservation of a two-thirds interest in mineral rights by Bost's grantor. Seventeen years after purchasing the land, Brown (P) contracted to sell the mineral rights for $6,000, but was forced to lower the price to $2,000 when the parties learned of the prior reservation of rights. Because the 10-year statute of limitations prevented Brown (P) from suing for breach of warranty, he chose to sue Bost's executor, Lober (D), for breach of the covenant of quiet enjoyment of the premises. In effect, Brown (P) claimed that the existence of the rights reservation constituted a constructive eviction. The trial court held for Lober (D) and the appellate court reversed. The case was then appealed to the Illinois Supreme Court.

ISSUE: Does the mere existence of a paramount title in a third-party constitute a breach of the covenant of quiet enjoyment by the vender of property?

HOLDING AND DECISION: (Underwood, J.) No. Brown (P) was in no way hindered from the peaceable possession and enjoyment of his property by someone holding superior title. The mere fact that he had to renegotiate his contract for the assignment of mineral rights does not constitute an interference with quiet enjoyment. Thus the suit was premature. The covenant of quiet enjoyment guarantees only possession and enjoyment of the premises, not a perfect title. Since there was no interference with the use of the property or assertion of an adverse title, there was no breach. The reservation of mineral rights was a matter of public record and Brown (P) could therefore have maintained an action for breach of warranty. However, he let the statute of limitations run and lost his opportunity. He may not now prevail on a premature claim of breach of quiet enjoyment. Reversed.

ANALYSIS

A general warranty deed typically contains the following five covenants: covenant of seisin, covenant of right to convey, covenant against encumbrances, covenant of quiet enjoyment, and covenant of warranty. Sometimes a sixth covenant, of further assurances, is included in the deed. This states that the covenantor will perform any reasonably necessary acts to perfect the purchaser's title. The general warranty deed covenants serve to warrant title against imperfections which occurred before the time which the grantor assumed his title, as well as during his time of title. The first three covenants (seisin, right to convey, and against encumbrances) are deemed present covenants. Thus a breach occurs, if at all, at the time the covenant is made and a cause of action arises at that time. In contrast, the last three covenants are future covenants and are not breached until the time the covenantee's possession is actually interfered with.

Quicknotes

COVENANT OF QUIET ENJOYMENT A promise contained in a lease or a deed that the tenant or grantee will enjoy unimpaired use of the property.

COVENANTEE A party for whom a promise is made pursuant to a written agreement.

FUTURE COVENANTS A written promise to do, or to refrain from doing, a particular activity in the future.

GENERAL WARRANTY DEED A deed that guarantees that the conveyor possesses that title that he purports to convey.

PRESENT COVENANTS Covenant to do an act at the present moment.

RESERVATION OF RIGHTS A clause in a deed or other instrument reserving particular rights to the grantor of the property.

Frimberger v. Anzellotti

Wetlands purchaser (P) v. Seller (D)

Conn. App. Ct., 25 Conn. App. 401, 594 A.2d 1029 (1991).

NATURE OF CASE: Appeal from award of damages for breach of warranty.

FACT SUMMARY: Anzellotti (D) contended that she did not breach the warranty against encumbrances and did not innocently misrepresent the condition of property purchased by Frimberger (P) and subsequently found to be in violation of wetlands statutes.

RULE OF LAW

Latent violations of state or municipal land use regulations (1) that do not appear on the land records, (2) that are unknown to the seller of the property, (3) as to which the agency charged with enforcement has taken no official action to compel compliance at the time the deed was executed, and (4) that have not ripened into an interest that can be recorded on the land records do not constitute an encumbrance for the purpose of the deed warranty.

FACTS: In 1978, Anzellotti's (D) brother, DiLoreto, subdivided a parcel of land for the purposes of constructing residences. The property abutted a tidal marshland and was, therefore, subject to the provisions of General Statutes §§ 22a-28 controlling the development of wetlands. DiLoreto built a bulkhead and filled that portion of the subject parcel immediately adjacent to the wetlands area and then proceeded with the construction of a dwelling on the property. DiLoreto then transferred the property to Anzellotti (D) by quit claim deed. Anzellotti (D), in turn, transferred the property to Frimberger (P) by warranty deed, free and clear of all encumbrances but subject to all building and zoning restrictions. Deciding to perform repairs on the land, Frimberger (P) requested a survey of the tidal wetlands from the state department of environmental protection (DEP). The survey discovered a violation of §§ 22a-30 of the General Statutes. DEP suggested that to correct the violation, Frimberger (P) submit an application to DEP, demonstrating the necessity of maintaining the bulkhead and fill within the tidal wetlands. Instead of filing the application, Frimberger (P) sued Anzellotti (D), claiming damages for breach of the warranty against encumbrances and innocent misrepresentation. The trial court found for Frimberger (P), holding that Anzellotti (D) breached the warranty against encumbrances and had innocently misrepresented the conditions. The court awarded Frimberger (P) $47,792.60, a figure that included costs to fix the land and diminution of value of the property caused by the violation. Anzellotti (D) appealed.

ISSUE: Does an alleged latent violation of a land use statute or regulation, existing on the land at the time title is conveyed, constitute an encumbrance such that the conveyance breaches the grantor's covenant against encumbrances?

HOLDING AND DECISION: (Lavery, J.) No. Latent violations of state or municipal land use regulations that do not appear on the land records, that are unknown to the seller of the property, as to which the agency charged with enforcement has taken no official action to compel compliance at the time the deed was executed, and that have not ripened into an interest that can be recorded on the land records do not constitute an encumbrance for the purpose of the deed warranty. The New Jersey Supreme Court in *Fahmie v. Wulster*, 81 N.J. 391, 408 A.2d 789 (1979), concluded that it was generally the law throughout the country that a claim for breach of a covenant against encumbrances cannot be predicated on the necessity to repair or alter the property to conform with land use regulations. By so doing, the *Fahmie* court refused to expand the concept of an encumbrance to include structural conditions existing on the property that constitute violations of a statute or governmental regulation. The case at bar raises the same issues as those raised in *Fahmie.* Here, in 1978 the wetlands area was filled without a permit and in violation of state statute. The alleged violation was unknown to Anzellotti (D), was not on the land records, and was discovered only after Frimberger (P) attempted to get permission to perform additional improvements to the wetlands area. The reasoning in *Fahmie* is correct, because to hold otherwise would create uncertainty in the law of conveyances, title searches, and title insurance. The parties to conveyance of real property can adequately protect themselves from such conditions by including protective language in the contract and by insisting on appropriate provisions in the deed. Frimberger (P), an attorney and land developer, who had previously developed waterfront property and was aware of wetlands statutes, could have adequately protected himself from any liability for wetlands violations. As for innocent misrepresentation, at no time was any representation made relating to the wetlands area. Because the warranty of a covenant against encumbrances was not violated, no misrepresentation could have been made. Reversed and remanded.

ANALYSIS

An encumbrance is defined as "every right to or interest in the land which may subsist in third persons, to the diminution of the value of the land, but consistent with the passing of the fee by the conveyance." All encumbrances may be classed as (1) a pecuniary charge against the

Continued on next page.

premises, such as mortgages, judgment liens, tax liens, or assessments, (2) estates or interests in the property less than the fee, like leases or life estates, or (3) easements or servitudes on the land, such as rights of way, restrictive covenants, and profits. It is important to note that the covenant against encumbrances cannot be breached unless the encumbrance existed at the time of the conveyance.

Quicknotes

WARRANTY AGAINST ENCUMBRANCES A guarantee in a contract that the interest in property being conveyed is unencumbered.

Rockafellor v. Gray

Remote grantees (P) v. Remote grantor (D)

Iowa Sup. Ct., 194 Iowa 1280, 191 N.W. 107 (1922).

NATURE OF CASE: Appeal from award of damages for breach of covenant of seisin.

FACT SUMMARY: Hansen & Gregerson (P), the remote grantees of a deed from Connelly (D), sued for a breach of the covenant of seisin.

RULE OF LAW

The breach of the covenant of seisin creates a chose in action which passes by assignment to subsequent grantees of the deed.

FACTS: Gray held a mortgage on a certain parcel of property which was obtained by Rockafellor. When payments were missed, Gray foreclosed on the mortgage. This resulted in the acquisition of the property by sheriff's deed by Connelly (D). Connelly (D) subsequently conveyed the property by warranty deed to Dixon in 1911 for $4,000. Dixon then sold it to Hansen & Gregerson (hereinafter Hansen) (P) for $7,000. In 1920, Rockafellor filed suit to vacate the foreclosure sale on the ground that the court lacked proper jurisdiction over him. Hansen (P) then filed a cross-petition, praying for a judgment against the remote grantor, Connelly (D), in the event that Rockafellor succeeded in vacating the foreclosure sale. The basis for Hansen's (P) claim was that Connelly (D) breached the covenant of seisin when he sold property to Dixon which in truth he did not own. The trial court vacated the foreclosure sale and rendered judgment on Hansen's (P) cross-complaint against Connelly (D) for $4,000. Connelly (D) appealed from the judgment against him only.

ISSUE: Does the breach of the covenant of seisin pass to remote grantees of the original covenantor as a chose in action?

HOLDING AND DECISION: (Faville, J.) Yes. The state of Iowa follows the English rule, which is the minority rule in America, that the covenant of seisin, runs with the land. Thus when the covenant is broken, it becomes a chose in action and is passed by assignment to subsequent grantees of the deed. Admittedly, there is an exception to this rule, arising from the situation where the original covenantor has neither title nor possession of the premises at the time the deed is executed and delivered. In such a case, the cause of action for the breach of the covenant of seisin arises immediately and is imbued in the immediate grantee. When the grantee subsequently assigns the deed to others, the cause of action for the breach is transferred along with the property. However, because the cause of action accrued immediately, the statute of limitations, which in Iowa is ten years, applies. Thus in the present case, it is irrelevant whether or not the remote grantor, Connelly (D), had title and possession at the time he delivered the deed to Dixon since the suit was brought nine years after the cause of action accrued, and is therefore valid. Since Hansen (P) acquired the right to sue for the breach of covenant as either a chose in action or a cause of action at the time he acquired the deed, he is entitled to judgment in this case. This is because Connelly (D) warranted that he was properly seized of the property when in fact he was not, as the foreclosure sale by which he acquired the deed was later judged invalid. Finally, the lower court's award of $4,000 was proper despite Connelly's (D) argument to the contrary. He offered evidence that despite the recital of $4,000 as consideration in the deed, the amount actually paid was nominal. Therefore, since Hansen's (P) cause of action accrues through the immediate grantee, he may not recover more damages than the immediate grantee would be entitled to. However, Hansen (P) was entitled to rely on the amount specified in the deed from Connelly (D) to Dixon. Even though Connelly (D) would be entitled to raise the discrepancy between the deed price and the price actually paid in an action against Dixon, it would be unfair to allow him to do so against a remote grantee. Affirmed.

ANALYSIS

In the majority of jurisdictions, the breach of the covenant of seisin (a present covenant) occurs at the time of conveyance and therefore cannot be said to run with the land. The cause of action for the breach arises at the time of conveyance and is subject to the restrictions of the statute of limitations. Under the common law, there was no implied assignment of the cause of action when the title was conveyed. However, some jurisdictions follow the English rule, under which such an assignment is implied.

Quicknotes

CHOSE IN ACTION The right to recover, or the item recoverable, in a law suit.

COVENANT OF SEISIN A promise that the conveyor of property has the lawful right to convey the interest he is attempting to transfer.

FORECLOSURE SALE Termination of an interest in property, usually initiated by a lienholder upon failure to tender mortgage payments, resulting in the sale of the property in order to satisfy the debt.

Sweeney v. Sweeney

Grantor's widow (P) v. Grantee (D)

Conn. Sup. Ct. of Errors, 126 Conn. 391, 11 A.2d 806 (1940).

NATURE OF CASE: Action to cancel a deed.

FACT SUMMARY: Maurice, Sweeney's (P) intestate, gave property to John Sweeney (D) by deed which was recorded, and John (D) deeded the property back to Maurice, who wished to be protected in the event John (D) predeceased him, but that deed was not recorded.

RULE OF LAW

Where a deed has been formally executed and delivered, the presumption that the grantee assented to delivery can be overcome only by evidence that no delivery was in fact intended.

FACTS: Sweeney (P) is Maurice Sweeney's widow and administratrix. Maurice deeded property to John Sweeney (D). This deed was recorded. Pursuant to Maurice's request, a second deed was executed which deeded the property back to him. This deed was not recorded. A week or two later, Maurice took John (D) the recorded deed, and a week or two after that he took John (D) the unrecorded deed. John (D) gave the second deed to his attorney. When the latter's office was burned, the deed was destroyed. Maurice's purpose in making the second deed was so that he would be protected if John (D) predeceased him. Maurice continued to live on the deeded property until his death. He made leases in regard to it and exercised full control over it without interference from John (D). The trial court concluded that there was no intention to deliver John's (D) deed to Maurice and there was no delivery or acceptance thereof.

ISSUE: Has a deed been delivered where it was formally executed and manually delivered and where there is no evidence that no delivery was intended?

HOLDING AND DECISION: (Jennings, J.) Yes. It is true that physical possession of a duly executed deed is not conclusive proof that it was legally delivered. Delivery must be made with the intent to pass title if it is to be effective. However, where a deed has been manually delivered, there is a rebuttable presumption that the grantee assented since the deed was beneficial to him. Where deeds are formally executed and delivered, this presumption can be overcome only by evidence that no delivery was in fact intended. In this case the only purpose in making the deed expressed by either party was Maurice's statement that it was to protect him in case John (D) predeceased him. Since this purpose would have been defeated had there been no delivery with intent to pass title, this conclusively establishes the fact that there was legal delivery. John (D) also contended that the delivery was on the condition that John (D) predeceased Maurice. However, a conditional delivery can only be made by placing the deed in the hands of a third person to be kept until the happening of the condition. The court's ruling is reversed.

ANALYSIS

The delivery must be voluntary and must occur with the mutual intention of the parties to pass title. The term "escrow" is sometimes used as importing any deposit of a deed for delivery upon the performance of a condition. There can be no escrow without conditional delivery of the deed to a third person as depositary. "Conditional delivery to a grantee vests absolute title in the latter."

Quicknotes

DELIVERY The transfer of title or possession of property.

Rosengrant v. Rosengrant

Conveyance contestants (P) v. Alleged grantee (D)

Okla. Ct. App., 629 P.2d 800 (1981).

NATURE OF CASE: Petition to cancel a deed purporting to transfer real property to only one of the grantors' six nieces and nephews.

FACT SUMMARY: A retired couple tried to convey their farm to one of their nieces and nephews. After the couple died, the other nieces and nephews challenged the conveyance for lack of legal delivery.

RULE OF LAW

Grantors do not legally deliver a deed if they reserve the right to retrieve the deed, require that the delivery may become operative only when the grantors have died, and keep using the property as if it were still their own.

FACTS: A retired couple, Harold and Mildred Rosengrant, who had no children of their own, tried to convey their farm to J.W. ("Jay") Rosengrant (D), one of the couple's six nieces and nephews. Harold and Mildred both signed a deed transferring the property to Jay (D), but they also asked him to leave the deed at their bank, saying that he could record the deed after they died. Harold himself handed the deed to Jay (D) at the bank during their meeting with the banker, apparently in an effort to comply with the legal requirement that a deed be delivered. Jay (D) took the deed from Harold but then handed it to the banker. The banker then held the deed in a safety deposit box in an envelope marked as being for "J.W. Rosengrant or Harold Rosengrant." Six days after Harold died Jay (D) recorded the deed. Nineteen days after recordation, a petition to cancel the deed was filed [by other nieces and nephews of Harold and Mildred Rosengrant]. The petition to cancel alleged that the deed was not legally delivered, and was therefore void, or that the deed was only a testamentary instrument and therefore failed to comply with the Statute of Wills. The trial court agreed with the petitioners' first argument and voided the deed for lack of legal delivery. Jay (D) appealed.

ISSUE: Do grantors legally deliver a deed if they reserve the right to retrieve the deed, require that the delivery may become operative only when the grantors have died, and keep using the property as if it were still their own?

HOLDING AND DECISION: (Boydston, J.) No. Grantors do not legally deliver a deed if they reserve the right to retrieve the deed, require that the delivery may become operative only when the grantors have died, and keep using the property as if it were still their own. The grantor's intent at the time of delivery controls the question of whether legal delivery occurred. Here, as the writing on the envelope clearly signified, Harold could have retrieved the deed at any time. The same conclusion finds support in Harold and Mildred's conditioning the conveyance on two future events: their deaths and the deed's recordation by Jay (D) after they died. Also significant is that Harold and Mildred continued to live on the farm and kept using it as their own even after the alleged conveyance to Jay (D). Under these circumstances, the evidence supports the trial court's judgment finding the deed null and void for lack of delivery. Affirmed.

CONCURRENCE: (Brightmire, J.) Although the facts in cases like this one can be difficult to determine, the applicable law is clear: the grantor must actually or constructively deliver the deed to the grantee, and the grantor must evince an intent to divest himself of his interest. To help the courts determine the pertinent facts in this case, only one of the four people involved in the original conveyance meeting at the bank—Jay (D) himself—is still alive and able to testify. Jay's (D) self-serving statements at the trial in this case therefore suffer inherent problems with credibility. Harold and Mildred's conduct after the meeting only further implies that they did not intend to deliver the deed to Jay (D). Even if they did so intend, they also retained a right to revoke the conveyance. Either way, the deed was not validly delivered.

ANALYSIS

The legal requirement of delivery is not an empty formality, as the *Rosengrant* court emphasizes. Even though Harold and Mildred obviously intended to reward Jay (D) for his and his wife's kindness, the totality of the evidence just as clearly demonstrates in Harold and Mildred a hesitation, an indecision that contradicted a legally binding intent, to deliver.

Quicknotes

CONVEYANCE OF TITLE Any transfer or conveyance having an effect on title to an interest in real property.

NULLITY An act having no legal effect.

STATUTE OF WILLS An English law stating the requirements for a valid testamentary disposition.

TESTAMENTARY INSTRUMENT An instrument that takes effect upon the death of the maker.

Murphy v. Fin. Dev. Corp.

Defaulting mortgagor (P) v. Foreclosing mortgagee (D)

N.H. Sup. Ct., 126 N.H. 536, 495 A.2d 1245 (1985).

NATURE OF CASE: Appeal from order setting aside a foreclosure.

FACT SUMMARY: Murphy (P) contended that Financial Development Corporation (Financial) (D) failed to use due diligence in attempting to get a reasonable price for his property in a foreclosure sale.

RULE OF LAW

Mere compliance with statutory requirements may not discharge a mortgagee's duty to exercise good faith and due diligence in selling the property at foreclosure.

FACTS: Murphy (P) was the mortgagor of his residence, the mortgagee being Financial (D). Murphy (P) defaulted on loan payments and attempted several times to renegotiate and refinance the debt. Financial (D) cooperated by postponing the foreclosure sale at least once, but subsequently held the sale after proper notice. No one other than Murphy (P) appeared at the sale, at which Financial (D) pledged its mortgage and obtained title to the property. Murphy (P) sued to set aside the sale on the basis that Financial (D) failed to use due diligence in obtaining a fair price for the property. A special master was appointed who held for Murphy (P) and awarded attorney fees. Financial (D) appealed.

ISSUE: Does compliance with foreclosure sale statutes fulfill the mortgagee's duties to the mortgagor?

HOLDING AND DECISION: (Douglas, J.) No. Mere compliance with statutory requirements may not discharge a mortgagee's duty to exercise good faith and due diligence in selling the property at foreclosure. A mortgagee has an affirmative duty to act as a fiduciary toward the mortgagor's equity in the home. In this case, $27,000 was pledged for property worth twice that. No other bids were affirmatively solicited. Thus the base notice requirements did not discharge the mortgagee's duties. However, no bad faith was present, and thus no attorney fees were recoverable. Affirmed in part, reverse in part; and remanded.

ANALYSIS

The property was sold soon after the foreclosure sale, but before any controversy had arisen. The buyer clearly was a bona fide purchaser; thus title to the property was not at issue here. Damages were set at the difference between a fair price for the property and the price obtained at foreclosure. This differed from the master's ruling which used the fair market value as a starting point.

Quicknotes

BONA FIDE PURCHASER A party who purchases property in good faith and for valuable consideration without notice of a defect in title.

DUE DILIGENCE The standard of care as would be taken by a reasonable person in accordance with the attendant facts and circumstances.

FAIR MARKET VALUE The price of particular property or goods that a buyer would offer and a seller accept in the open market, following full disclosure.

FORECLOSURE An action to recover the amount due on a mortgage of real property where the owner has failed to pay their debt, terminating the owner's interest in the property which must then be sold to satisfy the debt.

POWER OF SALE MORTGAGE A clause contained in a mortgage granting the mortgagee the authority to sell the property that is the subject of the mortgage upon default of the mortgage payments.

PROMISSORY NOTE A written promise to tender a stated amount of money at a designated time and to a designated person.

Commonwealth v. Fremont Investment & Loan

Massachusetts (P) v. Industrial bank (D)

897 N.E.2d 548 (Mass. 2008).

NATURE OF CASE: Appeal from trial court's granting of preliminary injunction to state.

FACT SUMMARY: Fremont (D) was selling subprime, adjustable rate mortgages to thousands of Massachusetts residents. The Commonwealth's Attorney General's office brought suit alleging the sale of such mortgages was a violation of the state's consumer protection statute.

RULE OF LAW

Mortgage loans with the following four characteristics would likely be "unfair" under the Massachusetts consumer protection statute: (1) the loans were adjustable with a preliminary rate for three years; (2) the initial rate was typically three points lower than the usual mortgage rate on 30-year loans; (3) the debt to income ratio would exceed 50 percent after the introductory period expired; and (4) the loan-to-value ratio was 100 percent.

FACTS: Fremont (D) was selling loans to thousands of residents in Massachusetts. There is no dispute the loans in question had the four characteristics mentioned in the Rule of Law. In March 2007, Fremont (D) entered into an agreement with the Federal Deposit Insurance Corporation (FDIC) to cease granting subprime loans to customers without considering whether the customer would be able to pay the monthly loan amounts after the rate increased. Subsequently, Massachusetts entered into a similar agreement with Fremont. (D). Accordingly, Fremont (D) had to give the Attorney General's (P) office 90 days notice before any foreclosures. If the Attorney General (P) objected, Fremont (D) would attempt to resolve the matter short of foreclosure. As it turned out, the Attorney General (P) objected to all foreclosure requests. The Attorney General then filed this action to enjoin Fremont (D) from foreclosing on such loans because the loans were "unfair" under G.L. c. 93A, the Massachusetts consumer protection statute. The judge granted the preliminary injunction. The court ordered Fremont (D) to give notice to the Attorney General (P) prior to foreclosures and ordered Freemont (D) to resolve any foreclosure issues with the Attorney General (P). If there was no resolution, Fremont (D) was required to go to court for an order of foreclosure. Fremont (D) appealed on the grounds that its loans were customary in the industry and, therefore, the loans were not unfair.

ISSUE: Are mortgage loans with the following four characteristics likely to be "unfair" under the state's consumer protection statute: (1) the loans were adjustable with a preliminary rate for three years; (2) the initial rate was typically three points lower than the usual mortgage rate on 30-year loans; (3) the debt to income ratio would exceed 50 percent after the introductory period expired; and (4) the loan-to-value ratio was 100 percent?

HOLDING AND DECISION: (Botsford, J.) Yes. Mortgage loans with the following four characteristics would likely be "unfair" under the state's consumer protection statute: (1) the loans were adjustable with a preliminary rate for three years; (2) the initial rate was typically three points lower than the usual mortgage rate on 30-year loans; (3) the debt to income ratio would exceed 50 percent after the introductory period expired; and (4) the loan-to-value ratio was 100 percent. First, Fremont's (D) argument that the adjustable rate mortgage (ARM) loans were not unfair because they were standard practice in the industry is without merit. The record at the preliminary injunction stage revealed that Fremont (D) knew or should have known that loans that had the four characteristics stated above would most likely be difficult to repay. In addition, the record below reveals that Fremont (D) did not attempt to determine if borrowers would be able to pay the monthly loan amounts after the rate increased. FDIC's actions in this matter underscored its belief that these loans constitute unsafe and unsound banking practices. Regarding the Massachusetts Predatory Home Loan Practices Act, Fremont (D) is correct that the statute technically does not apply because that statute only applies to high-cost home mortgage loans. However, the trial court judge used the statute for policy support to conclude that loans are unfair where the lender should know the borrower will be unable to repay the loan. Lastly, that the loans in question are technically allowed by state and federal regulations does not mean they are not unfair. It has long been held that a determination of whether conduct is permitted by statute is just one aspect of the fairness analysis. It is not dispositive. The preliminary injunction is affirmed.

ANALYSIS

This case is an example of a successful government action against the subprime lenders in the wake of the mortgage crisis. However, surprisingly, other states have not followed Massachusetts's tactic of using a local consumer protection statute. Rather, a handful of other states have brought actions against subprime lenders under the federal Securities Act of 1933.

Continued on next page.

Quicknotes

MORTGAGE An interest in land created by a written instrument providing security for the payment of a debt or the performance of a duty.

PRELIMINARY INJUNCTION A judicial mandate issued to require or restrain a party from certain conduct; used to preserve a trial's subject matter or to prevent threatened injury.

Bean v. Walker

Home seller (P) v. Defaulting buyer (D)

N.Y. App. Div., Fourth Dept., 95 A.D.2d 70, 464 N.Y.S.2d 895 (1983).

NATURE OF CASE: **Appeal from summary judgment granting repossession of real property branch of a land purchase contract.**

FACT SUMMARY: **Bean (P), a vendor, contended that Walker (D), a defaulting vendee, had no rights pursuant to their land purchase agreement, and that he should be able to repossess the premises and retain all the money paid under the contract.**

RULE OF LAW

The vendee under a land sale contract acquires an interest in the property of such a nature that it must be extinguished before the vendor may resume possession.

FACTS: In January 1973, Bean (P) agreed to sell and Walker (D) agreed to buy a home for $15,000. The contract provided that this sum would be paid over a 15-year period at five % interest, in monthly installments of $118.62. Bean (P) retained legal title to the property, which they agreed to convey upon payment in full. The contract provided that in the event Walker (D) defaulted in making payments and failed to cure the default within 30 days, Bean (P) could elect to call the remaining balance immediately due or elect to declare the contract terminated and repossess the premises. If the latter alternative was chosen, Bean (P) could retain all the money paid under the contract as "liquidated" damages. For eight years, Walker (D) paid Bean (P) as provided in their agreement. In 1981, Walker (D) came on hard times due to an injury and defaulted on the contract, having already paid over $12,000 in principal and interest and having made substantial improvement to the house. Bean (P), after the required 30-day period, commenced an action for ejectment, to be adjudged the owner in fee granted possession. From summary judgment for Bean (P), Walker (D) appealed.

ISSUE: Does the vendee under a land sale contract acquire an interest in the property of such a nature that it must be extinguished before the vendor may resume possession?

HOLDING AND DECISION: (Doerr, J.) Yes. The vendee under a land sale contract acquires an interest in the property of such a nature that it must be extinguished before the vendor may resume possession. Such an interest exists since the vendee acquires equitable title and the vendor merely holds the legal title in trust for the vendee, subject to the vendor's equitable lien for payment of the purchase price in accordance with the terms of the contract. The vendor may not enforce his rights by the simple expedient of an action in ejectment but must instead proceed to foreclose the vendee's equitable title or bring an action at law for the purchase price, neither of which remedies Bean (P) sought. The effect of the judgment granted below is that Bean (P) will have regained the property with improvements made over the years by Walker (D), along with $12,000 in principal and interest. This result would be quite inequitable. Reversed and remanded.

ANALYSIS

If the only substantive law to be applied to this case was that of contracts, the result reached by the lower court would have been correct. However, under the facts presented in the case, the law with regard to the transfer of real property must also be considered. The doctrine that equity deems as done that which ought to be done is an appropriate concept which applies to the present case. Walker (D) did not abandon the property or pay a minimal balance before he defaulted. Unfortunate circumstances prevented him from continuing what he had previously and faithfully done for over eight years. Such factors will not be taken lightly.

Quicknotes

EQUITABLE TITLE Interest in property that is not recognized in a court of law but that is protected in equity.

FIDUCIARY Person holding a legal obligation to act for the benefit of another.

LEGAL TITLE Title such that is recognized by a court of law.

LIQUIDATED DAMAGES An amount of money specified in a contract representing the damages owed in the event of breach.

MORTGAGEE Party to whom an interest in property is given in order to secure a loan.

MORTGAGOR Party who grants an interest in property in order to secure a loan.

SUMMARY JUDGMENT Judgment rendered by a court in response to a motion by one of the parties, claiming that the lack of a question of material fact in respect to an issue warrants disposition of the issue without consideration by the jury.

CHAPTER 8

Title Assurance

Quick Reference Rules of Law

PAGE

1. **The Indexes.** An instrument, which describes the property to be conveyed as "all of the grantor's property in a certain county," is not sufficiently specific as to be effective against subsequent purchasers and mortgagees, unless they have actual knowledge of the transfer. (Luthi v. Evans) *78*

2. **The Indexes.** A misspelled name does not give constructive notice to title searchers under the doctrine of *idem sonans*. (Orr v. Byers) *79*

3. **Types of Recording Acts.** An unacknowledged deed does not qualify for recordation and therefore the recording does not give constructive notice to subsequent purchasers. (Messersmith v. Smith) *80*

4. **Chain of Title Problems.** The recording of a deed from a grantee in an unrecorded deed to a third person is not notice of the prior unrecorded deed to a subsequent purchaser. (Board of Education of Minneapolis v. Hughes) *81*

5. **Chain of Title Problems.** A grantee is bound by restrictions in deeds to its neighbors from a common grantor, even if it takes without actual notice and his deed does not mention them, if the grantor has placed in writing the same restrictions on his remaining land. (Guillette v. Daly Dry Wall, Inc.) *82*

6. **Persons Protected by the Recording System.** One cannot claim bona fide purchaser status if he receives actual notice of an unrecorded interest in real estate prior to taking title. (Daniels v. Anderson) *83*

7. **Persons Protected by the Recording System.** A person who records an interest in real estate after a bona fide purchaser (BFP) takes title thereto is inferior to the BFP, even if that BFP has not paid for the property. (Lewis v. Superior Court) *84*

8. **Inquiry Notice.** A deed which specifically refers to an earlier unrecorded deed puts a subsequent purchaser on notice of the existence of the earlier deed; thus, the purchaser claiming under the later deed is not entitled to priority, though the later deed was recorded first. (Harper v. Paradise) *85*

9. **Inquiry Notice.** Subsequent successors to legal title, after a contract to convey title has been executed, take title subject to all equitable interests of which they have notice. (Waldorff Insurance and Bonding, Inc. v. Eglin National Bank) *86*

10. **Title Insurance.** A title company's liability is limited to the policy, and the company is not liable in tort for negligence for searching records if it has not expressly contracted or implicitly agreed to do so. (Walker Rogge, Inc. v. Chelsea Title & Guaranty Co.) *87*

11. **Title Insurance.** A title insurance company is obligated to protect the insured against defects in title but not against loss arising from physical damage to property. (Lick Mill Creek Apartments v. Chicago Title Insurance Co.) *89*

Luthi v. Evans

Subsequent assignee of oil and gas leases (P) v. Prior assignee (D)

Kan. Sup. Ct., 223 Kan. 622, 576 P.2d 1064 (1978).

NATURE OF CASE: Appeal from award of lease interest.

FACT SUMMARY: Grace V. Owens assigned her interest in all her Coffey County leases "whether or not the same are specifically enumerated above . . . ." to International Tours, Inc. (D); Owens subsequently assigned a lease, unenumerated in the first assignment, to J.R. Burris (P).

RULE OF LAW

An instrument, which describes the property to be conveyed as "all of the grantor's property in a certain county," is not sufficiently specific as to be effective against subsequent purchasers and mortgagees, unless they have actual knowledge of the transfer.

FACTS: On February 1, 1971, Grace V. Owens assigned all her interests in seven oil and gas leases located in Coffey County, Kansas, to International Tours, Inc. (D). The instrument further assigned Owens's interest in all Coffey County oil and gas leases "whether or not the same are specifically enumerated above . . . ." (This is an example of a "Mother Hubbard" clause.) The assignment was recorded on February 16, 1971. On January 30, 1975, Owens assigned a Coffey County oil and gas lease that had not been specifically enumerated in the first instrument to J.R. Burris (P). Burris's (P) personal check of the records and his abstract of title did not reveal the prior assignment. The district court found the recording of the first assignment to be insufficient notice to a subsequent innocent purchaser of a lease not specifically enumerated therein. The court of appeals reversed, and this appeal followed.

ISSUE: Does the recording of an instrument which uses a "Mother Hubbard" clause to describe the property conveyed constitute constructive notice to a subsequent purchaser?

HOLDING AND DECISION: (Prager, J.) No. The purpose of statutes authorizing the recording of conveyances is to provide notice to subsequent purchasers of instruments affecting specific tracts of land. Thus, the land conveyed must be described with sufficient specificity, either in the instrument itself or by specific reference to other recorded conveyances. Instruments containing a "Mother Hubbard" clause, while valid as between parties, thereto, are not sufficient description of the land conveyed to be effective against subsequent purchasers and mortgagees, unless they have actual knowledge of the transfer. Here, the conveying instrument used a "Mother Hubbard" clause to describe the oil and gas lease in question. This was an insufficient description; further, Burris (P) had no actual knowledge of the transfer. Reversed.

ANALYSIS

Generally, the description in a recorded instrument must be sufficient to point out the property to one examining the record. If the property cannot be located and identified, as would be the case, for example, where the description is no more than "all other lands owned by the vendor in this state," then the sale is void as to third persons who deal upon the faith of the public records.

Quicknotes

ABSTRACT OF TITLE A summary of the history of title to a certain parcel of real property, including and transfers of, or liens against, such property.

CONVEYANCE The transfer of property, or title to property, from one party to another party.

RECORD AN INSTRUMENT The recording of a document in the public record.

Orr v. Byers

Lienholder (P) v. Subsequent purchaser (D)

Cal. Ct. App., Fourth Dist., 198 Cal. App. 3d 666, 244 Cal. Rptr. 13 (1988).

NATURE OF CASE: Appeal of denial of declaration of rights and duties of the parties.

FACT SUMMARY: Because Orr (P) had misspelled Elliott's (D) name when recording a judgment against him, when Elliott (D) sold property which was subject to the judgment, the title search did not reveal the cloud on title.

RULE OF LAW

A misspelled name does not give constructive notice to title searchers under the doctrine of *idem sonans.*

FACTS: Orr (P) obtained a judgment for more than $50,000 against Elliott (D). Orr's (P) attorney recorded the judgment in Orange County, California, but misspelled Elliott's (D) name as "Elliot" and "Eliot." Elliott (D) then sold property to Byers (D) that should have been subject to Orr's (P) lien. However, the title search failed to disclose the judgment because of the misspelling of Elliott's name. Orr (P) filed suit against Byers (D), Elliott (D), and the bank (D) which conducted the search, seeking a declaration of the rights and duties of the parties (and, in essence, judicial foreclosure of his judgment lien). He claimed that the name was constructive notice of alternate spellings and hence the search should have included alternate spellings, based on the doctrine of *idem sonans* (identity is presumed from the similarity of sounds). The trial court ruled against Orr (P), who appealed and was granted review.

ISSUE: Does the doctrine of *idem sonans* give constructive notice to title searchers where a judgment has been recorded under a misspelled, yet similar sounding, name?

HOLDING AND DECISION: (Sonenshine, J.) No. The rule of *idem sonans* does not give constructive notice to title searchers and good faith purchasers. The *idem sonans* doctrine allows for the identity of a person to be presumed where there is an inaccurately spelled name, but the misspelling would be pronounced similarly. The rule will not be applied where the burden to track down alternate spellings is unreasonable. It is unjustifiable to insist that Byers (D), the good faith purchaser, and the bank (D) which conducted the title search comb the judgment records for other spellings of the name. The burden is better placed on the party recording the judgment to take steps to ensure the name is spelled correctly. Affirmed.

ANALYSIS

The court was unpersuaded by the arguments put forth in *Green v. Myers*, 72 S.W. 128 (1903), which applied the rule of *idem sonans* to judgment records. The California court rejected the reasoning in *Green* because its effect was, essentially, to dispense with the formalities of record notice. While it was suggested that computer technology would reduce the burden of extensive title searches of multiple spellings, it was concluded that title searches should not require purchasers to hire highly trained specialists with expensive equipment to make certain that the seller of real property did not make a mistake when he recorded his deed. The decision is also in conflict with 4 American Law of Property, § 17.18 (1952), which states that similarly pronounced names beginning with the same letter give constructive notice to title searchers.

Quicknotes

ABSTRACT OF JUDGMENT Summary of the history of an action.

CONSTRUCTIVE NOTICE Knowledge of a fact that is imputed to an individual who was under a duty to inquire and who could have learned of the fact through the exercise of reasonable prudence.

GOOD FAITH PURCHASER FOR VALUE A party who purchases property in good faith and for valuable consideration without notice of a defect in title.

IDEM SONANS The doctrine that a name stated in a legal document need not be its exact spelling if the name as pronounced sounds sufficiently identical to the name in the document.

JUDGMENT LIEN Lien filed by a judgment creditor against the property of a judgment debtor pursuant to a judgment rendered in a civil case.

Messersmith v. Smith

Prior grantee (P) v. Subsequent purchaser (D)

N.D. Sup. Ct., 60 N.W.2d 276 (1953).

NATURE OF CASE: Action to quiet title.

FACT SUMMARY: In a race-notice recording statute jurisdiction, subsequent bona fide purchasers failed to record their deeds properly before a prior purchaser properly recorded.

RULE OF LAW

An unacknowledged deed does not qualify for recordation and therefore the recording does not give constructive notice to subsequent purchasers.

FACTS: Caroline Messersmith and her nephew, Frederick Messersmith (P), each owned an undivided one-half interest in land. On April 23, 1951, Smith (D) negotiated an oil and gas lease with Caroline Messersmith which was recorded on May 14, 1951. On May 7, 1951, Caroline Messersmith executed a mineral deed to the land which was recorded on May 26, 1951. On its face, the deed indicated that it had been acknowledged, but Caroline Messersmith had not, in fact, acknowledged it. On May 7, 1946, Caroline Messersmith delivered a quit-claim deed to Frederick Messersmith (P) for the land, and the deed was recorded on July 9, 1951. On May 9, 1951, Smith (D) executed the mineral deed he had received from Caroline Messersmith to Seale which was recorded on May 26, 1951. Seale asserted this deed which Smith (D) got from Caroline Messersmith and which was recorded on May 26, 1951, as cutting off Frederick Messersmith's (P) prior deed which was not recorded until July 9, 1951. The jurisdiction had a race-notice recording statute.

ISSUE: Does a deed which is unacknowledged, though recorded, impart constructive notice to the world so as to prevent a subsequent purchaser from being a bona fide purchaser without notice?

HOLDING AND DECISION: (Morris, C.J.) No. The recording of an instrument affecting title which does not meet the statutory requirements of the recording laws affords no constructive notice. The deed from Caroline to Smith (D) contained a certificate of acknowledgment on its face, but that is not conclusive as to its actual acknowledgment. Here, the grantor, Caroline, did not appear before an officer to acknowledge the execution of the instrument. Caroline did not acknowledge the deed to Smith (D) and, therefore, the deed was not properly recorded by Smith (D), and Seale (D) could not be a subsequent purchaser in good faith. Seale (D) must rely wholly upon his position as an innocent purchaser in compliance with the recording statutes. Therefore, Frederick Messersmith's (P) title was not cut off by the conveyance to Smith (D) and Seale. Reversed.

ANALYSIS

An unacknowledged deed does not give constructive notice because it does not qualify for recordation. Therefore, Smith's (D) deed and Seale's deed were not properly recorded. They did not prevail over Messersmith (P) because the jurisdiction had a race-notice statute, which means that the first to record a deed without actual or constructive notice of a prior deed will prevail.

Quicknotes

BONA FIDE PURCHASER A party who purchases property in good faith and for valuable consideration without notice of a defect in title.

CONSTRUCTIVE NOTICE Knowledge of a fact that is imputed to an individual who was under a duty to inquire and whom could have learned of the fact through the exercise of reasonable prudence.

RACE-NOTICE RECORDING STATUTE Statute determining priority of interests in real property whereby a person who records first has a preference over others receiving an interest in the property from the same source only if the party received no notice of the prior unrecorded conveyance.

Board of Education of Minneapolis v. Hughes

Subsequent purchaser (P) v. Prior grantee (D)

Minn. Sup. Ct., 118 Minn. 404, 136 N.W. 1095 (1912).

NATURE OF CASE: Action to determine adverse claims to certain real property.

FACT SUMMARY: Hughes (D) and Duryea & Wilson purchased the same lot from Hoerger. Hughes's (D) deed did not contain his name. He inserted it later. Duryea & Wilson sold to Board of Education of Minneapolis (P). Hughes's (D) deed was recorded before Duryea & Wilson's, but Board of Education of Minneapolis's (P) was recorded before either Hughes's (D) or Duryea & Wilson's.

RULE OF LAW

The recording of a deed from a grantee in an unrecorded deed to a third person is not notice of the prior unrecorded deed to a subsequent purchaser.

FACTS: On May 17, 1906, Hoerger executed and delivered a deed to convey certain land to Hughes (D). Hughes's (D) name was not inserted as grantee. He filled it in shortly before recording the deed on December 16, 1910. On April 27, 1909, Duryea & Wilson were delivered a deed by Hoerger for the same lot. This deed was recorded on December 21, 1910. On November 19, 1909, Duryea & Wilson delivered a deed to the Board of Education of Minneapolis (P) for the lot. This deed was recorded on January 27, 1910.

ISSUE: Where a grantor has made a prior deed which has not been recorded, does the recording of a deed from the grantee to a third person constitute notice of the unrecorded deed to a subsequent purchaser?

HOLDING AND DECISION: (Bunn, J.) No. There are two questions which must be decided here. The first is whether Hughes's (D) deed became operative, since his name was not inserted. A deed that does not name a grantee is inoperative as a conveyance until the grantee's name is legally inserted. Such a deed becomes operative without a new execution or acknowledgment if the grantee, with express or implied authority from the grantor, inserts his name in the blank space for the grantee. The authority may be parole and implied from the circumstances. In this case Hughes's (D) had such authority, in the absence of evidence showing the lack of it. Hence, Hughes's (D) deed became operative when he inserted his name. The second question to be decided is whether Hughes (D) is a subsequent purchaser whose deed was duly recorded. Hughes's (D) conveyance dates from the time he filled in the blank space, which was after the deed from Hoerger to Duryea & Wilson. Hence, Hughes (D) was a subsequent purchaser. Record of a deed from a prior grantee is not notice to a subsequent purchaser of a prior unrecorded conveyance by the grantor to the prior grantee. In this case the recording of Duryea's deed to Board of Education (P) did not act as notice to Hughes (D). It was necessary that the deed to Board of Education (P) be recorded before the deed to Hughes (D); it was also necessary that the deed to Duryea & Wilson be recorded first. Order reversed and new trial granted.

ANALYSIS

As between the parties, at least, a blank paper signed, sealed, and delivered and which is subsequently filled in without authority from the grantor will not pass title to any property. However, although blank when signed and sealed, if the deed is written with the grantor's authority and so delivered, it will be operative as a deed.

Quicknotes

CONVEYANCE The transfer of property, or title to property, from one party to another party.

ESTOPPEL An equitable doctrine precluding a party from asserting a right to the detriment of another whom justifiably relied on the conduct.

IMPLIED AUTHORITY Inferred power granted to an agent to act on behalf of the principal in order to effectuate the principal's objective.

NULLITY An act having no legal effect.

RECORDATION The recording of a document in the public record.

Guillette v. Daly Dry Wall, Inc.

Subdivision neighbors (P) v. Subsequent purchaser of unrestricted lot (D)

Mass. Sup. Jud. Ct., 367 Mass. 355, 325 N.E.2d 572 (1975).

NATURE OF CASE: Appeal from injunction in suit to enforce restrictive covenants.

FACT SUMMARY: Daly Dry Wall (Daly) (D), a grantee who took without knowledge of restrictions binding neighboring lots that had been deeded by a common grantor, proceeded to ignore the restrictions.

RULE OF LAW

A grantee is bound by restrictions in deeds to its neighbors from a common grantor, even if it takes without actual notice and his deed does not mention them, if the grantor has placed in writing the same restrictions on his remaining land.

FACTS: In 1967 and 1968, Guillette (P), the Walcotts (P), and the Paraskivas (P) bought individual lots in the same subdivision. Each of these three deeds either set out restrictions maintaining the subdivision as a residential area for single family dwellings, or incorporated such restrictions by reference. Additionally, the Guillette (P) deed provided that the lots retained by the seller were similarly restricted. Daly (D) purchased a lot in 1972 and the deed contained no restrictions; though the deed referred to the same recorded plan, this plan was also silent as to restrictions. After Daly (D) learned of the restrictions, it obtained a building permit for 36 apartment type units. Guillette (P) and the others sought to enjoin the construction. Daly (D) appealed the injunction and the case was transferred to this court.

ISSUE: Is a grantee bound by restrictions contained in deeds to its neighbors from a common grantor, even though he has no actual notice and his deed is silent as to restrictions, if the grantor has, in writing, placed the same restrictions on his remaining land?

HOLDING AND DECISION: (Braucher, J.) Yes. Although the Statute of Frauds prevents enforcement of restrictions against the grantor or subsequent purchasers of a lot not expressly restricted, where the common grantor has not bound his remaining land in writing, reciprocity of restriction between the grantor and grantee can be enforced. Therefore, if a grantor similarly restricts his remaining land by writing, a subsequent purchaser from the common grantor acquires title subject to the restrictions in the deed to the earlier purchaser. Further, each grantee within the scope of the common scheme may enforce the restrictions against other such grantees. Here, the Guillette (P) deed similarly restricted the grantor's remaining land. The deed was properly recorded. As a subsequent purchaser, Daly (D) took subject to these restrictions. Affirmed.

ANALYSIS

Cases are equally divided between the position illustrated by *Guillette v. Daly Dry Wall* and the position that restrictions on neighboring property deeded by a common grantor are not in the subsequent purchaser's chain of title.

Quicknotes

CHAIN OF TITLE Successive transfers of particular property.

COMMON GRANTOR Mutual conveyor of property.

RESTRICTIVE COVENANT A promise contained in a deed to limit the uses to which the property will be made.

STATUTE OF FRAUDS A statute that requires specified types of contracts to be in writing in order to be binding.

Daniels v. Anderson

Purchase option holder (P) v. Subsequent purchaser (D) and seller (D)

Ill. Sup. Ct., 162 Ill. 2d 47, 642 N.E.2d 128 (1994).

NATURE OF CASE: Appeal from judgment granting specific performance of a real estate purchase option.

FACT SUMMARY: Daniels (P) claimed that Zografos (D) could not claim bona fide purchaser status as to certain real estate because he had actual notice of Daniels's (P) interest therein prior to conveyance of title.

RULE OF LAW

One cannot claim bona fide purchaser status if he receives actual notice of an unrecorded interest in real estate prior to taking title.

FACTS: Daniels (P), besides purchasing two lots from Jacula (D), purchased a right of first refusal as to purchase of an adjacent parcel. This interest was not recorded. Jacula (D) later contracted with Zografos (D) to purchase the parcel. Daniels (P) was not notified of Zografos's (D) offer. The contract called for installment payments, with title to pass upon completion of payments. After Zografos (D) had paid several installments, but before title passed, Daniels (P) became aware of Zografos's purchase contract. He sued for specific performance of his purchase option. The trial court ordered Zografos (D) to convey the land to Daniels (P), and ordered Daniels (P) to reimburse Zografos (D) for the installments paid. The appellate court affirmed, and the Illinois Supreme Court granted review.

ISSUE: Can one claim bona fide purchaser status if he receives actual notice of an unrecorded interest in real estate prior to taking title?

HOLDING AND DECISION: (Freeman, J.) No. One cannot claim bona fide purchaser status if he receives actual notice of an unrecorded interest in real estate prior to taking title. A bona fide purchaser, by definition, is one who takes title to property without actual or constructive notice of another's rights therein. When one has not taken title, one is not a bona fide purchaser (BFP). That the putative BFP has made installment payments pursuant to a land sales contract is not sufficient to elevate him to BFP status. Here, Zografos (D) was given actual notice of Daniels's interest prior to title passing, so he was not a bona fide purchaser. His remedy was return of the monies paid, which is what the lower court ordered. Affirmed.

ANALYSIS

Zografos (D) argued, on appeal, that he had taken equitable title to the property upon payment of the first installment, so he actually did fit the definition of a BFP. The court refused to consider the argument because it had not been raised at trial. It is quite clear from the tone of the court's opinion that, even if it had considered the defense, it would have rejected it.

Quicknotes

ACTUAL NOTICE Direct communication of information that would cause an ordinary person of average prudence to inquire as to its truth.

BONA FIDE PURCHASER A party who purchases property in good faith and for valuable consideration without notice of a defect in title.

EQUITABLE TITLE Interest in property that is not recognized in a court of law but that is protected in equity.

SPECIFIC PERFORMANCE An equitable remedy whereby the court requires the parties to perform their obligations pursuant to a contract.

Lewis v. Superior Court

Purchasers (P) v. *Lis pendes* recorder (D)

Cal. App., Second Dist., 30 Cal. App. 4th 1850, 37 Cal. Rptr. 2d 63 (1994).

NATURE OF CASE: **Petition for writ of mandate following denial of motion for summary judgment in action seeking to quiet title.**

FACT SUMMARY: **Fontana Films (D) recorded a *lis pendens* on property before the Lewises (P), purchasers of real estate, took title thereto, but the *lis pendens* was not indexed until after the Lewises (P) acquired title.**

RULE OF LAW

A person who records an interest in real estate after a bona fide purchaser (BFP) takes title thereto is inferior to the BFP, even if that BFP has not paid for the property.

FACTS: Fontana Films (D) sought to record a *lis pendens* (notice of lawsuit affecting title) on certain property. However, the Lewises (P) purchased the property, and took title thereto, the day before the *lis pendens* was indexed. At the time they took title, the Lewises (P) had not paid for the property, as they were obligated under the land sale contract to make installments. The Lewises (P) filed an action to quiet title. They moved for summary judgment. The trial court denied the motion. The Lewises (P) petitioned for a writ seeking reversal of the denial.

ISSUE: Is a person who records an interest in real estate after a BFP takes title thereto inferior to the BFP, even if that BFP has not paid for the property?

HOLDING AND DECISION: (Woods, J.) Yes. A person who records an interest in real estate after a BFP takes title thereto is inferior to the BFP, even if that BFP has not paid for the property. Fontana Films (D) argues that a BFP who has not yet paid for property is not actually injured if he has not made a payment for property prior to recordation of an interest, and therefore the mere fact that title has passed should not make one in the Lewises' (P) position superior to the *lis pendens* recorder. While some old authority arguably supports this position, it is totally contrary to current practice in the real estate market. One who engages a title search, pays a down payment, and receives title to property has every right to expect that his right to the property is secure. The logical conclusion of Fontana's (D) position is that a person buying real estate under a typical 30-year mortgage would have to do a title search prior to each payment, a total of 360 searches over the life of the note. This is a ludicrous result that cannot be supported in any realistic view of real estate law. Therefore, the rule must be that, to defeat a claim of BFP status, the party challenging the BFP's status must have recorded his interest before the BFP took legal title, irrespective of when payments are made. Here, the *lis pendens* was not properly recorded until it was indexed, the day after title passed to the Lewises (P). Since the Lewises (P) took legal title before Fontana Films (D) recorded its interest, the Lewises (P) had superior title and entitled to summary judgment on this issue. Petition granted.

ANALYSIS

The generally accepted definition of a BFP is a person who takes title for value without actual or constructive notice of another's claim thereto. In this instance, the Lewises (P) had made a down payment. It is possible that if title were to pass without payment, BFP status could be defeated. (It is also unusual that this would happen in a normal real estate transaction.)

Quicknotes

BONA FIDE PURCHASER A party who purchases property in good faith and for valuable consideration without notice of a defect in title.

LEGAL TITLE Title such that is recognized by a court of law.

LIS PENDENS A pending action.

QUIET TITLE Equitable action to resolve conflicting claims to an interest in real property.

RECORDATION The recording of a document in the public record.

SUMMARY JUDGMENT Judgment rendered by a court in response to a motion by one of the parties, claiming that the lack of a question of material fact in respect to an issue warrants disposition of the issue without consideration by the jury.

WRIT OF MANDAMUS A court order issued commanding a public or private entity, or an official thereof, to perform a duty required by law.

Harper v. Paradise

Remaindermen (P) v. Subsequent grantees (D)

Ga. Sup. Ct., 233 Ga. 194, 210 S.E.2d 710 (1974).

NATURE OF CASE: Appeal from directed verdict in title dispute.

FACT SUMMARY: After Maude Harper's death, her children (P) claimed some land under a deed which had named Maude as life tenant and her children (P) as remaindermen, and the Paradises (D) claimed title to the same land, through a security deed executed by Maude to secure a loan which became in default.

RULE OF LAW

A deed which specifically refers to an earlier unrecorded deed puts a subsequent purchaser on notice of the existence of the earlier deed; thus, the purchaser claiming under the later deed is not entitled to priority, though the later deed was recorded first.

FACTS: Susan Harper conveyed a farm in 1922 to Maude Harper, her daughter-in-law, for life with remainder in fee to Maude's children (P). The deed was misplaced and so not recorded until 1957. While the deed was presumed lost, Susan Harper died, and her heirs gave Maude a quitclaim deed in 1928 "to take the place of the deed made . . . by Mrs. Susan Harper . . . ." On February 27, 1933, Maude executed a security deed, recorded the same day, which purported to convey the entire fee to Ella Thornton to secure a loan. When the loan became in default, Thornton foreclosed. Lincoln and William Paradise (D) were grantees in an unbroken chain of record title tracing back to Thornton. They also claim as adverse possessors. When Maude died in 1972, her children (P) brought an action to recover the land. They appealed from the trial court's finding that the Paradises (D) had superior title.

ISSUE: Does a deed which refers to an earlier unrecorded deed put a subsequent purchaser on inquiry notice regarding the existence of the earlier deed?

HOLDING AND DECISION: (Ingram, J.) Yes. If the Paradises (D) relied on the 1922 deed, they could have no interest except in the life estate, for a life tenant cannot sell anything more. As for the 1928 deed, heirs might join in a deed to an innocent person acting without notice of an earlier deed, and thereby convey a fee simple. But here the grantee of the quitclaim was Maude Harper, who surely had notice of the earlier deed. Furthermore, the 1928 deed stated it was intended to replace the earlier, missing deed. A deed which specifically refers to an earlier unrecorded deed puts a subsequent purchaser on notice of the existence of the earlier deed; thus, the purchaser claiming under the later deed is not entitled to priority, though the later deed was recorded first. Here, the recital in the 1928 deed put the Paradises (D) on inquiry notice, so they are not entitled to priority. Finally, the Paradises (D) have not gained title by adverse possession, as prescription did not start to run until the life estate ended in 1972. Reversed.

ANALYSIS

The majority rule is that the record affords notice not only of those facts recited therein, but also material matters suggested thereby, which might be disclosed by reasonable inquiry. Compare this to the uniform simplification of Land Transfers Act, which states that, unless a document refers to another document by its record location, a grantee is not charged with knowledge of the document or an adverse claim founded upon it.

Quicknotes

ADVERSE POSSESSION A means of acquiring title to real property by remaining in actual, open, continuous, exclusive possession of property for the statutory period.

DIRECTED VERDICT A verdict ordered by the court in a jury trial.

INQUIRY NOTICE The communication of information that would cause an ordinary person of average prudence to inquire as to its truth.

PRIORITY The relative preference of different claims to specific property.

QUITCLAIM A deed whereby the grantor conveys whatever interest he or she may have in the property without any warranties or covenants as to title.

REMAINDERMAN A person who has an interest in property to commence upon the termination of a present possessory interest.

Waldorff Insurance and Bonding, Inc. v. Eglin National Bank

Condo owner (P) v. Foreclosing-manager (D)

Fla. Dist. Ct. App., First Dist., 453 So. 2d 1383 (1984).

NATURE OF CASE: Appeal from foreclosure judgment.

FACT SUMMARY: **Eglin National Bank (Eglin) (D) contended it had no notice of Waldorff Insurance and Bonding, Inc.'s (Waldorff's) (P) ownership of the condominium unit, and thus it obtained good title upon foreclosure.**

RULE OF LAW

Subsequent successors to legal title, after a contract to convey title has been executed, take title subject to all equitable interests of which they have notice.

FACTS: Choctaw Partnership (Chocktaw) mortgaged a condominium project to Eglin (D). It sold a single unit to Waldorff (P), which occupied the unit and paid all expenses and rent. Choctaw executed a second mortgage in favor of Eglin (D) on which it defaulted. Eglin (D) foreclosed on the project, including the unit occupied by Waldorff (P). Waldorff (P) sued, contending it had better title. The trial court held Eglin (D) had no notice of Waldorff's (P) ownership merely because of possession. Waldorff (P) appealed.

ISSUE: Do subsequent successors to legal title take subject to all equitable interests, of which they have notice?

HOLDING AND DECISION: (Shivers, J.) Yes. Subsequent successors to legal title take subject to all equitable interests of which they have notice. A contract to convey legal title on payment of the purchase price creates an equitable interest in the purchaser. Beneficial ownership passes to the purchaser while the seller retains mere naked title. The occupancy of the unit placed Eglin (D) on notice of Waldorff's (P) interest. Thus Waldorff (P) retained greater title. Reversed and remanded.

ANALYSIS

Choctaw owed Waldorff (P) $35,000 in insurance premiums on the project. The parties agreed that Waldorff (P) would receive full title to the unit in return for a cancellation of the debt. The court rejected Eglin's (D) argument that because Waldorff (P) wrote the Choctaw debt off for tax purposes, no consideration supported the purchase. Choctaw's receipt of cancellation of a debt constituted sufficient consideration.

Quicknotes

BENEFICIAL OWNERSHIP A party holding equitable but not legal title to property that is held by a third party for his benefit.

CONSIDERATION Value given by one party in exchange for performance, or a promise to perform, by another party.

EQUITABLE INTEREST A beneficiary's interest in a trust.

Walker Rogge, Inc. v. Chelsea Title & Guaranty Co.

Tract purchaser (P) v. Title-company (D)

N.J. Sup. Ct., 116 N.J. 517, 562 A.2d 208 (1989).

NATURE OF CASE: Appeal from award of damages for negligence.

FACT SUMMARY: When Walker Rogge, Inc. (Rogge) (P) discovered by survey that its property contained 5.5 less acres than the seller had represented, it sued Chelsea Title & Guaranty Co. (Chelsea Title) (D) for failing to discover and disclose the correct acreage contained in Chelsea Title's (D) files.

RULE OF LAW

A title company's liability is limited to the policy, and the company is not liable in tort for negligence for searching records if it has not expressly contracted or implicitly agreed to do so.

FACTS: While negotiating to sell a tract of land, Kosa, the seller, showed Rogge (P), the prospective buyer, a Price Walker survey indicating that the tract was 18.33 acres. Rogge (P) ordered a title policy, but not a title search, from Chelsea Title (D). Chelsea Title (D) had issued two prior title policies on the same property and had a deed in its files that showed that the tract actually consisted of only 12.48 acres. Neither the Kosa-to-Rogge (P) deed nor the title policy issued by Chelsea Title (D) included an acreage count, but both referenced the Price Walker survey. The title policy stated that Chelsea Title (D) insured against loss or damage from defects in title or unmarketability of title. It also stated that Chelsea Title (D) did not insure against any matters which could be disclosed by an accurate survey and inspection of the property. Six years after closing, in preparation for subdividing the land, Rogge (P) hired a new surveyor, who concluded that the actual quantity of acreage in the property was 12.43 acres. Rogge (P) filed suit against Chelsea Title (D), alleging that the 5.5-acre shortage was an insurable loss under the policy, and that Chelsea Title (D) was liable in negligence for failing to disclose documents in its files revealing that the property contained fewer than 18 acres. The trial court concluded that the shortage constituted a defect in title, rendering it unmarketable, and assessed damages at $88,000. Finding that Rogge (P) did not contract for a title search, however, the court dismissed the negligence charge against Chelsea Title (D). The appeals court affirmed, and Chelsea Title (D) appealed.

ISSUE: Is a title company liable in tort for negligence for searching records if it has not expressly contracted or implicitly agreed to do so?

HOLDING AND DECISION: (Pollock, J.) No. A title company is not liable in tort for negligence for searching records if it has not expressly contracted or implicitly agreed to do so. A title company's liability is limited to the policy, and a company is not liable in contract for an acreage shortage, if no acreage is stated in a deed, or in tort for failure to search records, if it has not agreed to do so. A title insurance policy is a contract of indemnity under which the insurer agrees to indemnify the insured against loss through defects of title to or liens or encumbrances upon realty owned by the insured. However, title insurance is no substitute for a survey. If no acreage is stated on a deed, a title company does not insure the quantity of land. In this case, Chelsea Title's (D) insurance policy contained an enforceable survey exception which placed the risk of paying for nonexistent acres on Rogge (P). Had Rogge (P) obtained the survey prior to closing, rather than six years later, he could have eliminated the survey exception from the policy, and transferred the risk of an acreage shortage to Chelsea Title (D). Since he did not, Chelsea Title (D) is not liable in contract. It may, however, be subject to a negligence action if the failure to assure the quantity of acreage was the direct result of duties voluntarily assumed by it in addition to the mere contract to insure title. A title company is not liable in tort for negligence in searching records unless it agreed to conduct a search and to provide the insured with an abstract of title in addition to the title policy. Although Rogge (P) did not order a separate abstract of title, Chelsea Title (D) had insured the property before and had the correct amount of acreage in its files. On remand, the trial court must determine whether, under the circumstances, Chelsea Title (D) assumed an independent duty to assure the quantity of acreage, whether it breached that duty, or whether the breach caused any damage to Rogge (P). Affirmed in part; reversed in part; and remanded.

ANALYSIS

In some jurisdictions, statutes require a title search to be performed prior to the issuance of any policies regardless of whether the insurance company has contracted to conduct such a search. In the absence of a statute, the majority rule holds that the title insurance company owes a duty to its insured to search the records. This rule assumes that the issuance of a policy is predicated upon a careful examination of the title and an exhaustive study of the applicable law. It also assumes that a person seeking title insurance expects to obtain a professional title search as well as an opinion as the condition of that title. *Rogge*, on the other hand, represents the minority rule that

Continued on next page.

any duty on the part of the insurance company to search the records must be expressed in or implied from the policy.

Quicknotes

DEFEAT IN TITLE Termination or annulment of a title.

INDEMNIFY Securing against potential injury; compensation for injury suffered.

TITLE POLICY A policy insuring against loss incurred as the result of a defective title.

TITLE SEARCH An examination of records of title documents in order to ascertain whether title to a particular property is defective.

Lick Mill Creek Apartments v. Chicago Title Insurance Co.

Developer (P) v. Title insurance company (D)

Cal. App., Sixth Dist., 283 Cal. Rptr. 231, 231 Cal. App. 3d 1654 (1991).

NATURE OF CASE: Appeal from dismissal of action for indemnification for hazardous waste cleanup costs.

FACT SUMMARY: After paying for removal and cleanup of hazardous substances existing but unknown at the time a title insurance policy was issued on its property, Lick Mill Creek Apartments (Lick Mill) (P) sued Chicago Title Insurance Co. (Chicago Title) (D) for reimbursement, contending that the presence of hazardous waste rendered the title unmarketable and constituted an encumbrance on title.

RULE OF LAW

A title insurance company is obligated to protect the insured against defects in title but not against loss arising from physical damage to property.

FACTS: While acquiring lots for development, Lick Mill (P) purchased title insurance from Chicago Title (D). Before issuing the policy, Chicago Title (D) commissioned a survey and inspection of the entire site. Unbeknownst to Chicago Title (D) or Lick Mill (P), the government had been keeping records documenting the presence of hazardous substances in the soil, subsoil, and groundwater of the property. After Lick Mill (P) purchased the property, it incurred costs for removal and cleanup of the hazardous materials. It then sought indemnity from Chicago Title (D) for the cost of the cleanup, arguing that the presence of hazardous substances rendered the title defective or unmarketable within the terms of the title insurance policy. Lick Mill (P) also contended that liability for the costs of the cleanup constituted an encumbrance on title. The trial court concluded that Chicago Title's (D) insurance policy did not cover the costs of removing hazardous substances. Lick Mill (P) appealed.

ISSUE: Is a title insurance company obligated to protect the insured against defects in title but not against loss arising from physical damage to property?

HOLDING AND DECISION: (Agliano, J.) Yes. A title insurance company is obligated to protect the insured against defects in title but not against loss arising from physical damage to property. Title insurance covers title marketability, which relates to defects affecting legally recognized rights and incidents of ownership. Title insurance does not cover market value. It is possible to hold perfectly marketable title to valueless, unmarketable land. Here, the presence of hazardous material may affect the market value of Lick Mill's (P) land, but it does not affect the title to the land. Chicago Title (D) was obligated, under its policy, to insure Lick Mill (P) against unmarketability of title. But since marketability of title and the market value of the land itself are separate and distinct, Lick Mill (P) could not claim coverage, under the policy, for the property's physical condition. Furthermore, it could not claim coverage for an encumbrance where no lien has been filed against the property. "Encumbrances" include only liens, easements, restrictive covenants, and other such interests in or rights to the land that are held by third persons. The mere possibility that the state may attach a lien in the future to secure payment of cleanup costs is not sufficient to create an encumbrance on title. Affirmed.

ANALYSIS

Title insurance reflects the faith of the insurer in the validity of title, not the physical condition of the property. Title insurance policies are contractual devices. Most courts will construe policies to insure only what they say they insure. This will be true even if the court subscribes to the presumption that policies are to be strictly construed in favor of the insured and against the title insurance company.

Quicknotes

ENCUMBRANCE An interest in property that operates as a claim or lien against its title making it potentially unmarketable.

INDEMNITY The duty of a party to compensate another for damages sustained.

LIEN A claim against the property of another in order to secure the payment of a debt.

TITLE INSURANCE A policy insuring against loss incurred as the result of a defective title.

TITLE MARKETABILITY Title that, although not perfect, would be acceptable to a reasonably well-informed buyer exercising ordinary business prudence.

CHAPTER 9

Judicial Land Use Controls

Quick Reference Rules of Law

	PAGE
1. **The Substantive Law.** Lawful conduct which is non-negligent may constitute a nuisance if it is intentional and unreasonable under the circumstances. (Morgan v. High Penn Oil Co.)	*92*
2. **Remedies.** Even though a jury finds facts constituting a nuisance, equities must be balanced in order to determine if an injunction should be granted. (Estancias Dallas Corp. v. Schultz)	*93*
3. **Remedies.** Although the rule in New York is that a nuisance will be enjoined even when there is a marked disparity shown in economic consequence between the effect of the injunction and the effect of the nuisance, an injunction should not be applied if the result is to close down a plant. Permanent damages may be awarded as an alternative. (Boomer v. Atlantic Cement Co.)	*94*
4. **Remedies.** The doctrine of coming to the nuisance does not prohibit granting injunctive relief against the nuisance. (Spur Industries, Inc. v. Del E. Webb Development Co.)	*95*

Morgan v. High Penn Oil Co.

Homeowners (P) v. Polluting-refinery (D)

N.C. Sup. Ct., 238 N.C. 185, 77 S.E.2d 682 (1953).

NATURE OF CASE: Appeal from award of damages and injunction in nuisance suit.

FACT SUMMARY: The Morgans (P) sought to enjoin High Penn Oil Co. (High Penn) (D) from emitting gas and odors from its refinery, and to recover damages for past impairment of the use and enjoyment of their property due to refinery emissions.

RULE OF LAW

Lawful conduct which is non-negligent may constitute a nuisance if it is intentional and unreasonable under the circumstances.

FACTS: The Morgans (P) had resided on their property since August 1945, and had since established a trailer park and restaurant thereon, which supplemented their income. High Penn (D) had operated its oil refinery, located approximately 1,000 feet from the Morgans' (P) dwelling, since October 1950. The Morgans (P) offered evidence to show that the refinery regularly emitted nauseating gases and odors in large quantities, which invaded neighboring property and made people sick. Further, High Penn (D) disregarded the Morgans' (P) demand to abate the nuisance. The trial court awarded damages and an injunction, and High Penn (D) appealed.

ISSUE: If one conducts a lawful enterprise on one's own property may that enterprise only constitute a nuisance if it is operated or constructed negligently?

HOLDING AND DECISION: (Ervin, J.) No. Private nuisances may be nuisances per se, that is, at all times and under any circumstances, or they may be nuisances per accidens, that is, nuisances by reason of their location or manner of construction or operation. A lawful enterprise cannot be a nuisance per se, but may be one per accidens, and this is so even if it is constructed and operated non-negligently. A private nuisance exists whenever one uses one's own property in a way which substantially interferes with another's interest in the private use and enjoyment of that other's land. Liability arises, if the conduct was unintentional, when the actions are negligent, reckless, or ultrahazardous. But if the conduct was intentional, a person is liable if his actions were unreasonable under the circumstances. This is the case where the person acts for the purpose of causing the nuisance, or where he knows it is resulting or substantially certain to result from his conduct. In this case, the evidence supports a finding that High Penn (D) intentionally and unreasonably caused noxious gas and odors to escape the refinery, and that an injunction was required to avoid irreparable injury to the Morgans (P). Affirmed.

ANALYSIS

Great confusion exists regarding the legal basis of liability in the law of nuisance. *Morgan v. High Penn Oil Co.* states the Restatement rule: An interference with the use and enjoyment of another's land gives rise to liability if it is substantial and either intentional and unreasonable, or the unintentional result of negligence, recklessness or abnormally dangerous activity. But the application of this rule is difficult because, as Professor Prosser notes, the courts work in an ad hoc fashion to resolve land-use conflicts in a way that makes compatible dissimilar needs and desires. 10 Prosser, *The Law of Torts 571* (4th ed. 1971).

Quicknotes

INJUNCTION A remedy imposed by the court ordering a party to cease the conduct of a specific activity.

NUISANCE PER ACCIDENS An action, occupation or building that becomes a nuisance due to its location or method of operation.

NUISANCE PER SE An action, occupation or building that is a nuisance at any time and under any condition.

PRIVATE NUISANCE An unlawful use of property interfering with the enjoyment of the private rights of an individual or a small number of persons.

Estancias Dallas Corp. v. Schultz

Apartment complex (D) v. Homeowners (P)

Tex. Civ. App., 500 S.W.2d 217 (1973).

NATURE OF CASE: Appeal from grant injunction in nuisance suit.

FACT SUMMARY: The Schultzes (P) sought to enjoin Estancias Dallas Corp. (D) from operating air conditioning equipment on the property adjoining the Schultzes' (P) residence.

RULE OF LAW

Even though a jury finds facts constituting a nuisance, equities must be balanced in order to determine if an injunction should be granted.

FACTS: Estancias Dallas Corp. (D) completed construction of an apartment complex in 1969. An air conditioning unit, which serviced the entire complex, was located about five feet from the Schultzes' (P) property line. The Schultzes (P) testified that the neighborhood was a quiet one prior to the construction of these apartments, that they could not converse or sleep due to the tremendous noise of the unit, and that it had decreased the value of their property from $25,000 to about $10,000. The jury found that a continuous and permanent nuisance existed, although it failed to find that the nuisance proximately caused material personal discomfort, inconvenience, annoyance, and impairment of health to the Schultzes (P). When the trial court granted a permanent injunction, Estancias Dallas Corp. (D) appealed.

ISSUE: Do nuisance cases require a balancing of equities by the court, even though a jury finds facts constituting a nuisance?

HOLDING AND DECISION: (Stephenson, J.) Yes. Texas law requires a balancing of equities in nuisance cases, even if the jury has found that a nuisance exists. *Storey v. Central Hide & Rendering Co.*, 148 Tex. 509, 226 S.W.2d 615 (1950). The *Storey* court noted that if the injury to the public in enjoining the nuisance would be great, the nuisance might be permitted to exist "of necessity." Here, it is implied by the entering of the judgment granting the injunction that the court balanced the equities in favor of the Schultzes (P). Furthermore, the existence of the unit is of no public benefit, and so the enjoining of its operation would cause no public injury. Affirmed.

ANALYSIS

An owner of real property is entitled to the full beneficial use of that property, provided that he does not invade the corresponding property rights of others. When determining liability for the use of one's own property, the test is one of reasonableness. It follows that an owner is liable only for injury to others resulting from his "unreasonable" use, and this must be determined as a question of fact in light of the particular circumstances of the case. Hence, balancing is required in every nuisance case.

Quicknotes

BALANCING TEST Court's balancing of an individual's constitutional rights against the state's right to protect its citizens.

INJUNCTION A court order requiring a person to do or prohibiting that person from doing a specific act.

NECESSITY A defense to liability for unlawful activity where the conduct is unavoidable and is justified by preventing the injury to life or health.

NUISANCE An unlawful use of property that interferes with the lawful use of another's property.

PROXIMATE CAUSE Something that causes a result in the natural sequence of events without which an injury would not have been sustained.

Boomer v. Atlantic Cement Company

Land owners (P) v. Cement plant (D)

N.Y. Ct. App., 26 N.Y.2d 219, 257 N.E.2d 870, 309 N.Y.S.2d 312 (1970).

NATURE OF CASE: Action to enjoin maintenance of nuisance and for damages.

FACT SUMMARY: Trial court refused to issue injunction which would close down plant, but awarded permanent damages instead.

RULE OF LAW

Although the rule in New York is that a nuisance will be enjoined even when there is a marked disparity shown in economic consequence between the effect of the injunction and the effect of the nuisance, an injunction should not be applied if the result is to close down a plant. Permanent damages may be awarded as an alternative.

FACTS: A group of land owners (P), complaining of injury to their property from dirt, smoke, and vibration emanating from a neighboring cement plant (D), brought an action to enjoin the continued operation of the plant and for damages. The trial court held that the plant constituted a nuisance, found substantial damage but, because an injunction would shut down the plant's operation, refused to issue one. Permanent damages of $185,000 were awarded the group of land owners (P) instead.

ISSUE: Where the issuance of an injunction to enjoin the maintenance of a business would shut down a business, may permanent damages be issued as an alternative?

HOLDING AND DECISION: (Bergan, J.) Yes. Damages may be awarded as an alternative to an injunction in nuisance cases. Another alternative would be to grant the injunction but postpone its effect to a specified future date to give opportunity for technical advances to permit the company (D) to eliminate the nuisance. However, there is no assurance that any significant technical improvement would occur. Moreover, the problem is universal, and can only be solved by an industry-wide effort. Permanent damages would themselves be a spur to conduct more research. Future owners of this land would not be able to recover additional damages, since the award is to the land. Reversed and remanded.

DISSENT: (Jasen, J.) The majority approach is licensing a continuing wrong. Furthermore, permanent damages alleviate the need for more research and decrease incentive.

ANALYSIS

The reasoning advanced here has been carried one step further by other courts. In *Pennsylvania Coal Co. v. Sanderson*, 113 Pa. St. 126, 6 A. 453 (1886), a suit for damages was frowned upon by the Supreme Court which said, "To encourage the development of the great natural resources of a country, trifling inconveniences to particular persons must sometimes give way to the necessities of a great community."

Quicknotes

INJUNCTION A court order requiring a person to do or prohibiting that person from doing a specific act.

NUISANCE An unlawful use of property that interferes with the lawful use of another's property.

TEMPORARY DAMAGES Monetary compensation awarded by the court to a party for injuries sustained as the result of another party's occasional wrongful actions.

Spur Industries, Inc. v. Del E. Webb Development Co.

Developer (P) v. Feed lot (D)

Ariz. Sup. Ct., 108 Ariz. 178, 494 P.2d 700 (1972).

NATURE OF CASE: Appeal from permanent injunction.

FACT SUMMARY: **Del E. Webb Development Co. (Webb) (P) sought to enjoin Spur Industries, Inc. (Spur) (D) from running a cattle feedlot near its Sun City retirement community.**

RULE OF LAW

The doctrine of coming to the nuisance does not prohibit granting injunctive relief against the nuisance.

FACTS: In 1956, Spur's (D) predecessors in interest developed feedlots in an area some 15 miles west of the urban area of Phoenix, Arizona. In May 1959, Webb (P) began to plan the development of an urban retirement area to be known as Sun City, by purchasing 20,000 acres of farmland near Spur's (D) feedlots. In 1960, Spur (D) purchased the property in question and began a rebuilding and expansion program extending to the north and south of the original feedlot facilities. Homes were first offered for sale by Webb (P) in 1960, when odors from the Spur (D) feedlot were not considered to be a problem. In December 1967, Webb (P) filed suit, complaining that in excess of 1,000 lots in its development were unfit for sale because of the operation of the Spur (D) feedlot. Webb (P) alleged that the Spur (D) feeding operation was a public nuisance because of the flies and odor which were drifting over Sun City. The trial court permanently enjoined Spur (D) from operating a cattle feedlot near Sun City, and Spur (D) appealed.

ISSUE: Does the doctrine of coming to the nuisance prohibit granting injunctive relief against the nuisance?

HOLDING AND DECISION: (Cameron, J.) No. Spur's (D) operation was an enjoinable public nuisance as far as the people in the southern portion of Webb's (P) Sun City were concerned. Spur's (D) operation, which constituted a breeding place for flies, was a public nuisance dangerous to the public health, and Webb (P), having shown a special injury in the loss of sales, has standing to bring suit to enjoin the nuisance. However, there was no indication here at the time Spur (D) and its predecessors located in Maricopa County that a new city would spring up, full-blown, alongside the feeding operation, and that the developer of that city would ask the court to order Spur (D) to move because of the new city. Spur (D) is required to move not because of any wrongdoing on the part of Spur (D), but because of a proper and legitimate regard of the courts for the rights and interests of the public. Having brought people to the nuisance to the foreseeable detriment of Spur (D), Webb (P) must indemnify Spur (D) for a reasonable amount of the cost of moving or shutting down. Affirmed in part, reversed in part, and remanded for further proceedings.

ANALYSIS

The majority view is that coming to a nuisance does not completely bar a suit for damages or injunctive relief, but is a factor to be considered in adjudicating the action. The position taken by the court in this case attempts to promote both ideas of fairness to the parties, and a concern over the most efficient use of the property in question. The court's remedy, abating the nuisance accompanied by compensatory damages to Spur (D), attempts to effectuate these concerns.

Quicknotes

"COMING TO THE NUISANCE" A claim may be weakened when a plaintiff moves to the defendant's established locale.

COMPENSATORY DAMAGES Measure of damages necessary to compensate victim for actual injuries suffered.

INJUNCTION A court order requiring a person to do or prohibiting that person from doing a specific act.

NUISANCE An unlawful use of property that interferes with the lawful use of another's property.

CHAPTER 10

Private Land Use Controls

Quick Reference Rules of Law

PAGE

1. **Creation of Easements.** Contrary to the ancient common-law rule, modernly, a grantor, in deeding property to one person, may effectively reserve and vest an interest in the same property in a third party. (Willard v. First Church of Christ, Scientist) *99*

2. **Creation of Easements.** A right to the use of a roadway over the land of another may be established by estoppel. (Holbrook v. Taylor) *100*

3. **Creation of Easements.** Whether there is an implied easement on certain property will be inferred from the intentions of the parties, and such inference will be drawn from the circumstances under which the conveyance was made. Parties to a conveyance will be assumed to know and to contemplate the continuance of reasonably necessary uses which have so altered the premises as to make them apparent upon reasonably prudent investigation. (Van Sandt v. Royster) *101*

4. **Creation of Easements.** In order to create an easement by necessity, the necessity must have existed at the time that the estate was created. (Othen v. Rosier) *103*

5. **Creation of Easements.** Under the public trust doctrine, sands upland from the high water mark must be available for use by the general public, subject to a reasonable fee for costs incurred for management services. (Raleigh Avenue Beach Assn. v. Atlantis Beach Club) *104*

6. **Assignability of Easements.** An easement in gross may arise by prescription and is assignable if the parties to its creation so intend. (Miller v. Lutheran Conference & Camp Association) *105*

7. **Scope of Easements.** If an easement is appurtenant to a particular parcel of land, any extension thereof to other parcels is a misuse of the easement, unless the servient estate does not overburden it. (Brown v. Voss) *106*

8. **Termination of Easements.** A change in use of an easement from a rail line to a recreational path constitutes a taking. (Preseault v. United States) *107*

9. **Covenants Enforceable in Equity: Equitable Servitudes.** Privity of estate notwithstanding, a person who acquires real property with notice of a restriction placed upon it will not be allowed, in equity, to violate its terms. (Tulk v. Moxhay) *108*

10. **Creation of Covenants.** If the owner of two or more lots, which are situated so as to bear a relation to each other, sells one with restrictions which are of benefit to the land retained, during the period of restraint, the owner of the lot or lots retained can do nothing forbidden to the owner of the lot sold. This is the doctrine of reciprocal negative easements. (Sanborn v. McLean) *109*

11. **Validity and Enforcement of Covenants.** A covenant in deed subjecting land to an annual charge for improvements to the surrounding residential tract is enforceable by the property owners' association against subsequent purchasers if: (1) grantor and grantee so intended; (2) it appears that the covenant is one touching or concerning the land; and (3) privity of estate is shown between the party claiming benefit of the covenant and the party under the burden of such covenant. (Neponsit Property Owners' Association, Inc. v. Emigrant Industrial Savings Bank) *110*

12. **Discriminatory Covenants.** State court enforcement of private, discriminatory restrictive covenants constitutes state action under the Fourteenth Amendment. (Shelley v. Kraemer) *112*

13. **Termination of Covenants.** A restrictive covenant is enforceable so long as its provisions remain of substantial value. (Western Land Co. v. Truskolaski) *113*

14. **Termination of Covenants.** Courts will not engage in a balancing of equities but will enforce restrictive covenants unless there is a substantial change of conditions in the general neighborhood. (Rick v. West) *114*

15. **Termination of Covenants.** A landowner cannot abandon property to which he holds perfect title. (Pocono Springs Civic Association, Inc. v. MacKenzie) *115*

16. **Common Interest Communities.** A recorded use restriction imposed by a common interest development in California must be enforced uniformly against all residents of the development unless the restriction is unreasonable. (Nahrstedt v. Lakeside Village Condominium Association, Inc.) *116*

17. **Common Interest Communities.** Under the business judgment rule, courts will defer to the residential cooperative's vote and findings as competent evidence that the tenant is objectionable and subject to eviction. (40 West 67th Street Corp. v. Pullman) *118*

Willard v. First Church of Christ, Scientist

Subsequent purchaser (P) v. Third-party easement beneficiary (D)

Cal. Sup. Ct., 7 Cal. 3d 473, 498 P.2d 987 (1972).

NATURE OF CASE: Appeal in a quiet title action.

FACT SUMMARY: Although when Petersen bought a lot from McGuigan, the deed reserved an easement on the lot for the use of First Church of Christ, Scientist (the Church) (D), Petersen then sold the lot to the Willards (P) without the easement.

RULE OF LAW

Contrary to the ancient common-law rule, modernly, a grantor, in deeding property to one person, may effectively reserve and vest an interest in the same property in a third party.

FACTS: Having bought lot 19 from McGuigan, Petersen also offered to purchase the abutting lot 20 from her in order to sell both lots to the Willards (P). However, McGuigan, a member of the First Church of Christ, Scientist (D), had always allowed the Church (D) to use the lot for parking. Accordingly, she had a clause included in the deed to Petersen whereby lot 20 was subject to an easement for church (D) parking to run with the land as long as used for Church (D) purposes. Petersen bought the lot and recorded the deed. However, Petersen did not include the easement in his deed to the Willards (P). When the Willards (P) became aware of it, they brought this quiet title action. At trial, McGuigan testified that she had originally bought lot 20 to provide church (D) parking and would not have sold it without the easement. The trial court found that, although McGuigan and Petersen intended to convey an easement, the clause was invalidated under the common-law rule that the grantor, in deeding property to one person, cannot reserve an interest in the same property to a third party. The Church (D) appealed.

ISSUE: May a grantor, in deeding property to one person, effectively reserve and vest an interest in the same property in a third party?

HOLDING AND DECISION: (Peters, J.) Yes. Contrary to the ancient common-law rule, modernly, a grantor, in deeding property to one person, may effectively reserve and vest an interest in the same property in a third party. Today, courts primarily try to give effect to the grantor's intent, whereas the common-law rule would defeat that intent. Also, it must be recognized that due to the encumbrance on the property, the grantee paid a reduced price for it. Therefore, it would be inequitable to allow him to remove the third party's interest, thereby greatly increasing the property's value. The determination of whether the common-law rule should still be used involves a balancing of equitable and policy considerations. In this case, despite the Willards' (P) contrary contentions that the grantees and title insurers relied on the common-law rule, we believe the modern position applies. Reversed.

ANALYSIS

Because easements are interests to land, they normally must be in compliance with the Statute of Frauds. However, easements may also exist by implication in those instances where the parties have not expressly reserved or granted them in writing. Since these easements are created by operation of law, no writing under the Statute of Frauds is necessary. However, easements by implication arise only when common title to land is severed.

Quicknotes

EASEMENT The right to utilize a portion of another's real property for a specific use.

EASEMENT BY IMPLICATION An easement that is not expressly stated in a deed, but which is inferred upon conveyance, that a portion of one parcel had been used to benefit the other parcel and that upon sale the buyer of the benefited parcel could reasonably expect such benefits to continue.

ENCUMBRANCE An interest in property that operates as a claim or lien against its title making it potentially unmarketable.

QUIET TITLE Equitable action to resolve conflicting claims to an interest in real property.

STATUTE OF FRAUDS A statute that requires specified types of contracts to be in writing in order to be binding.

Holbrook v. Taylor

Property owner (D) v. Roadway user (P)

Ky. Sup. Ct., 532 S.W.2d 763 (1976).

NATURE OF CASE: Appeal from denial of right to the use of a roadway.

FACT SUMMARY: Taylor (P) used a road which ran across Holbrook's (D) property.

RULE OF LAW

A right to the use of a roadway over the land of another may be established by estoppel.

FACTS: In 1944, Holbrook (D) gave permission for a road to be constructed across his property, to be used by a coal company for moving coal from a newly opened mine. The roadway was so used until 1949, when the mine closed. In 1964, Taylor (P) bought a three-acre site adjoining Holbrook's (D) land and in 1965, built a home on that site. During the period in which Taylor's (P) home was being constructed, Taylor (P) was allowed to use the roadway for construction purposes, and later, Taylor (P) was given express permission by Holbrook (D) to use and repair the roadway. Subsequently, a dispute arose, and suit was filed to declare the right of Taylor (P) to use the roadway without interference. Taylor (P) appealed from a decision for Holbrook (D).

ISSUE: May a right to the use of a roadway over the land of another be established by estoppel?

HOLDING AND DECISION: (Sternberg, J.) Yes. A right to the use of a roadway over the lands of another may be established by estoppel. One may acquire a license to use a roadway where, with the permission of the licensor, the licensee makes substantial expenditures, erects improvements, or uses it for other purposes in reliance on the licensor's grant of permission. Under these conditions, the license becomes in reality a grant through estoppel, and it becomes irrevocable and continues for so long a time as the nature of the license calls for. Here, the use of the roadway by Taylor (P) to get to his home from a public highway, the use of the roadway in constructing Taylor's (P) home, the improvements made to the roadway, the maintenance of the roadway, and the construction by Taylor (P) of a residence, all with the actual consent of Holbrook (D), indicated that the license to use the roadway may not be revoked. Affirmed.

ANALYSIS

Although in the usual case, a license is freely revocable, a license which is combined with an interest in land cannot be revoked. This type of interest is very similar to an easement, which is an interest in land allowing a person to make use of the property of another. Oral licenses, however, are not treated as interests in land which are subject to the Statute of Frauds.

Quicknotes

ESTOPPEL An equitable doctrine precluding a party from asserting a right to the detriment of another, who justifiably relied on the conduct.

LICENSE A right that is granted to a person allowing him or her to conduct an activity that without such permission he or she could not lawfully do, and which is unassignable and revocable at the will of the licensor.

Van Sandt v. Royster

Subsequent purchaser (P) v. Quasi-easement grantees (D)

Kan. Sup. Ct., 148 Kan. 495, 83 P.2d 698 (1938).

NATURE OF CASE: Action to enjoin Royster (D) and Gray (D) from using an underground sewer drain across Van Sandt's (P) property.

FACT SUMMARY: Van Sandt (P) found his cellar flooded with sewage and discovered for the first time the existence of a sewer drain across his property. Royster (D) and Gray (D) refuse to stop using the drain.

RULE OF LAW

Whether there is an implied easement on certain property will be inferred from the intentions of the parties, and such inference will be drawn from the circumstances under which the conveyance was made. Parties to a conveyance will be assumed to know and to contemplate the continuance of reasonably necessary uses which have so altered the premises as to make them apparent upon reasonably prudent investigation.

FACTS: Bailey owned three adjoining lots numbered 4, 20, and 19. In 1904, a private lateral drain was built running from the house on Lot 4 across Lots 20 and 19. Bailey conveyed Lot 20 to Murphy by a general warranty deed without exceptions or reservations in 1904. Title passed to Royster (D). In 1904, Bailey also conveyed Lot 19 to Jones by a general warranty deed without exceptions or reservations. Jones conveyed part of Lot 19 to Reynolds, who in 1924 conveyed to Van Sandt (P). Gray (D) succeeded title to Lot 4. In 1936, Van Sandt (P) discovered his basement flooded with sewage and filth. Upon investigation, he discovered for the first time the existence of a sewer drain running on, across, and through his property. Royster (D) and Gray (D) refuse to stop using the sewer. Van Sandt (P) argues that no easement has been created on his land, and even assuming there was an easement created, he took the land free from the burden of the easement because he was a bona fide purchaser, without notice.

ISSUE: Can a purchaser be charged with notice of a prior necessary use so as to create an implied easement where the use was not visible, but a reasonable inspection would have made the use apparent?

HOLDING AND DECISION: (Allen, J.) Yes. When one utilizes part of his land for the benefit of another, a quasi-easement exists. The part of the land being benefited is referred to as the quasi-dominant tenement, and the part being utilized is referred to as the quasi-servient tenement. If the owner of land, one part of which is subject to a quasi-easement, conveys the quasi-dominant tenement, an easement corresponding to such quasi-easement is vested in the grantee, provided such quasi-easement is apparent and continuous. An implied easement, in favor of either the grantor or the grantee arises as an inference of the intentions of the parties. This inference is drawn from the circumstances under which the conveyance is made. Factors to consider include whether the claimant is the grantee or grantor, the terms of the conveyance, the consideration given, the extent of necessity of the easement and the extent to which the use, which is the subject of the easement, was or might have been known to the parties. Parties to a conveyance will be assumed to know and to contemplate the continuance of reasonably necessary uses which have so altered the premises as to make them apparent upon reasonably prudent investigation. The degree of necessity required to imply an easement in favor of the grantor is greater than that required in the case of the grantee. But where land may be used without an easement, but cannot be used without disproportionate effort and expense, an easement may be implied in favor of either the grantor or grantee on the basis of necessity alone. In this case, the trial court found that Jones was aware of the sewer at the time he purchased Lot 19. It further found that the easement was necessary to the comfortable enjoyment of the grantor's (Bailey) land. Van Sandt (P) cannot claim that he purchased without notice. He inspected the property at the time of purchase, and knew the house was equipped with modern plumbing which had to drain into a sewer. The majority view is that appearance and visibility of easements is not synonymous, and the fact that the pipe, sewer or drain is hidden underground does not make it nonapparent. Here the easement was apparent within this meaning, and Van Sandt (P) is charged with notice of its existence. Affirmed.

ANALYSIS

The law does not favor implied easements since they are in derogation of the rule that written instruments speak for themselves. They also retard building and improvements, and violate the policy of recording acts. The implication of easements is based an the theory that when one conveys property he includes, or intends to include, in the conveyance whatever is necessary for its beneficial use and enjoyment and to retain whatever is necessary for the use and enjoyment of the land retained. In view of the rule that a conveyance is to be construed most strongly against the grantor, an easement in favor of the grantee

Continued on next page.

will be implied more readily than one in favor of the grantor.

Quicknotes

IMPLIED EASEMENT An easement that is not expressly stated in a deed, but which is inferred upon conveyance, that a portion of one parcel had been used to benefit the other parcel and that upon sale the buyer of the benefited parcel could reasonably expect such benefits to continue.

QUASI-DOMINANT TENEMENT Property whose owners benefit from the use of another's property.

QUASI-SERVIENT TENEMENT Property that is burdened in some aspect for the benefit of a dominant estate.

Othen v. Rosier

Road user (P) v. Property owner (D)

Tex. Sup. Ct., 148 Tex. 485, 226 S.W.2d 622 (1950).

NATURE OF CASE: Appeal from judgment denying the existence of an easement by either prescription or necessity.

FACT SUMMARY: Othen (P) alleged that he had acquired an easement across the land of Rosier (D), after Rosier (D) erected a levee on the land.

RULE OF LAW

In order to create an easement by necessity, the necessity must have existed at the time that the estate was created.

FACTS: Othen (P) and Rosier (D) own tracts of land which were formerly part of one larger parcel. In order to reach any public highways, Othen (P) must cross over someone else's property. Othen (P) had used a road which ran across Rosier's (D) property, which Rosier (D) kept in repair. As a result of encroaching surface waters, Rosier (D) erected a levee on his property, which made the road so muddy that for weeks at a time it was impassable except by horseback. Othen (P) filed suit for injunctive and declaratory relief, and for damages. The trial court found that Othen (P) had acquired an easement by necessity. However, the appellate court reversed, holding that Othen (P) had acquired neither an easement by necessity nor one by prescription.

ISSUE: In order to create an easement by necessity, must the necessity have existed at the time that the estate was created?

HOLDING AND DECISION: (Brewster, J.) Yes. Before an implied easement by necessity can be held to be created, it must be shown that there was a unity of ownership of the alleged dominant and servient estates; that the roadway is a necessity and not a mere convenience; and that the necessity existed at the time of severance of the two estates. Here, there was unity of ownership of the lands now owned by Othen (P) and Rosier (D). However, no easement may be implied for the road because the original owner did not reserve such an easement when he first sold the property now owned by Rosier (D). The record does not indicate that the roadway was a necessity as of the date of the original grant deed, rather than a mere convenience. Othen (P) has additionally not acquired an easement by prescription, because his use of the road was not under claim of right. Othen's (P) use of the roadway was merely permissive and therefore constituted only a license, which could not and did not ripen into a prescriptive right. Affirmed.

ANALYSIS

Several states have attempted to solve the problems posed by landlocked property through statutory provisions providing for condemnation of private ways. While the statutory provisions vary from state to state, all jurisdictions require payment to be made for the land taken by the owner of the benefited property. The degree of necessity required for condemnation also varies; some states require a showing of strict necessity; while others only require that the necessity be reasonable under all the circumstances.

Quicknotes

CLAIM OF RIGHT Person claiming a right in property is in possession and intends to claim ownership of that property without regard to the record title owner.

CONDEMNATION The taking of private property for public use so long as just compensation is paid therefor.

DOMINANT ESTATE Property whose owners benefit from the use of another's property.

EASEMENT BY NECESSITY An easement that arises by operation of law without which the owner of the benefited property is deprived of the use and enjoyment of his property.

EASEMENT BY PRESCRIPTION A manner of acquiring an easement in another's property by continuous and uninterrupted use in satisfaction of the statutory requirements of adverse possession.

LICENSE A right that is granted to a person allowing him or her to conduct an activity that without such permission he or she could not lawfully do, and which is unassignable and revocable at the will of the licensor.

PRESCRIPTIVE RIGHTS Rights to an easement in another's property acquired by continuous and uninterrupted use in satisfaction of the statutory requirements of adverse possession.

SERVIENT ESTATE Property that is burdened in some aspect for the benefit of a dominant estate.

Raleigh Avenue Beach Assn. v. Atlantis Beach Club

Beach association (P) v. Private club (D)

879 A.2d 112 (N.J. 2005).

NATURE OF CASE: Defendant's appeal of decision granting beach access to plaintiffs.

FACT SUMMARY: Atlantis Beach Club (Atlantis) (D) owned land on the New Jersey shore including a 480-foot-wide stretch of upland sands. Atlantis (D) limited public access to the beach by charging a $700 membership fee. Raleigh Avenue Beach Assn. (the Association) (P), a neighborhood beach association, sought both vertical and horizontal access to the beach under the public trust doctrine.

RULE OF LAW

Under the public trust doctrine, sands upland from the high water mark must be available for use by the general public, subject to a reasonable fee for costs incurred for management services.

FACTS: Atlantis (D) owned beachfront property that it operated as a private beach club. Atlantis (D) also owned a 480-foot-wide stretch of beach in front the club. Beginning in 1996, after a ten-year period where the beach was open to the public, Atlantis (D) restricted public access and began charging membership fees. As of 2003, the membership fee was $700 for six beach tags. The Association (P) sought access to the beach. Specifically, the Association (P) sought vertical access across the Atlantis (D) beach from Raleigh Avenue down to the ocean. The Association (P) also sought horizontal access to a portion of the beach just inland from the high water mark, as a place for members to sit and rest when not swimming. The trial court ruled in favor of the Association (P), granting it vertical access down to the beach, as well as a three-foot-wide horizontal access just above the high water mark. An intermediate appellate court affirmed, but also allowed Atlantis (D) to charge reasonable fees to the public. Atlantis (D) appealed.

ISSUE: Under the public trust doctrine, must sands upland from the high water mark be available for use by the general public subject to a reasonable fee for costs incurred for managerial services?

HOLDING AND DECISION: (Poritz, C.J.) Yes. Under the public trust doctrine, sands upland from the high water mark must be available for use by the general public, subject to a reasonable fee for costs incurred for managerial services. The public trust doctrine guarantees public access to the ocean and waters between the high and low water marks. Moreover, the doctrine assumes some reasonable right of access over privately owned, upland beach areas in order to access the ocean. Without such access, the public's right to swim in the ocean would be meaningless. However, public access to privately owned upland sands is subject to an accommodation of the interests of the owner. Precisely how much of the privately owned land must be made available to the public will depend on circumstances present in each case. Location of the sand in relation to the beachfront, availability of other publicly owned beaches, extent of the public demand, and usage of the sand by the owner are all factors to be weighed in determining the extent of the public right's to use the upland sand. In this matter, there is no publicly owned beachfront in the town. There is enormous public interest in beaches in general in New Jersey. Moreover, a residential condominium complex next door also had a permit to use a portion of the beach in question. In addition, the beach was open to the public for ten years prior to 1996. Based on all of these factors, we hold that the Atlantis (D) beach, in its entirety, must be made available to the public. However, we agree the state Department of Environmental Protection has jurisdiction to review any fees proposed by Atlantis (D). At the least, Atlantis (D) may charge for expenses incurred for managerial services related to the beach. Affirmed.

DISSENT: (Wallace, J.) I dissent on the grounds the beach just north of Atlantis's (D) beach is open to the public. Providing the public with vertical access down to the water and the minimal strip of dry stand, just above the water line, would more properly balance the private owner's right to use its land as it sees fit and the public right of access to the ocean.

ANALYSIS

This decision was a major victory for advocates of public access to local beaches. However, its holding is limited to the factual circumstances present in the case. In these circumstances, the most significant factor leading to the court's decision was the prior history of the beach as one fully open to the public.

Quicknotes

PUBLIC TRUST DOCTRINE The government holds lands that are submerged beneath the water, or that are capable of being submerged, in trust for the public's benefit.

Miller v. Lutheran Conference & Camp Association

Easement-in-gross owners (P) v. Easement assignees (D)

Pa. Sup. Ct., 331 Pa. 241, 200 A. 646, 130 A.L.R. 1245 (1938).

NATURE OF CASE: Appeal from issuance of injunction.

FACT SUMMARY: Miller (P) sought to prevent the Lutheran Conference & Camp Association (the Association) (D) from using a lake for swimming or boating.

RULE OF LAW

An easement in gross may arise by prescription and is assignable if the parties to its creation so intend.

FACTS: In September 1895, Frank C. Miller and his brother Rufus W. Miller, formed the Pocono Spring Water Ice Company, to have the exclusive use of the waters of Lake Naomi, a man-made lake. By deed dated March 20, 1899, the Company granted to "Frank C. Miller, his heirs and assigns forever, the exclusive right to fish and boat in all the waters" of Lake Naomi. On February 17, 1900, Frank C. Miller (his wife Katherine (P) not joining) granted to Rufus W. Miller, his heirs and assigns forever, a one-fourth interest in the "fishing, boating and bathing rights" of Lake Naomi. On July 13, 1929, the executors of Rufus W. Miller's estate granted a one-year license to the Association (D) to boat, bathe, and fish in the lake. Frank C. Miller and his wife, Katherine D. Miller (P), then filed suit to enjoin the Association (D) from using the lake, on the grounds that the rights to use the lake were easements in gross and therefore inalienable and indivisible. The trial court issued the injunction, and the Association (D) appealed.

ISSUE: May an easement in gross arise by prescription, and is it assignable if the parties to its creation so intend?

HOLDING AND DECISION: (Stern, J.) Yes. The deed of 1899 from the Pocono Springs Water Ice Company to Frank C. Miller clearly did not convey any bathing rights. However, Frank C. Miller did establish title to the bathing rights by prescription because the rights were used systematically for commercial purposes. An adverse enjoyment of an easement in gross may ripen into title thereto by prescription; and therefore Frank C. Miller and Rufus W. Miller acquired title to the bathing rights by prescription. Further, Frank C. Miller made a valid assignment of a one-fourth interest in all rights to Rufus W. Miller. The rights of fishing and boating were conveyed to Frank C. Miller, his heirs and assigns, thus showing that the grantor, the Pocono Spring Water Ice Company, intended to attach the attribute of assignability to the privilege granted. However, even though the easements may be divided amongst different title holders, the easements must be used or exercised as an entirety. They cannot be commercially used and licenses, thereunder, cannot be granted without the common consent and joinder of the Millers (P), who own a portion of the easements. It follows that the executors of the estate of Rufus W. Miller did not have the right, in and by themselves, to grant a license to the Association (D). Affirmed.

ANALYSIS

The modern trend rejects the old notion that the benefit of an easement in gross was not assignable. The Restatement view is that "easements in gross, if of a commercial character, are, alienable property interests." Commercial character is defined as "when the use authorized by it results in economic benefit rather than personal satisfaction." See, 5 Restatement of Property, § 489; and § 489, Comment C (1944).

Quicknotes

ASSIGNABLE Capable of being transferred or conveyed.

EASEMENT IN GROSS A right to use the land of another that is specific to a particular individual and which expires upon the death of that person.

INJUNCTION A court order requiring a person to do or prohibiting that person from doing a specific act.

LICENSE A right that is granted to a person allowing him or her to conduct an activity that without such permission he or she could not lawfully do, and which is unassignable and revocable at the will of the licensor.

PRESCRIPTION The acquisition of an easement in or on another's property as a result of continuous use for the statutory period.

Brown v. Voss

Easement grantee (P) v. Easement grantor (D)

Wash. Sup. Ct., 105 Wash. 2d 366, 715 P.2d 514 (1986).

NATURE OF CASE: Appeal from denial of injunctive relief.

FACT SUMMARY: The court of appeals held that an easement granted for the benefit of one dominant estate could be used for two dominant estates where no increased burden to the servient estate is shown.

RULE OF LAW

If an easement is appurtenant to a particular parcel of land, any extension thereof to other parcels is a misuse of the easement, unless the servient estate does not overburden it.

FACTS: In 1952, Voss (D) granted an easement to Brown (P) to allow ingress and egress to Voss's (D) property. Brown (P) subsequently obtained title to a third parcel and attempted to use the easement to gain access thereto. Brown (P) sued to establish the right to so use the easement, yet Voss (D) sought an injunction to forbid such use. The trial court denied the injunction, the court of appeals reversed, and Voss (D) appealed.

ISSUE: If an easement is appurtenant to a particular parcel of land, is any extension thereof to other parcels a misuse of the easement, unless the easement is not overburdened?

HOLDING AND DECISION: (Brachtenbach, J.) Yes. If an easement is appurtenant to a particular parcel of land, any extension thereof to other parcels is a misuse of the easement, unless the use does not overburden the easement. The easement received no greater use as a result of Brown's (P) acquisition of the second parcel. Brown (P) reasonably developed his property, and thus the injunction was correctly denied. Reversed.

DISSENT: (Dore, J.) Any extension of this easement is a misuse. Thus, injunctive relief should have been granted.

ANALYSIS

This case illustrates that while the law of easements can be traced back to common law, it is subject to judicial interpretation. Here, the reasonableness of the development, in the eyes of the court, served as the basis for denying the injunction.

Quicknotes

APPURTENANT A burden attached to real property that either benefits or burdens the owner's right to utilize that property.

DOMINANT ESTATE Property whose owners benefit from the use of another's property.

EASEMENT The right to utilize a portion of another's real property for a specific use.

INJUNCTIVE RELIEF A court order issued as a remedy, requiring a person to do, or prohibiting that person from doing, a specific act.

SERVIENT ESTATE Property that is burdened in some aspect for the benefit of a dominant estate.

Preseault v. United States

Right-of-way owners (P) v. Federal government (D)

100 F.3d 1525 (Fed. Cir. 1996).

NATURE OF CASE: Appeal from judgment rejecting claim for compensation due to exercise of eminent domain.

FACT SUMMARY: The Preseaults (P) contended that the federal Government (D) took their property when it authorized the conversion of a former railroad right-of-way over their property to public trail use.

RULE OF LAW

A change in use of an easement from a rail line to a recreational path constitutes a taking.

FACTS: An agreement executed in 1899 gave the federal government an easement across three parcels of land owned by the Preseaults' (P) predecessor for use as a rail line. The line began operating not long thereafter, but by 1970, rail operations had ceased. In 1975, the switches and tracks were removed. In 1986, under the Federal Rails-to-Trails Act, the land on which the rail line had once run was converted into a recreational trail. The Preseaults (P) filed suit in the Court of Federal Claims, contending that the new use constituted a taking for which they were entitled to compensation. The Court of Federal Claims rejected this contention, and they appealed.

ISSUE: Does a change in use of an easement from a rail line to a recreational path constitute a taking?

HOLDING AND DECISION: (Plager, J.) Yes. A change in use of an easement from a rail line to a recreational path constitutes a taking. Typically, an easement does not contain a specific termination date, but usually ends by way of abandonment. Abandonment is not effected merely by nonuse, but rather by acts that are inconsistent with the use for which the easement exists. Here, in 1975, the railroad took out the rail hardware, an act inconsistent with use as a rail line. At that point, then, abandonment was effected. At this point, the interest the Government (D) had in the Preseaults' (P) property was extinguished. The creation of the recreational path, therefore, was not a legitimate expansion of the original easement, but, rather, a taking of the Preseaults' (P) property, which, under the Fifth Amendment, required compensation. Reversed and remanded.

ANALYSIS

It is not uncommon for strips of land to be deeded for transport purposes. The drafters of these documents are not always careful in the language utilized, and the question often arises as to whether it was an easement or fee simple that was conveyed. As a rule, courts tend to view "right-of-way" language in such instruments as conveying easements, not fees.

Quicknotes

ABANDONMENT The voluntary relinquishment of a right without the intent of reclaiming it.

EASEMENT The right to utilize a portion of another's real property for a specific use.

EMINENT DOMAIN The governmental power to take private property for public use so long as just compensation is paid therefor.

FEE SIMPLE An estate in land characterized by ownership of the entire property for an unlimited duration and by absolute power over distribution.

RIGHT-OF-WAY The right of a party to pass over the property of another.

TAKING A governmental action that substantially deprives an owner of the use and enjoyment of his or her property, requiring compensation.

Tulk v. Moxhay

Original covenantor (P) v. Subsequent purchaser (D)

Ct. Ch., 2 Phillips 774, 41 Eng. Rep. 1143 (1848).

NATURE OF CASE: Bill for injunction to enforce covenant in deed.

FACT SUMMARY: Moxhay (D) indicated an intention to build upon a park-like piece of land, even though he was aware of an original, prohibitive covenant passed on by Tulk (P), 40 years earlier, which forbade any construction on the ground.

RULE OF LAW
Privity of estate notwithstanding, a person who acquires real property with notice of a restriction placed upon it will not be allowed, in equity, to violate its terms.

FACTS: Tulk (P), owner in fee of a square garden containing a statue, as well as adjacent houses, sold the property to Elms. A covenant in the deed of conveyance prohibited Elms and his assigns from ever constructing upon the ground. The piece of land eventually came into the hands of Moxhay (D), whose purchase deed contained no similar covenant, yet Moxhay (D) admitted he knew of the original covenant. When Moxhay (D) indicated he wanted to build on the piece of ground, Tulk (P) successfully obtained an injunction.

ISSUE: Can the purchaser of a deed of conveyance containing a restriction violate the restriction if he has notice of the original covenant?

HOLDING AND DECISION: (Cottenham, Lord Chan.) No. To hold otherwise would make it impossible for an owner of land to sell part of it without running the risk of seeing the part he retained rendered worthless. At issue is not whether the covenant "runs" with the land, but whether a party may violate a contract entered into by his vendor by using the land in an inconsistent manner. If there was mere agreement and no covenant, a court would enforce it against a party purchasing with notice; so long as equity is attached by an owner, no one purchasing with notice can stand in a different situation than the original purchaser.

ANALYSIS

Notice is the key element of the principle, commonly referred to as "the doctrine of *Tulk v. Moxhay*," enunciated in this case. Notice of the restriction may be either actual, inquiry, or record. The rights and obligations recognized here are variously named, but are generally known as "equitable servitudes." The restriction in the transfer of land need not be embodied in covenant—an informal contract or agreement is sufficient. A party intended to receive the benefit, as well as the original covenantor, can bring the suit in equity. However, proof of notice is essential to the doctrine.

Quicknotes

CONVEYANCE The transfer of property, or title to property, from one party to another party.

COVENANT A written promise to do, or to refrain from doing, a particular activity.

***DIVERS MESNE* CONVEYANCE** A conveyance falling between the original owner and the present owner in the chain of title.

EQUITABLE SERVITUDE Land use restriction enforceable in equity.

EQUITY Fairness; justice; the determination of a matter consistent with principles of fairness and not in strict compliance with rules of law.

INJUNCTION A court order requiring a person to do or prohibiting that person from doing a specific act.

OWNER IN FEE An owner of an absolute and unlimited interest in property.

PRIVITY OF ESTATE Common or successive relation to the same right in property.

Sanborn v. McLean

Neighbor (P) v. Gas station owner (D)

Mich. Sup. Ct., 233 Mich. 227, 206 N.W. 496 (1925).

NATURE OF CASE: Action to enjoin erection of gasoline filling station.

FACT SUMMARY: Sanborn (P) and McLean (D) trace the titles to their adjoining lots to the proprietor of the subdivision. Residences are built on all the surrounding lots. Sanborn (P) objected to McLean's (D) erection of a gas station on her lot.

RULE OF LAW

If the owner of two or more lots, which are situated so as to bear a relation to each other, sells one with restrictions which are of benefit to the land retained, during the period of restraint, the owner of the lot or lots retained can do nothing forbidden to the owner of the lot sold. This is the doctrine of reciprocal negative easements.

FACTS: On December 28, 1892, McLaughlin, who was then owner of the lots on Collingwood Avenue, deeded four of the lots with the restriction that only residences would be built on the lots. On July 24, 1893, McLaughlin conveyed several more lots with the same restriction. Sanborn (P) traces title to McLaughlin. McLean's (D) title runs back to a deed dated September 7, 1893, which does not contain the restrictions. No buildings other than residences have been erected on any of the lots of the subdivision.

ISSUE:

(1) If the owner of two or more lots, which are situated so as to bear a relation to each other, sells one with restrictions which are of benefit to the land retained, during the period of restraint, can the owner of the lot or lots retained do anything forbidden to the owner of the lot sold?

(2) Is a reciprocal negative easement personal to owners?

HOLDING AND DECISION: (Wiest, J.)

(1) No. The doctrine of reciprocal negative easements makes restrictions which are of benefit to the land retained mutual so that the owner can do nothing upon the land he has retained that is forbidden to the owner of the lot sold. In this case McLaughlin deeded lots with the restriction that only residences may be built on them. Such restrictions were imposed for the benefit of the lands retained by McLaughlin to carry out the scheme of a residential district, and a restrictive negative easement attached to the lots retained. Since his was one of the lots retained in the December 1892 and July 1893 deeds, a reciprocal negative easement attached to the lot which later became McLean's (D).

(2) No. Reciprocal negative easements are not personal to owners but are operative upon use of the land by any owner having actual or constructive notice thereof. In this case the reciprocal negative easement attached to McLean's (D) lot may now be enforced by Sanborn (P) provided McLean (D) had constructive knowledge of the easement at the time of purchase. At the time of purchase, McLean (D) had an abstract of title showing the subdivision and the 97 companion lots adjacent to his lot. He could not avoid noticing the strictly uniform residence character of the companion lots, and the least inquiry would have revealed the fact that his lot was subject to a reciprocal negative easement. The injunction is granted and the decree in the Circuit is affirmed.

ANALYSIS

Reciprocal negative easements must start with common owners. They cannot arise and fasten upon one lot by reason of other lot owners conforming to a general plan. Such easements are never retroactive, and as demonstrated here, they pass their benefits and carry their obligations to all purchasers of land provided the purchaser has constructive notice of the easement.

Quicknotes

CONSTRUCTIVE NOTICE Knowledge of a fact that is imputed to an individual who was under a duty to inquire and who could have learned of the fact through the exercise of reasonable prudence.

INJUNCTION A court order requiring a person to do or prohibiting that person from doing a specific act.

RECIPROCAL NEGATIVE EASEMENTS An implied covenant that arises when a common grantor conveys property and fails to contain a restriction placed on prior conveyances, pursuant to a general development scheme, to the present one and the grantee has either actual or constructive notice of such restrictions.

TITLE ABSTRACT Summary of the history of a title to property.

Neponsit Property Owners' Association, Inc. v. Emigrant Industrial Savings Bank

Covenantor's assignees (P) v. Subsequent purchaser (D)

N.Y. Ct. App., 278 N.Y. 248, 15 N.E.2d 793 (1938).

NATURE OF CASE: Action to foreclose a lien upon land.

FACT SUMMARY: **Neponsit Property Owners (P) claim that Emigrant Bank's (D) deed to certain property conveyed such property subject to a covenant contained in the original deed which provided for the payment by all subsequent purchasers of an annual improvements charge.**

RULE OF LAW

A covenant in deed subjecting land to an annual charge for improvements to the surrounding residential tract is enforceable by the property owners' association against subsequent purchasers if: (1) grantor and grantee so intended; (2) it appears that the covenant is one touching or concerning the land; and (3) privity of estate is shown between the party claiming benefit of the covenant and the party under the burden of such covenant.

FACTS: Neponsit Property Owners' (P) assignor, Neponsit Realty Company, conveyed the land now owned by Emigrant Bank (D) to R. Deyer and wife by deed. That original deed contained a covenant providing: (1) that the conveyed land should be subject to an annual charge for improvements upon the entire residential tract then being developed; (2) that such charge should be a lien; (3) such charge should be payable by all subsequent purchasers to the company or its assigns, including a property owners' association which might thereafter be organized; and (4) such covenant runs with the land. Neponsit Property Owners (P) brought action based upon the above covenant to foreclose a lien upon the land which Emigrant Bank (D) now owns, having purchased it at a judicial sale. Emigrant Bank (D) appealed from an order denying their motion for judgment on the pleadings.

ISSUE: Does a covenant in the original deed subjecting land to an annual charge for improvements run with the land and create a lien which is enforceable against subsequent owners by Neponsit Property Owners (P)?

HOLDING AND DECISION: (Lehman, J.) Yes. A covenant will run with the land and will be enforceable against a subsequent purchaser if: (1) the grantor and grantee intend that the covenant run with the land; (2) the covenant touches or concerns the land with which it runs; (3) there is privity of estate between the party claiming benefit of the covenant and the party who rests under the burden of the covenant. In the instant case the grantor and grantee manifested their intent that the covenant run with the land by so stating in the original deed. The covenant touches or concerns the land in substance if not in form, i.e., the covenant alters the legal rights of ownership of the land, by providing that the burden of paying the cost of maintaining public improvements is inseparably attached to the land which enjoys the benefits of such improvements. The concept of privity of estate between parties usually requires that the party claiming benefit from the enforcement of a covenant own the property which benefits from such enforcement. Although Neponsit Property Owners (P), the corporation, does not own the property which would benefit from enforcement, the corporation is acting as the agent of property owners and should therefore be considered in privity in substance if not in form. Since the covenant complies with the legal requirements for one which runs with the land and is enforceable against subsequent purchasers, the order which denied Emigrant Bank's (D) motion for judgment on the pleadings is affirmed.

ANALYSIS

It has been suggested that the technical requirements that determine the enforceability of covenants as to future parties, e.g., *Neponsit*, might well be abandoned and that the intention of the covenanting parties be the sole criterion. This suggestion is supported by the following developments: (1) the benefit of a contract may now be assigned, or even created, initially for the benefit of a third person; (2) recording systems, though imperfect, afford much protection to the purchaser of land against outstanding burdens of which he may be unaware. It should be noted, however, that the unrestricted enforcement of covenants may seriously impair the usefulness of land. A student reading this case should keep in mind that *Neponsit* is not concerned with the enforcement of covenants between original covenanting parties. That question of enforceability is left to the contracts course.

Quicknotes

COVENANT A written promise to do, or to refrain from doing, a particular activity.

FORECLOSURE An action to recover the amount due on a mortgage of real property where the owner has failed to pay their debt, terminating the owner's interest in the property which must then be sold to satisfy the debt.

Continued on next page.

JUDICIAL SALE A sale of property by a sheriff pursuant to a judgment.

LIEN A claim against the property of another in order to secure the payment of a debt.

PRIVITY OF ESTATE Common or successive relation to the same right in property.

"RUN WITH THE LAND" Covenants that are binding on successor in interest to the property to which they are attached.

Shelley v. Kraemer

Home buyer (D) v. Neighbors (P)

334 U.S. 1 (1948).

NATURE OF CASE: Appeal from state high court decision in favor of defendants.

FACT SUMMARY: Shelley (D), an African-American, sought to purchase a home. A group of neighbors sought to uphold a restrictive covenant that prohibited the sale of any neighborhood homes to any person "not of the Caucasian race."

RULE OF LAW

State court enforcement of private, discriminatory restrictive covenants constitutes state action under the Fourteenth Amendment.

FACTS: On February 16, 1911, 30 of 39 owners of property in a neighborhood of St. Louis executed an agreement prohibiting the sale of any of the homes to any person "not of the Caucasian race." In 1945, Shelley (D), an African-American, sought to buy one of the homes covered by the agreement. The other homeowners, led by Kraemer (P), brought suit to uphold the restrictive covenant and to prevent the sale. The Missouri Supreme court upheld the validity of the restrictive covenant. Shelley (D) appealed to the U.S. Supreme Court.

ISSUE: Does state court enforcement of private, discriminatory restrictive covenants constitute state action under the Fourteenth Amendment?

HOLDING AND DECISION: (Vinson, C.J.) Yes. State court enforcement of private, discriminatory restrictive covenants constitutes state action under the Fourteenth Amendment. First, the Fourteenth Amendment requires equality in the enjoyment of property rights. Moreover, if the prohibition in the private agreement was contained in a state statute or local ordinance, the Fourteenth Amendment would bar such prohibition because state action would be present. Here, the restrictive covenant is contained in an agreement between private individuals. We therefore conclude that without any state court intervention, private, restrictive covenants, even if discriminatory, do not run afoul of the Fourteenth Amendment because no state action is present. However, in the instant case, state courts have entered the fray and upheld the validity of the clearly discriminatory, private agreement. We have long held that "state action" includes action of the state courts and judicial officials. Therefore, the state court's intervention to uphold the covenants constitutes state action. That action is a violation of Shelley's (D) right to equal protection under the laws. Reversed.

ANALYSIS

Shelley was the first case to strike down private, race-based restrictive covenants. The Civil Rights Act, plus a host of other state and local ordinances now outlaw discrimination in the private, residential housing market.

Quicknotes

FOURTEENTH AMENDMENT Declares that no state shall make or enforce any law that shall abridge the privileges and immunities of citizens of the United States. No state shall deny to any person within its jurisdiction the equal protection of the laws.

RESTRICTIVE COVENANT A promise contained in a deed to limit the uses to which the property will be made.

Western Land Co. v. Truskolaski

Subdivision homeowners (P) v. Subdivision developer (D)

Nev. Sup. Ct., 88 Nev. 200, 495 P.2d 624 (1972).

NATURE OF CASE: Appeal from order enjoining construction.

FACT SUMMARY: Western Land Co. (D) wanted to build a shopping center near property owned by Truskolaski (P), who argued that such construction would violate a restrictive covenant.

RULE OF LAW

A restrictive covenant is enforceable so long as its provisions remain of substantial value.

FACTS: In 1941, Western Land Co. (D) subdivided and developed a 40-acre parcel in Reno, Nevada. At that time, Western Land Co. (D) subjected the individual lots to certain restrictive covenants which specifically restricted the entire 40 acres of the subdivision to single family dwellings and further prohibited any stores, butcher shops, grocery, or mercantile business of any kind. In 1969, Truskolaski (P) and other homeowners in the subdivision sued to enjoin Western Land Co. (D) from constructing a shopping center on a parcel of land located within the subdivision. In holding for Truskolaski (P), the trial court found that the restrictive covenants remained of substantial value to the homeowners in the subdivision, despite the growth of commercial development in the area.

ISSUE: Is a restrictive covenant enforceable so long as its provisions remain of substantial value?

HOLDING AND DECISION: (Batjer, J.) Yes. So long as the original purpose of restrictive covenants can be accomplished and substantial benefit inure to the restricted area by their enforcement, the covenants will stand even though the subject property has a greater value if used for other purposes. Even though nearby streets have become heavily traveled, restrictive covenants are still enforceable if the single-family residential character of the neighborhood has not been adversely affected, and the purpose of the restrictions has not been thwarted. Here, Western Land Co. (D) has not carried its burden of showing that the subdivision is not now suitable for residential purposes because of the growth of commercial activities. Further, even though the Reno City Council considered rezoning the area around the subdivision, a zoning ordinance cannot override privately placed restrictive covenants. Affirmed.

ANALYSIS

Several states have now enacted statutes which terminate restrictive covenants or limit their application by requiring that they be re-recorded after a specified period of time. Perhaps typical of the duration to be accorded these covenants are provisions contained in the statutes of Georgia (20 years) and Massachusetts (30 years). In a few states, restrictive covenants will not be enforced if the covenant carries no substantial benefit, or where there has been substantial compliance for a reasonable period of time.

Quicknotes

RESTRICTIVE COVENANT A promise contained in a deed to limit the uses to which the property will be made.

Rick v. West

Subsequent purchaser (P) v. Servitude proponent (D)

N.Y. Sup. Ct., Westchester County, 228 N.Y.S.2d 195(1962).

NATURE OF CASE: Appeal from judgment enforcing restrictive covenant.

FACT SUMMARY: West (D), owner of a half-acre lot in a residential subdivision, refused to consent to a release of a covenant in her favor restricting the lots to single-family dwellings, thereby frustrating Rick's (P) plans to construct a hospital in the subdivision.

RULE OF LAW

Courts will not engage in a balancing of equities but will enforce restrictive covenants unless there is a substantial change of conditions in the general neighborhood.

FACTS: When Rick's (P) predecessor in title, the owner of 62 acres of vacant land, first subdivided the land, he filed a declaration of covenants, restricting the land to single-family dwellings. West (D) purchased a half-acre lot and built her house on it. Rick's predecessor (P) attempted to sell 45 acres for industrial use, but West (D) refused to release the covenant in her favor. After purchasing the remaining acreage, Rick (D) attempted to sell a 15-acre tract for construction of a hospital. Again West (D) refused to release the covenant. Rick (P) sued to have the covenant declared unenforceable, claiming changed conditions. The trial court held for West (D), and Rick (P) appealed.

ISSUE: Will courts enforce restrictive covenants, notwithstanding the parties' relative equities, so long as there is no substantial change of conditions in the general neighborhood?

HOLDING AND DECISION: (Hoyt, J.) Yes. Courts will enforce restrictive covenants, notwithstanding the parties' relative equities, so long as there is no substantial change of conditions in the general neighborhood. In this case, Rick's (P) predecessor in title chose to promote a residential development, imposing the residential restriction, upon which West (D) relied. She has a right to continue to rely on the restrictive covenant. The court will not engage in a balancing of equities, regardless of the location's suitability for a hospital. Because the restriction is not outmoded and affords real benefit to West (D), West (D) may not be awarded damages in lieu of enforcement. Affirmed.

ANALYSIS

If this case had been litigated in Massachusetts, the outcome might have been different. Massachusetts has a statute which requires that the person seeking to enforce the servitude show that the restriction actually benefits her. However, damages are the only remedy and will be awarded if there have been changes in the neighborhood which reduce the need for the restriction, or if continuation of the restriction would impede reasonable use of the land for purposes for which it is most suitable or would impair the growth of the neighborhood. Therefore, if Massachusetts law had been applied in the case above, even if West (D) could have demonstrated such a benefit, she probably could not have actually enforced the restriction but would have instead received an award of money damages.

Quicknotes

CHANGED CONDITIONS A defense to a claim of ameliorative waste, based on the theory that a change in the surrounding area warranted the alterations to the property.

RESTRICTIVE COVENANT A promise contained in a deed to limit the uses to which the property will be made.

SERVITUDE Land use restriction enforceable in equity.

Pocono Springs Civic Association, Inc. v. MacKenzie

Development association (P) v. Vacant-lot owners (D)

Pa. Super. Ct., 446 Pa. Super. 445, 667 A.2d 233 (1995).

NATURE OF CASE: Appeal from judgment awarding back homeowner's fees against a property owner.

FACT SUMMARY: The MacKenzies (D) contended that their nonuse of their property, refusal to pay taxes, and offers to sell created abandonment.

RULE OF LAW

A landowner cannot abandon property to which he holds perfect title.

FACTS: The MacKenzies (D) purchased a vacant lot in a development known as Pocono Springs, which was under the control of the Pocono Springs Civic Association, Inc. (Association) (P). The MacKenzies (D) planned to build on the property. However, it turned out that the property was unable to support a sewage system. Believing their investment to be worthless, they tried to deed the property to the Association (P), which refused to accept it. They then stopped paying taxes on it, and the local government tried to sell it at a foreclosure sale, but there were no takers. The MacKenzies (D) then mailed a "notice of abandonment" to all interested parties, notifying them that they were renouncing all claim to the land. The Association (P) later filed an action seeking to collect delinquent association dues. The trial court entered summary judgment awarding the dues. The MacKenzies (D) appealed.

ISSUE: Can a landowner abandon property to which he has perfect title?

HOLDING AND DECISION: (Rowley, J.) No. A landowner cannot abandon property to which he holds perfect title. Abandoned property is defined as property to which the owner has abandoned all right, title, claim, and possession. When the owner still has title, the property has not been abandoned. Here, the MacKenzies (D) remain owners of real property in fee simple, with a recorded deed and perfect title, so they have not effected abandonment. Consequently, they are still liable for association dues. Affirmed.

ANALYSIS

The law at issue here seems to leave the MacKenzies (D) with little in the way of options. It seems that even not paying taxes will not get them out of the property. This would appear to be a good illustration of the concept of *caveat emptor*.

Quicknotes

ABANDONMENT The voluntary relinquishment of a right without the intent of reclaiming it.

CAVEAT EMPTOR Let the buyer beware; doctrine that a buyer purchases something at his own risk.

PERFECT TITLE Total right of possession and disposition over particular property.

Nahrstedt v. Lakeside Village Condominium Association, Inc.

Cat lover (P) v. Homeowners association (D)

Cal. Sup. Ct., 878 P.2d 1275 (1994).

NATURE OF CASE: Suit challenging the validity of a provision in a common interest development's Covenants, Conditions and Restrictions (CC&Rs) that prohibited the keeping of pets in the development.

FACT SUMMARY: A resident of a common interest development in California kept three cats in her condominium in violation of the development's governing CC&Rs. The homeowners association therefore assessed continuing penalties against her for the violations.

RULE OF LAW

A recorded use restriction imposed by a common interest development in California must be enforced uniformly against all residents of the development unless the restriction is unreasonable.

FACTS: Nahrstedt (P) owned and lived in a condominium in Lakeside Village, a 530-unit common interest development in Los Angeles County overseen by the Lakeside Village Condominium Association ("the homeowners association") (D). Nahrstedt's (P) ownership of her condominium gave her membership in the homeowners association (D). One of the homeowners association's (D) duties was to enforce Lakeside Village's governing, duly recorded CC&Rs. One clause of the CC&Rs provided that "[n]o animals (which shall include dogs and cats) . . . shall be kept in any unit." Nahrstedt (P), who alleged that she did not know of the pet restriction when she bought her condominium, lived in her unit with her three cats, but she did not let her cats have free run of Lakeside Village's common areas. When the homeowners association (D) learned that Nahrstedt (P) was keeping the cats in her home, it started assessing monthly fines against her for violating the CC&Rs. Nahrstedt (P) sued the homeowners association (D), asking the trial court to invalidate the assessments already imposed against her, to enjoin the homeowners association (D) from making such assessments against her in the future, and to declare the pet restriction in the CC&Rs "unreasonable" as applied to situations involving non-disturbing, essentially entirely in-home pet ownership like hers. The homeowners association (D) filed a demurrer to Nahrstedt's (P) complaint [i.e., the homeowners association (D) moved to dismiss her complaint for failing to state a claim upon which relief could be granted]. The trial court agreed with the homeowners association (D) and dismissed Nahrstedt's (P) complaint. On Nahrstedt's (P) appeal, the intermediate appellate court reversed the trial court's judgment, agreeing with Nahrstedt (P) that the reasonableness of a recorded use restriction in a common interest development must be determined on a case-by-case basis. The homeowners association (D) petitioned the California Supreme Court for further review.

ISSUE: Must a recorded use restriction imposed by a common interest development in California be enforced uniformly against all residents of the development unless the restriction is unreasonable?

HOLDING AND DECISION: (Kennard, J.) Yes. A recorded use restriction imposed by a common interest development in California must be enforced uniformly against all residents of the development unless the restriction is unreasonable. Homeowners in a common interest development sacrifice certain freedoms in exchange for, among other things, their ability to enforce restrictive covenants against other homeowners in the development. These restrictions are enforceable, though, only if they qualify as equitable servitudes or as covenants running with the land. In Section 1354(a) of the California Civil Code, California's legislature has established the test for determining whether a common interest development's use restrictions are enforceable: under Section 1354(a), a recorded declaration's use restrictions are "enforceable . . . unless unreasonable." Some states have reached similar conclusions through the courts. For example, in *Hidden Harbour Estates v. Basso*, 393 So. 2d 637 (Fla. Ct. App. 1981), a Florida appellate court held that a recorded declaration's stated use restrictions are entitled to a heavy presumption of validity, so much so that even somewhat unreasonable restrictions should nevertheless be enforced. The *Hidden Harbour Estates* court concluded further that arbitrary restrictions or those that violate public policy or a fundamental constitutional right should not be enforced. In a case involving a pet restriction, *Noble v. Murphy*, 612 N.E.2d 266 (Mass. App. Ct. 1993), the court agreed with the *Hidden Harbour Estates* rationale that otherwise-valid use restrictions should be enforced unless they violate constitutional rights or public policy. This court concludes, then, that recorded restrictive covenants should not be enforced when they violate public policy, as in *Shelley v. Kramer*, 334 U.S. 1 (1948) (racial restriction), or when they are arbitrary and bear no rational relation to a purpose involving the land. In such cases, the harm resulting from enforcement of arbitrary use restrictions or restrictions that violate fundamental public policy always outweighs any benefit that such restrictions might confer. Such principles also inform Section 1354(a) of the California Civil Code, which this court interprets as requiring enforcement of use restrictions unless they are arbitrary, violate public policy,

Continued on next page.

or impose burdens outweighing any benefit. This presumption of validity for recorded restrictive covenants means that homeowners associations can enforce their covenants without fear of instigating litigation. The presumption also relieves the judicial system from making case-by-case determinations of whether covenants are reasonable as applied to a particular homeowner. The presumption thus in turn means that homeowners in common interest developments will have the assurance that their covenants will be enforced uniformly and predictably. In this particular case, the appellate court failed to apply the pertinent rules governing equitable servitudes and erroneously relied on two opinions, *Portola Hills Community Assn. v. James*, 5 Cal. Rptr. 2d 580 (Cal. Ct. App. 1993), and *Bernardo Villas Management Corp. v. Black*, 235 Cal. Rptr. 509 (Cal. Ct. App. 1987), both of which are hereby disapproved because those courts did not use appropriately deferential review of the covenants at issue in those cases. Whether a use restriction is reasonable or unreasonable must be determined by referring to the entire common interest development, not by referring to the particular facts of a specific complaining homeowner. More specifically, the court holds that the Lakeside Village pet restriction is not arbitrary because it rationally promotes the other owners' legitimate concerns about health, sanitation, and noise; Nahrstedt (P) has failed to allege that the restriction's burden is so disproportionate to the legitimate benefits that the pet restriction is unreasonable. Moreover, no fundamental public policy requires that pets be kept in a condominium development, and no constitutional provision or California statute grants the right to keep pets in such a situation, either. Reversed and remanded.

DISSENT: (Arabian, J.) The majority's reasoning has technical merit, but the application of that analysis to these facts reveals a narrow understanding of the relationship between the law and the human spirit. The pet restriction at issue here violates Section 1354(a). It is arbitrary and unreasonable, within the meaning of Section 1354(a), because it imposes an undue burden on owners who keep their pets within their units and do not permit their pets to disturb the use of other homeowners' properties. The restriction's burden on such homeowners outweighs those homeowners' quality of life in the common interest development, and indeed the restriction only worsens the breakdown of our social fabric. All that the majority has done today is to accept, uncritically, the homeowners association's (D) assurances that uniform enforcement will promote all owners' "health and happiness." The first question in an appropriately probing inquiry should be to recognize that the burden on the particular use at issue here goes well beyond the impersonal and mundane issues normally covered by restrictive covenants. The majority instead asks only whether the use restriction at issue was stated in the original recorded declaration. If it was, it now shall be presumed valid unless it violates public policy. Such a standard means that almost all recorded use restrictions are valid, a status that only the commandments issued by Moses have enjoyed before today. Further, the proscribed activity here, pet ownership that is wholly confined to one's own home, deprives homeowners of the American dream, a notion that has always included the ownership and full enjoyment of one's home. Courts should rule with more humanity and strive to create harmony, not division, within the populace.

ANALYSIS

Despite the emotionalism of Justice Arabian's dissent, and despite the intermediate appellate court's contrary ruling (relying on two now-invalidated opinions), today this case seems relatively easy for all the reasons cited by the majority. Public policy argues heavily against Nahrstedt's (P) position because that position would create great instability within homeowners associations, and because the burden of deciding enforceability of use restrictions on a case-by-case basis would substantially increase the caseloads of a judicial system that is already over-burdened. Under the rationale of *Nahrstedt* and cases like it, homeowners now can know that, when they sign a development's recorded covenants and use restrictions, those covenants and restrictions will almost certainly be enforced.

Quicknotes

CC&Rs Covenants, conditions, and restrictions that residents of a condominium development agree to abide by when they take ownership of a unit in that development.

DECLARATORY RELIEF A judgment of the court establishing the rights of the parties.

40 West 67th Street Corp. v. Pullman

Residential cooperative (P) v. Tenant (D)

790 N.E.2d 1174 (N.Y. 2003).

NATURE OF CASE: Appeal from intermediate appellate court decision in favor of plaintiff.

FACT SUMMARY: Pullman (D) engaged in a series of acts objectionable to the residential cooperative corporation (P), of which Pullman (D) was a member tenant. The cooperative (P) voted to evict him from his apartment.

RULE OF LAW

Under the business judgment rule, courts will defer to the residential cooperative's vote and findings as competent evidence that the tenant is objectionable and subject to eviction.

FACTS: The cooperative (P) owns the building at 40 West 67th Street in Manhattan. Pullman (D) rented one of the apartments in the building and signed a lease subjecting him to the rules and regulations of the cooperative (P). After moving in, Pullman (D) began complaining, without merit, about the loud noise from the television of the tenants above him, an elderly couple that had lived there for twenty years. After a physical altercation with the husband from that apartment, Pullman (D) also distributed flyers in the building stating that there was a "psychopath in our midst." In a separate flyer, Pullman (D) accused the same gentleman as having an affair with the wife of the cooperative's board president. Lastly, Pullman (D) made physical alterations to his apartment without proper approval. The cooperative called for a vote to evict Pullman (D) based on his "objectionable conduct." The cooperative (P), with 75% of the tenants present, voted unanimously to evict Pullman (D). After Pullman (D) refused to leave, the cooperative (P) brought this action to evict him. The trial court held that the business judgment rule did not apply. It held that the cooperative (P) had to prove its claim of objectionable conduct by competent evidence in a court of law. The intermediate appellate court reversed and held that the business judgment rule did apply here. Pullman (D) appealed.

ISSUE: Under the business judgment rule, will courts defer to the residential cooperative's vote and findings as competent evidence that the tenant is objectionable and subject to eviction?

HOLDING AND DECISION: (Rosenblatt, J.) Yes. Under the business judgment rule, courts will defer to the residential cooperative's vote and findings as competent evidence that the tenant is objectionable and subject to eviction. The parties disagree on the standard to be applied to the cooperative's (P) vote to evict Pullman (D). Pullman (D) believes Real Property Actions and Proceedings Law 711 (RPAPL 711) requires a court to make its own evaluation of the cooperative's conduct using a reasonableness standard. The cooperative (P) believes the business judgment rule applies, where courts defer to the good faith decisions made by boards of directors in business settings. We hold the business judgment rule applies. The rule balances the competing interests of the cooperative in governing itself while providing a limited judicial review in the case of abuses. Moreover, application of the business judgment rule does not conflict with RPAPL 711's requirement of a finding of competent evidence that a tenant is objectionable before facing eviction. We hold that the cooperative's own determination whether a tenant is objectionable constitutes competent evidence under the statute. Accordingly, in these contexts, courts must defer to the cooperative's determination pursuant to the business judgment rule. However, there are certain instances when courts may inquire further into a cooperative's actions. Those instances are when the cooperative acts: (1) outside the scope of its authority; (2) in a manner that does not further the cooperative's purpose; and (3) in bad faith. In this matter, we find that none of these circumstances are present. The intermediate appellate court's decision is affirmed. Affirmed.

ANALYSIS

Only a small handful of states apply the business judgment rule to decisions by residential cooperatives or similar homeowner's associations. The majority of states use a less deferential reasonableness standard based on the court's independent review of the cooperative's actions. This case only applies to eviction actions by residential cooperatives. Different standards apply in other forms of housing, most notably in the public housing sector.

Quicknotes

BUSINESS JUDGMENT RULE Doctrine relieving corporate directors and/or officers from liability for decisions honestly and rationally made in the corporation's best interests.

CHAPTER 11

Legislative Land-Use Controls

Quick Reference Rules of Law

PAGE

1. **Historical Background.** A zoning ordinance, as a valid exercise of the police power, will only be declared unconstitutional where its provisions are clearly arbitrary and unreasonable, having no substantial relation to the public health, safety, morals or general welfare. (Village of Euclid v. Ambler Realty Co.) *120*

2. **The Nonconforming Use.** A zoning ordinance which requires the amortization and discontinuance of a lawful preexisting nonconforming use is confiscatory and violative of the state constitution as a taking of property without just compensation. (PA Northwestern Distributors, Inc. v. Zoning Hearing Board) *122*

3. **Aesthetic Regulation.** The protection of property values is a legitimate objective of zoning ordinances. (State ex rel. Stoyanoff v. Berkeley) *123*

4. **Aesthetic Regulation.** A building code cannot consist of design criteria that are strictly subjective in nature. (Anderson v. City of Issaquah) *124*

5. **Aesthetic Regulation.** A municipality may not enact a blanket prohibition against signs on residential property. (City of Ladue v. Gilleo) *125*

6. **Protection of Religious Establishments and Uses.** Under the Religious Land Use and Institutionalized Persons Act of 2000 (RLUIPA), no government shall apply a land-use regulation in a manner that imposes a substantial burden on a person or a religious assembly or institution. (Guru Nanak Sikh Society of Yuba City v. County of Sutter) *126*

7. **Environmental Protection.** A court will not overturn an agency determination regarding the requirement of an environmental impact statement unless the decision was affected by an error of law or was arbitrary, capricious or constituted an abuse of discretion. (Fisher v. Giuliani) *127*

8. **Controls on Household Composition.** A city may pass an ordinance which prohibits unrelated individuals from living in one location. (Village of Belle Terre v. Boraas) *129*

9. **Controls on Household Composition.** A family composition zoning rule is not exempt from Fair Housing Act scrutiny. (City of Edmonds v. Oxford House, Inc.) *130*

10. **Exclusionary Zoning.** Municipal land-use regulations must provide a realistic opportunity for low and moderate income housing. (Southern Burlington County NAACP v. Township of Mount Laurel) *131*

Village of Euclid v. Ambler Realty Co.

Municipal corporation (D) v. Tract owner (P)

272 U.S. 365 (1926).

NATURE OF CASE: Action to enjoin enforcement of a zoning ordinance.

FACT SUMMARY: Euclid (D) zoned property of Ambler Realty (P) in a manner which materially reduced its potential value.

RULE OF LAW

A zoning ordinance, as a valid exercise of the police power, will only be declared unconstitutional where its provisions are clearly arbitrary and unreasonable, having no substantial relation to the public health, safety, morals, or general welfare.

FACTS: Ambler Realty (P) was the owner of 68 acres in the village of Euclid (D). Though surrounded primarily by residential neighborhoods, the 68 acres also is bounded by a major thoroughfare to the south and a railroad to the north. Euclid (D) instituted zoning ordinances placing use, height, and area restrictions. Restrictions were placed on Ambler Realty's (P) property prohibiting (1) apartment houses, hotels, churches, schools, or any other public or semi-public buildings for the first 620 feet from Euclid Avenue, the above-described major thoroughfare, and (2) industry, theatres, banks, shops, etc., for the next 130 feet after that. As a result of this zoning, the value of Ambler Realty's (P) property has declined from $10,000 per acre to $2,500 per acre. Ambler Realty (P) brought an action to enjoin Euclid (D) from enforcing the ordinance on the ground that it constitutes a violation of Fourteenth Amendment due process. From a decree in favor of Amber Realty (P), Euclid (D) appeals, contending that the ordinance was a valid exercise of the police power of the state.

ISSUE: Is a zoning ordinance unconstitutional as a deprivation of property without due process because it results in a diminution of value in the property zoned?

HOLDING AND DECISION: (Sutherland, J.) No. A zoning ordinance, as a valid exercise of the police power, will only be declared unconstitutional where its provisions are clearly arbitrary and unreasonable, having no substantial relation to the public health, safety, morals, or general welfare. Zoning ordinances, and all similar laws and regulations, must find their justification in some aspect of the police power, asserted for the public welfare. Until recent years, urban life was comparatively simple; but with the great increase and concentration of population, problems have developed which require new restrictions on the use and occupation of private lands in urban communities. There is no serious difference of opinion on the state power to avoid the nuisances which industry may cause in a residential area. As for residential regulation, many considerations point toward their validity. Segregation of residential business and industrial buildings makes it easier to provide appropriate fire apparatus, for example. Further, it is often observed that the construction of one type of building destroys an area for other types. In light of these considerations, the court is not prepared to say that the end of public welfare here is not sufficient to justify the imposition of this ordinance. It clearly cannot be said that it "... passes the bounds of reason and assumes the character of a merely arbitrary fiat." The decree must be reversed.

ANALYSIS

Village of Euclid v. Ambler Realty is the landmark Supreme Court decision on zoning ordinances as valid exercises of the police power. Essentially, any zoning ordinance which is tied to public health, safety, morals, or welfare will be upheld unless clearly arbitrary and unreasonable. So-called *Euclidian* Zoning, which resulted from this decision, usually consists in the division of areas into zones, in which building use, height, and area are regulated in a manner designed to guarantee homogeneity of building patterns. All too often, however, zoning operates not so much to protect the public interest as to protect the vested interests in a community. Building restrictions may all too easily be used as an economic sanction by which social segregation is perpetuated. (Barring low-cost housing keeps out economically deprived segment of the population.) Note, however, that *Euclid* did not foreclose the possibility that government land-use regulations may constitute a "taking" which requires compensation. In *Pennsylvania Coal Co. v. Mahon*, 260 U.S. 393 (1922), the U.S. Supreme Court held that an anti-mining restriction, which totally destroyed the interest of the party who owned only the mineral rights, constituted a taking as to that person for which compensation had to be paid. In the *Mahon* case, the diminution in value of the party's property was total, and was thus clearly a "taking."

Quicknotes

INJUNCTION A court order requiring a person to do or prohibiting that person from doing a specific act.

POLICE POWER The power of a government to impose restrictions on the rights of private persons, as long as those restrictions are reasonably related to the promotion and protection of public health, safety, morals, and the general welfare.

PUBLIC WELFARE The well-being of the general community.

Continued on next page.

TAKING A governmental action that substantially deprives an owner of the use and enjoyment of his or her property, requiring compensation.

ZONING ORDINANCE A statute that divides land into defined areas and which regulates the form and use of buildings and structures within those areas.

PA Northwestern Distributors, Inc. v. Zoning Hearing Board

Adult bookstore owner (P) v. Zoning board (D)

Pa. Sup. Ct., 526 Pa. 186, 584 A.2d 1372 (1991).

NATURE OF CASE: Appeal from dismissal of action challenging constitutionality of amortization ordinance.

FACT SUMMARY: Three weeks after PA Northwestern Distributors, Inc. (PA Northwestern) (P) opened an adult book store in Moon Township, Pennsylvania, the Board of Supervisors adopted an ordinance restricting permissible locations for bookstores and allowing only 90 days for nonconforming uses to either comply or shut down.

RULE OF LAW

A zoning ordinance which requires the amortization and discontinuance of a lawful preexisting nonconforming use is confiscatory and violative of the state constitution as a taking of property without just compensation.

FACTS: After obtaining the necessary permits, PA Northwestern (P) opened an adult book store in Moon Township. Three weeks later, following a public meeting, the Moon Township Board of Supervisors amended the zoning ordinances to impose extensive restrictions on the location and operation of "adult commercial enterprises." Any preexisting use in conflict with the new amendments was given 90-days' grace period, designed as a period of amortization, to either come into compliance with the ordinance or discontinue business. PA Northwestern (P) could not meet the place restrictions set forth in the ordinance because it was not located in an area designated for adult commercial enterprises. It filed an appeal with the Zoning Hearing Board (D), challenging the validity of the amortization provision, but the Hearing Board (D) validated the provision. PA Northwestern (P) appealed to the Court of Common Pleas, which dismissed the appeal. The Commonwealth Court affirmed applying the criteria set forth in *Sullivan v. Zoning Bd.*, 83 Pa. Commw. 228, 478 A.2d 912 (1984), comparing the impact of the provision on the property to the beneficial effects that would accrue to the community as a result of a discontinuance of the use. PA Northwestern (P) appealed.

ISSUE: Is a zoning ordinance which requires the amortization and discontinuance of a lawful preexisting non-conforming use confiscatory and violative of the state constitution as a taking of property without just compensation?

HOLDING AND DECISION: (Larsen, J.) Yes. A zoning ordinance which requires the amortization and discontinuance of a lawful preexisting nonconforming use is confiscatory and violative of the state constitution as a taking of property without just compensation. Contrary to the appellate court's interpretation, Sullivan is not a correct statement of Pennsylvania law regarding amortization provisions. The usual presumption of a zoning ordinance's validity must be tempered by the fact that zoning involves governmental restrictions on a property owner's constitutionally guaranteed right to use his property, except where the use violates a law or creates a nuisance. Municipalities lack the power to compel a change in the nature of an existing lawful use of property. A lawful nonconforming use establishes in the property owner a vested property right which cannot be abrogated or destroyed. A "taking" under the Pennsylvania Constitution is not limited to actual physical possession or seizure of property. If the effect of the zoning law is to deprive an owner of the lawful use of his property, it amounts to a taking for which he must be compensated. In this case, the amortization ordinance deprived PA Northwestern (P) of the lawful use of its property because it forced it to cease using its property as an adult book store within 90 days. Therefore, the amortization provision was unconstitutional on its face because it effected a taking of PA Northwestern's (P) property without just compensation. Reversed.

CONCURRENCE: (Nix, C.J.) Although the amortization provision in this case is unreasonable and must be struck down because it failed to provide adequate time for elimination of the nonconforming use, the per se prohibition against amortization provisions advanced by the majority is too restrictive. Amortization provisions that provide adequate notice to the property owner so that he is not deprived of the property or its use are an effective way to reconcile community interests with business needs.

ANALYSIS

Pennsylvania is part of a small minority of states that forbid amortization ordinances altogether. In most states, a requirement that a nonconforming use cease within a certain time period does not constitute a taking, so long as the time period is reasonable. If the time period gives the owner adequate time to make new plans, any loss he suffers may be offset by the monopoly position he occupies for as long as the nonconforming business remains in place.

Quicknotes

AMORTIZATION The satisfaction of a debt by the tendering of regular, equal payments over a period of time.

TAKING A governmental action that substantially deprives an owner of the use and enjoyment of his or her property, requiring compensation.

State ex rel. Stoyanoff v. Berkeley

Landowner (P) v. Architectural board (D)

Mo. Sup. Ct., 458 S.W.2d 305 (1970).

NATURE OF CASE: Appeal from finding of property deprivation without due process.

FACT SUMMARY: Stoyanoff (P) desired to build a house of unusual shape in a St. Louis, Missouri, suburb.

RULE OF LAW

The protection of property values is a legitimate objective of zoning ordinances.

FACTS: Stoyanoff (P) desired to build a home in the City of Ladue, which is one of the finer suburbs in the St. Louis area. The plans called for the home to be of pyramid shape, with a flat top, and with triangular-shaped windows or doors at one or more corners. A city ordinance established an architectural board to ensure that new residences "conform to certain minimum architectural standards of appearance and conformity with surrounding structures, and that unsightly, grotesque and unsuitable structures detrimental to the . . . welfare of surrounding property . . . be avoided." The homes surrounding Stoyanoff's (P) lot were virtually all two-story houses of conventional architectural design. After the architectural board (D) denied Stoyanoff's (P) application for a building permit, a trial court issued a peremptory writ of mandamus to compel the City of Ladue to issue Stoyanoff (P) a residential building permit.

ISSUE: Is the protection of property values a legitimate objective of zoning ordinances?

HOLDING AND DECISION: (Pritchard, Commr.) Yes. The stabilizing of property values and giving some assurance to the public that, if property is purchased in a residential district, its value will be preserved, is a legitimate objective for zoning ordinances. Property use that offends sensibilities and decreases property values affects not only the adjoining property owners in that vicinity, but the general public as well. When property values are destroyed or seriously impaired, the tax base of the community is affected, and the public suffers economically as a result. Here, the denial of a building permit for Stoyanoff's (P) highly modernistic residence in an area where traditional Colonial, French Provincial, and English Tudor styles of architecture are erected does not appear to be arbitrary and unreasonable when the basic purpose to be served is that of the general welfare of persons in the entire community. Reversed.

ANALYSIS

The court in this case rested its decision on the objective of protecting property values. This is because many early cases held that aesthetic concerns were insufficient to support restrictive zoning regulations. The modern trend, though, shows that many courts are inclined to accept the legitimacy of zoning based exclusively on aesthetic considerations.

Quicknotes

WRIT OF MANDAMUS A court order issued commanding a public or private entity, or an official thereof, to perform a duty required by law.

ZONING ORDINANCE A statute that divides land into defined areas and which regulates the form and use of buildings and structures within those areas.

Anderson v. City of Issaquah

Developer (P) v. Municipality (D)

Wash. Ct. App., 70 Wash. App. 64, 851 P.2d 744 (1993).

NATURE OF CASE: Appeal from denial of building permit.

FACT SUMMARY: The building code of the City of Issaquah, Washington (the City) (D) included criteria with respect to building design that were strictly subjective in nature.

RULE OF LAW

A building code cannot consist of design criteria that are strictly subjective in nature.

FACTS: The City (D) included, as part of its municipal building code, certain design criteria to be followed in new building developments. The code mandated, inter alia, that buildings be "harmonious" with surrounding architecture and that building proportions be "appropriate." Anderson (P), intending to develop certain commercial property, submitted his building design to the Development Commission. During several hearings, the members expressed dissatisfaction with the design, although the members themselves did not seem to agree on what could be done to make the design more acceptable. After several revisions, Anderson (P) submitted his final plans, which were not approved. He appealed to the city council, which also denied approval. He filed suit seeking an injunction mandating approval. The trial court dismissed the complaint, and Anderson (P) appealed.

ISSUE: Can a building code consist of design criteria that are strictly subjective in nature?

HOLDING AND DECISION: (Kennedy, J.) No. A building code cannot consist of design criteria that are strictly subjective in nature. A statute that either forbids or requires the doing of an act in terms so vague that persons of common intelligence must necessarily guess at its meaning and differ as to its application violates due process. It is inherent in due process that laws be crafted in such a fashion that a person can reasonably be able to understand them. Terms that are totally subjective cannot meet this standard. The ordinance at issue here is an example of this. It mandates that design be "harmonious" and "appropriate." Obviously, what might or might not meet these standards is strictly in the eye of the beholder. This is borne out by the fact that the individual Commission members seemed to have had differing ideas as to what Anderson (P) had to do to bring his design into compliance, which left him in a totally impossible situation. Since the ordinance was clearly unconstitutionally vague, the City (D) should have issued the building permit. So ordered.

ANALYSIS

Private developments, such as condominium complexes, often have similar design criteria and their own architectural committees. Courts, as a general rule, have been much more deferential to decisions of private developments. Of course, the state constitution applies to state actions only, so the Due Process Clause is generally inapplicable in such situations.

Quicknotes

BUILDING CODE Local ordinances that govern requirements for residential housing.

DUE PROCESS CLAUSE Clauses found in the Fifth and Fourteenth Amendments to the United States Constitution providing that no person shall be deprived of "life, liberty, or property, without due process of law."

INJUNCTION A court order requiring a person to do or prohibiting that person from doing a specific act.

STATE ACTION Actions brought pursuant to the Fourteenth Amendment claiming that the government violated the plaintiff's civil rights.

City of Ladue v. Gilleo

Municipality (D) v. Antiwar homeowner (P)

512 U.S. 43 (1994).

NATURE OF CASE: Review of order striking down municipal land-use regulation.

FACT SUMMARY: The City of Ladue (the City) (D) enacted a zoning ordinance that prohibited all signs on residential property, with the exception of "for sale"-type placards.

RULE OF LAW
A municipality may not enact a blanket prohibition against signs on residential property.

FACTS: The City (D) enacted an ordinance that prohibited all signs on residential property, with a few narrow exceptions, the main one being "for sale"-type signs of no greater than a specified size. Gilleo (P) had erected a sign protesting the Gulf War. When City (D) authorities cited her for violation of the ordinance, she filed an action in district court challenging the constitutionality of the ordinance. The district court held the ordinance unconstitutional, and the court of appeals affirmed. The Supreme Court granted review.

ISSUE: May a municipality enact a blanket prohibition against signs on residential property?

HOLDING AND DECISION: (Stevens, J.) No. A municipality may not enact a blanket prohibition against signs on residential property. Signs are clearly a form of expression protected by the First Amendment. However, they do implicate the rights of local government police power, as they take up space and may obstruct views. Therefore, local government does have some regulatory power over sign placement. Any regulation of this nature, however, will have to walk a fine line between legitimate health and safety concerns and freedom of expression. The regulation at issue here, however, clearly does not. The ordinance forecloses a venerable means of communication that is both unique and important. Residential signs often play an important role in political campaigns. They are also a low-cost means of expression, and may be the only practical mode of expression for persons of modest means. While municipalities can regulate the time, place, and manner of speech, they cannot cut off an entire mode without leaving reasonable alternative means. A blanket prohibition at issue here does not do so, and as such, runs afoul of the First Amendment. Affirmed.

ANALYSIS

This case is almost the mirror image of an earlier case, *Linmark Associates, Inc. v. City of Willingboro*, 431 U.S. 85 (1977). In that case, a city had forbade "for sale" signs on the theory that such signs lowered property values and encouraged "white flight." The Court there found the ordinance unconstitutional. Given this precedent, it would have been hard for the Court to have ruled otherwise in the present case, which involved a much more severe restriction on signs.

Quicknotes

BLANKET PROHIBITION A prohibition that is absolute.

FIRST AMENDMENT Prohibits Congress from enacting any law respecting an establishment of religion, prohibiting the free exercise of religion, abridging freedom of speech or the press, the right of peaceful assembly, and the right to petition for a redress of grievances.

ZONING ORDINANCE A statute that divides land into defined areas and which regulates the form and use of buildings and structures within those areas.

Guru Nanak Sikh Society of Yuba City v. County of Sutter

Non-profit (P) v. State county (D)

456 F.3d 978 (9th Cir. 2006).

NATURE OF CASE: Appeal from granting of summary judgment to the plaintiff.

FACT SUMMARY: Guru Nanak Sikh Society of Yuba City (Nanak) (P) applied twice in Sutter County for a permit to build a Sikh temple. The County (D) denied both applications.

RULE OF LAW

Under the Religious Land Use and Institutionalized Persons Act of 2000 (RLUIPA), no government shall apply a land-use regulation in a manner that imposes a substantial burden on a person or a religious assembly or institution.

FACTS: Nanak (P), a non-profit organization set up to teach the practices of the Sikh religion, first applied for a permit in Sutter County (D) in 2001. The Planning Commission denied the conditional use permit because of concerns over increased noise and traffic in the residential area. In 2002, Nanak (P) applied for a second permit in an area of the same county zoned for agricultural use. This site was much larger, and Nanak (P) also agreed to a 25-foot no-development buffer, to a requirement that all ceremonies be held indoors, and to landscaping requirements. After an initial approval, the County's (D) board of supervisors denied the application. One supervisor found the property was for agricultural uses only. Another supervisor suggested the temple was too far removed from the city and would not promote orderly growth. Another supervisor agreed, calling it "leapfrog development." Nanak (P) filed suit under RLUIPA, and the federal district court granted summary judgment to Nanak (P). The County (D) appealed.

ISSUE: Under RLUIPA, may a government apply a land-use regulation in a manner that imposes a substantial burden on a person or a religious assembly or institution?

HOLDING AND DECISION: (Bea, J.) No. Under RLUIPA, no government shall apply a land-use regulation in a manner that imposes a substantial burden on a person or a religious assembly or institution. RLUIPA is the most recent attempt by Congress to craft a constitutionally valid mechanism to protect rights of discrete religions. The statute applies if a government entity imposes a substantial burden on the free exercise of religion by making an individualized assessment of the proposed use of the property at issue. The requirement of an individualized assessment is significant. It distinguishes those permit or zoning procedures that are neutral laws of general applicability. If there is no individualized assessment present, a plaintiff may not avail itself of the statute's protections. The County (D) made an individualized assessment of Nanak's (P) second application. The County's (D) own zoning code requires a comprehensive review for conditional use permits, which should be reviewed "under the circumstances of the particular case." Turning to the substantial burden analysis, Nanak (P) bears the burden of proof. For a land-use regulation to constitute a substantial burden, it must be "oppressive to a significantly great extent." We agree with the lower court that the County (D) imposed a substantial burden upon Nanak (P). In this matter, the parcel in the agricultural zone left a great deal of space between the proposed temple and neighbors. Moreover, the County's (D) concern with leapfrog development could apply to all future permit requests by religious organizations. In addition, other churches already exist in the same area, including another Sikh temple one mile away in the same agricultural zone. The County's (D) permitting is simply not consistent. Lastly, Nanak (P) agreed to all of the county planning board's conditions, including the set back provisions. All of these facts support the lower court's conclusion that the County's (D) denial constituted a substantial burden upon Nanak's (P) free exercise of religion. Summary judgment affirmed.

ANALYSIS

Several circuit courts of appeals have agreed with the Ninth Circuit's definition of "substantial burden," that the regulation at issue must be "oppressive to a great extent." As the text notes, the Supreme Court has yet to consider RLUIPA's standard for determining whether a land-use regulation burdens the free exercise of religion.

Quicknotes

FREE EXERCISE CLAUSE The guarantee of the First Amendment to the United States Constitution prohibiting Congress from enacting laws regarding the establishment of religion or prohibiting the free exercise thereof.

SUMMARY JUDGMENT Judgment rendered by a court in response to a motion made by one of the parties, claiming that the lack of a question of material fact in respect to an issue warrants disposition of the issue without consideration by the jury.

Fisher v. Giuliani

City residents (P) v. New York City (D)

720 N.Y.S.2d 50 (N.Y. App. Div. 2001).

NATURE OF CASE: Appeal from trial court's decision in favor of plaintiffs.

FACT SUMMARY: In 1998, New York City (D) amended its zoning laws for the Theater District to allow transfer of development rights to any possible site within the district, not just nearby parcels. Residents of an adjoining district brought suit, alleging the City (D) was obligated to prepare an environmental impact statement before modifying the zoning laws.

RULE OF LAW

A court will not overturn an agency determination regarding the requirement of an environmental impact statement unless the decision was affected by an error of law or was arbitrary, capricious or constituted an abuse of discretion.

FACTS: New York City (D) amended its zoning laws for the Theater District, including Broadway, in 1998 to allow certain theaters to transfer development rights to any sites within the theater subdistrict. Previously, such transfers could only be made to nearby parcels, not to anywhere within the district. The transfer of the development rights included a 20 percent increase in the floor-to-area ratio (FAR) of the receiving site. In addition, the new amendments created a discretionary mechanism where a developer could obtain the same 20 percent increase of the FAR amount. Prior to submitting the amendments for public review, the city conducted an environmental assessment of the transfer of rights amendment required by the State Environmental Quality Review Act (SEQRA). This Environmental Assessment Statement would state whether or not the zoning amendment would have a significant effect on the environment. If the answer was in the affirmative, the local zoning agency would have to then prepare a separate Environmental Impact Statement. Accordingly, at the preliminary stage, the City (D) reviewed the development trends for a ten-year period into the future and concluded that zoning capacity would accommodate demand twice over. Also, the City (D) reviewed the amendment's effect on traffic, transit, and air quality and determined the amendment would not have a significant effect. The City (D) therefore decided, in a 75-page single-spaced report, that no additional Environmental Impact Statement was necessary. There was no separate environmental review conducted for the other zoning amendment regarding the discretionary review mechanism. The plaintiffs, a group of city residents in a nearby district, brought suit, alleging the City's (D) preparation of the preliminary Environmental Assessment Statement was deficient in several respects. The trial court agreed with the plaintiffs and invalidated the new zoning amendments due to the deficient Environmental Assessment Statement.

ISSUE: May a court overturn an agency determination regarding the requirement of an environmental impact statement if the decision was not affected by an error of law or was not arbitrary, capricious, or an abuse of discretion?

HOLDING AND DECISION: (Friedman, J.) No. A court may not overturn an agency determination regarding the requirement of an environmental impact statement unless the decision was affected by an error of law or was arbitrary, capricious, or constituted an abuse of discretion. It is not a court's role to weigh desirability of the proposed rules or competing considerations. Instead, in regards to environmental decisions of city or state agencies, courts should review whether the agency identifies the relevant areas of environmental concern and takes a "hard look" at them. The petitioners' claim that the City (D) did not thoroughly review the environmental impact is without merit. First, the City's (D) determination that market demand and consequent development will remain constant is rational and based upon reasonable forecasting methods of future development. Second, the City's (D) use of a ten-year future projection was "hardly an irrational examination" of the future development prospects. Therefore, the City (D) was correct that a further Environmental Impact Statement was not required. Separately, however, the amendment's discretionary mechanism for approval of FAR increases for individual theaters is invalid. The City (D) erroneously believed that because environmental impact reviews would occur when individual owners applied for the FAR permit, the City (D) did not need to conduct an environmental assessment prior to the adoption of that amendment. Under SEQRA, there must be an environmental assessment completed prior to adoption of the zoning amendments in all respects. Accordingly, that portion of the amendments is hereby severed and annulled. Reversed.

ANALYSIS

Fisher is an example of judicial deference to the expertise of a particular agency. In several different areas of the law, courts often decline to overturn agency decisions, particularly when the agency is interpreting its own governing regulations. Here, the facts supported the finding that the City (D) had addressed the relevant environmental concerns present in the case.

Continued on next page.

Quicknotes

ARBITRARY AND CAPRICIOUS STANDARD Standard imposed in reviewing the decision of an agency or court when the decision may have been made in disregard of the facts or law.

Village of Belle Terre v. Boraas

Municipality (D) v. Unrelated tenants (P)

416 U.S. 1 (1974).

NATURE OF CASE: Appeal from judgment invalidating zoning ordinance.

FACT SUMMARY: Belle Terre (D) passed an ordinance restricting land use to one-family dwellings.

RULE OF LAW

A city may pass an ordinance which prohibits unrelated individuals from living in one location.

FACTS: Belle Terre (D) is a village on Long Island's north shore of about 220 homes inhabited by 700 people. Its total land area is less than one square mile. It has restricted land use to one family dwellings excluding, lodging houses, boarding houses, fraternity houses, or multiple-dwelling houses. Boraas (P) and five other students at State University at Stony Brook, who were not related to each other by blood, adoption, or marriage, rented a home in Belle Terre (D) in December 1971. When Belle Terre (D) served the owners of the home with an "Order to Remedy Violations" of the ordinance, the owners plus three tenants brought an action under the Civil Rights Act for an injunction and a judgment declaring the ordinance unconstitutional. The court of appeals held that the law was unconstitutional, and Belle Terre (D) appealed.

ISSUE: May a city pass an ordinance which prohibits unrelated individuals from living in one location?

HOLDING AND DECISION: (Douglas, J.) Yes. The concept of the public welfare is broad and inclusive. The ordinance here does not burden any fundamental rights guaranteed by the Constitution, nor does it inflict procedural disparities on some but not on others. Rather, this ordinance is in the field of economic and social legislation and will be upheld if it bears a rational relationship to a permissible state objective. A quiet place where yards are wide, people few, and motor vehicles restricted are legitimate guidelines in a land-use project addressed to family needs. The police power is not confined to elimination of filth, stench, and unhealthy places. It is ample to lay out zones where family values, youth values, and the blessings of quiet seclusion and clean air make the area a sanctuary for people. Reversed.

DISSENT: (Marshall, J.) The ordinance in this case unnecessarily burdens the First Amendment freedom of association and the right to privacy. The First and Fourteenth Amendments protect the freedom to choose one's associates. Constitutional protection is extended, not only to modes of association that are political in the usual sense, but also to those that pertain to the social and economic benefit of the members. The choice of household companions involves deeply personal considerations as to the kind and quality of intimate relationships within the home. That decision surely falls within the ambit of the right to privacy protected by the Constitution.

ANALYSIS

The Supreme Court, in a later decision invalidating an ordinance which defined "family" to include no more than one set of grandchildren, limited the holding of this case. "The ordinance (in *Belle Terre*) affected only unrelated individuals . . . East Cleveland, in contrast, has chosen to regulate the occupancy of its housing by slicing deeply into the family itself . . . (The) freedom of personal choice in matters of marriage and family life is one of the liberties protected by the Due Process Clause of the Fourteenth Amendment . . . ." *Moore v. City of East Cleveland*, 431 U.S. 494 (1977).

Quicknotes

EUCLIDEAN ZONING A zoning scheme whereby zoning districts are established based on the uses permitted pursuant to local ordinance.

FIRST AMENDMENT Prohibits Congress from enacting any law respecting an establishment of religion, prohibiting the free exercise of religion, abridging freedom of speech or the press, the right of peaceful assembly, and the right to petition for a redress of grievances.

POLICE POWER The power of a state or local government to regulate private conduct for the health, safety, and welfare of the general public.

PUBLIC WELFARE The well-being of the general community.

ZONING ORDINANCE A statute that divides land into defined areas and which regulates the form and use of buildings and structures within those areas.

City of Edmonds v. Oxford House, Inc.

Municipality (P) v. Halfway house (D)

514 U.S. 725 (1995).

NATURE OF CASE: Review of order striking down municipal land-use regulation.

FACT SUMMARY: The City of Edmonds (the City) (P) contended that its limitation of residences to single-family use was exempt from the ambit of the Fair Housing Act.

RULE OF LAW

A family composition zoning rule is not exempt from Fair Housing Act scrutiny.

FACTS: The City (P) had enacted a zoning ordinance which, among other things, limited occupancy of certain areas of resident property to "single family" use. "Single family" was defined as a group of people related by blood, marriage, or adoption, or any group of five or fewer unrelated persons living in the same household. Oxford House, Inc. (D), instituted at a dwelling covered by the ordinance a halfway house for recovering alcoholics and drug addicts. The City (P) cited Oxford (D) for violating the regulation. It then sued in federal court, seeking a declaration that the Fair Housing Act did not constrain its family definition rule. Oxford (D) counterclaimed, contending that the City (P) had not made a reasonable accommodation for its group home as required by the Fair Housing Act. The district court ruled that the ordinance was a reasonable restriction on the maximum number of occupants, which was exempt from the Fair Housing Act per § 3607(b)(1) of the Act. The Ninth Circuit reversed, and held the ordinance to violate the Fair Housing Act. The Supreme Court granted review.

ISSUE: Is a family composition zoning rule exempt from the Fair Housing Act?

HOLDING AND DECISION: (Ginsburg, J.) No. A family composition zoning rule is not exempt from the Fair Housing Act. Section 3607(b)(1) of the Fair Housing Act exempts from its ambit laws or ordinances that limit the number of persons living in a household. This exemption was inserted into the Act as recognition that localities have an interest in preventing overcrowding. Here, the district court, apparently looking at the portion of the ordinance defining a "family" as, among other things, "five or fewer individuals," concluded that the ordinance fell within the exemption. This was an incorrect analysis. "Family" is also defined in the ordinance as persons related by blood, marriage, or adoption, without regard to number of persons. Consequently, the rule at issue here is not in any real sense a limitation on the number of persons living in a dwelling. The district court therefore erred in so holding. Affirmed.

ANALYSIS

The Court's decision here was a rather narrow one. It did not decide whether or not the City's (P) ordinance actually violated the Fair Housing Act; rather, it simply decided that § 3607's exemption did not apply. The present decision will most likely be of little import in future Fair Housing Act cases.

Quicknotes

FAIR HOUSING ACT 42 U.S.C. § 3601 Prohibits housing discrimination on the basis of familial status.

LAND-USE REGULATION Regulation governing the development and/or zoning of real estate.

SINGLE-FAMILY USE With respect to zoning refers to area restricted to single-family housing.

ZONING ORDINANCE A statute that divides land into defined areas and which regulates the form and use of buildings and structures within those areas.

Southern Burlington County NAACP v. Township of Mount Laurel

Civil rights organization (P) v. Municipality (D)

N.J. Sup. Ct., 67 N.J. 151, 336 A.2d 713, *appeal dismissed and cert. denied,* 423 U.S. 808 (1975).

NATURE OF CASE: Appeal from invalidation of zoning ordinance.

FACT SUMMARY: The trial court held that a bona fide attempt by a municipality to provide zoned land for low-cost housing fulfilled its constitutional obligations.

RULE OF LAW

Municipal land-use regulations must provide a realistic opportunity for low and moderate income housing.

FACTS: The NAACP (P) sued Mount Laurel (D), contending the municipality's zoning scheme violated the New Jersey constitution by failing to provide for low income housing outside of depressed areas. The New Jersey Supreme Court invalidated the ordinances and remanded for further proceedings. The trial court held that it was sufficient that Mount Laurel (D) had made a bona fide attempt to comply with the Supreme Court decision and upheld the new ordinance enacted in response. The NAACP (P) appealed, contending a mere attempt to provide such zoning did not discharge Mt. Laurel's (D) constitutional obligations.

ISSUE: Must municipal land-use regulations provide a realistic opportunity for low and moderate income housing?

HOLDING AND DECISION: (Hall, J.) Yes. Municipal land-use regulations must provide a realistic opportunity for low and moderate income housing. Such obligation extends beyond attempting to provide for such housing. The housing must be in direct proportion to the percentage of lower income residents in the city. To reach this goal, affirmative governmental action may be required. The elimination of some obstacles and the creation of a new zoning scheme may be frustrated by other restrictions which effectively deprive the poor of adequate housing. Therefore, the zoning scheme which merely manifested intent to abide by the original Supreme Court holding was insufficient to discharge Mount Laurel's (D) constitutional obligations. Reversed and judgment of the Law Division modified.

ANALYSIS

The rationale behind the *Mount Laurel* case is that the use of all land is controlled by the state. The state has constitutional obligations to all its residents whether rich or poor. Municipalities, as state subjects, must set aside a fair share of its land for lower income housing. They cannot allocate only dilapidated land for the poor and retain valuable land for the rich exclusively. While this rationale appears clear in theory, in execution it has proven very difficult. The main difficulty is in developing an equitable formula for determining "fair share." Until a definitive formula is developed, this will prevent widespread application of this rule.

Quicknotes

AFFIRMATIVE ACTION A form of benign discrimination designed to remedy existing discrimination by favoring one group over another.

LAND-USE REGULATION Regulation governing the development and/or zoning of real estate.

ZONING ORDINANCE A statute that divides land into defined areas and which regulates the form and use of buildings and structures within those areas.

CHAPTER 12

Eminent Domain and the Problem of Regulatory Takings

Quick Reference Rules of Law

PAGE

1. **The Public-Use Puzzle.** A city's proposed taking of private property for general economic development qualifies as a public use consistent with the Takings Clause of the Fifth Amendment to the U.S. Constitution. (Kelo v. City of New London) *134*

2. **Physical Occupations and Regulatory Takings—Two Categorical Rules.** Any permanent physical occupation of an owner's property which is governmentally authorized constitutes a taking of property for which just compensation must be paid. (Loretto v. Teleprompter Manhattan CATV Corp.) *136*

3. **Physical Occupations and Regulatory Takings.** A municipality may regulate business operations to prevent harm to the public. (Hadacheck v. Sebastian) *137*

4. **Rules Based on Measuring and Balancing.** Private property may be regulated pursuant to the police power of the state to protect public health, safety, or morals; but if such regulation goes so far as to destroy or appropriate a property right, it becomes a "taking" under the Fifth and Fourteenth Amendments, requiring just compensation therefor. (Pennsylvania Coal Co. v. Mahon) *138*

5. **Rules Based on Measuring and Balancing.** A city may place restrictions on the development of individual historic landmarks without effecting a taking requiring just compensation. (Penn Central Transportation Company v. City of New York) *139*

6. **A Third Categorical Rule.** The state must compensate a landowner when a regulatory action denies an owner economically viable use of his land, unless the prohibited use of the land constitutes a nuisance under state common law. (Lucas v. South Carolina Coastal Council) *140*

7. **A Third Categorical Rule.** A purchaser or successive title holder is not barred from bringing a takings claim by the mere fact that the title was acquired after the effective date of the state regulation. (Palazzolo v. Rhode Island) *142*

8. **A Third Categorical Rule.** A moratorium on development imposed during the process of devising a comprehensive land-use plan does not constitute a per se taking of property requiring compensation under the Takings Clause. (Tahoe-Sierra Preservation Council, Inc. v. Tahoe Regional Planning Agency) *143*

9. **The Problem of Exactions.** A state may not condition a property use permit on an act not addressing the problem caused by the permitted use. (Nollan v. California Coastal Commission) *145*

10. **The Problem of Exactions.** A city may condition a land-use permit upon dedication of the land to a public use if such dedication is roughly proportional to the impact upon the community caused by the proposed land use. (Dolan v. City of Tigard) *146*

Kelo v. City of New London

Landowners (P) v. Municipality (D)

545 U.S. 469 (2005).

NATURE OF CASE: Suit for orders enjoining a city from taking private properties to promote the city's planned economic revitalization.

FACT SUMMARY: A city adopted a development plan designed to revitalize the local economy. To implement its plan, the city sought to condemn 15 properties owned by nine private landowners who refused to sell their properties to the city.

RULE OF LAW

A city's proposed taking of private property for general economic development qualifies as a public use consistent with the Takings Clause of the Fifth Amendment to the U.S. Constitution.

FACTS: In 1990, a Connecticut state agency officially designated the City of New London ("the City" or "New London") (D) as a "distressed municipality." New London's (D) economy worsened in 1996 when the federal government closed a facility that employed 1,500 people. The City's (D) unemployment rate almost doubled that for the rest of the state, and its population had dwindled to its lowest level in almost 80 years. State and local officials therefore targeted the City (D) for economic revitalization. Eventually a development plan focused on a 90-acre area known as Fort Trumbull as the center of the City's (D) revitalization efforts. The drafters designed the development plan to coincide with the expected arrival of a major company, Pfizer Inc., and to rejuvenate the local economy with jobs, tax revenue, and a generalized momentum for future growth and recreational activities. Most landowners in the Fort Trumbull area agreed to sell their properties to the City (D). Nine owners, however, refused to sell their 15 properties, and the City (D) initiated condemnation proceedings for the 15 properties. The City (D) condemned the properties purely because they were within the area designated for development; the City (D) never alleged that the properties were in any degree of substandard condition. Susette Kelo (P) and the other eight resisting owners sued the City (D) in state court, where the trial judge permanently enjoined the City (D) from taking 11 of the contested properties but permitted the taking of the other four properties. Both sides appealed to the Connecticut Supreme Court, which held that all 15 properties could properly be taken by New London (D). Applying state statute, that court held that the proposed taking was for a public use that satisfied both state and federal constitutional requirements. Kelo (P) and her fellow landowners petitioned the U.S. Supreme Court for further review.

ISSUE: Does a city's proposed taking of private property for general economic development qualify as a public use consistent with the Takings Clause of the Fifth Amendment to the U.S. Constitution?

HOLDING AND DECISION: (Stevens, J.) Yes. A city's proposed taking of private property for general economic development qualifies as a public use consistent with the Takings Clause of the Fifth Amendment to the U.S. Constitution. A government may not take private property merely to transfer it to another private owner; conversely, private property may be taken if the taking is legitimately for "use by the public." Neither of these general propositions controls this case, though, because the question here narrows to whether a proposed taking for general economic development serves a "public purpose," which is the broader reading of "public use" that this Court has consistently used for more than a century. The Court upheld the redevelopment plan at issue in *Berman v. Parker*, 348 U.S. 26 (1954), because creating a "better balanced, more attractive community" was a valid public purpose. Similarly, in *Hawaii Housing Authority v. Midkiff*, 467 U.S. 229 (1984), the Court upheld a state statute that took fee title from lessors and vested title in lessees to eliminate the "social and economic evils of land oligopoly." These cases show that the determinative question is the proposed taking's purpose, not the specific means by which the government proposes to achieve its purpose. Under this appropriately deferential standard of review, New London's (D) proposed takings here do meet the public-use requirement imposed by the Takings Clause. Kelo's (P) request that the Court reject economic development as an acceptable public use contradicts not only precedent but also logic because no principled distinction exists between economic development and other accepted public uses. Further, her objection that economic development confuses the distinction between public and private use also contradicts precedent; public use often benefits specific private owners, too. Finally, Kelo's (P) objection that nothing would stop a city from transferring land from one private owner to another specific private owner for a public purpose presents issues that are not before the Court in this case. Accordingly, this Court's takings jurisprudence provides no basis for enjoining the City of New London (D) from taking the 15 properties in the Fort Trumbull area. Affirmed.

CONCURRENCE: (Kennedy, J.) Deferential review should not become so deferential that it ignores a taking

Continued on next page.

designed primarily to favor another private party. Furthermore, a more stringent standard of review might apply in cases where economic development is the asserted public use.

DISSENT: (O'Connor, J.) Past cases have recognized three kinds of takings that meet the public-use requirement: transferring private property to public ownership, to private ownership for common public use, and to private ownership within a program serving a public purpose. The third category, represented by *Midkiff* and *Berman,* raises the most questions. The takings in those two cases addressed identifiable public harms (oligopoly and blight, respectively), but this case goes beyond curing a public harm—and it goes too far.

ANALYSIS

Despite the firestorm of criticism that greeted the *Kelo* decision, the majority opinion fits only the most naive definitions of judicial activism. Indeed, at least in the casebook excerpts, it is Justice O'Connor's reasoning in dissent that seems the more ill-considered: If New London's (D) chronic and deepening economic demise does not qualify as a public harm, what does?

Quicknotes

EMINENT DOMAIN The governmental power to take private property for public use so long as just compensation is paid therefore.

FIFTH AMENDMENT Provides that no person shall be compelled to serve as a witness against himself, or be subject to trial for the same offense twice, or be deprived of life, liberty, or property without due process of law.

PUBLIC USE Basis for governmental taking of property pursuant to its power of eminent domain so that property taken may be utilized for the benefit of the public at large.

TAKING A governmental action that substantially deprives an owner of the use and enjoyment of his property, requiring compensation.

TAKINGS CLAUSE Provision of the Fifth Amendment to the United States Constitution prohibiting the government from taking private property for public use without providing just compensation therefor.

Loretto v. Teleprompter Manhattan CATV Corp.

Fee owners (P) v. State (D)

458 U.S. 419 (1982).

NATURE OF CASE: Appeal from enforcement of state statute.

FACT SUMMARY: Loretto (P) contended that a New York law requiring apartment house owners to allow for the installation of cable television equipment allowed a taking of property without just compensation.

RULE OF LAW

Any permanent physical occupation of an owner's property which is governmentally authorized constitutes a taking of property for which just compensation must be paid.

FACTS: New York enacted a statute which required apartment house owners to provide tenants with access to cable television reception. Loretto (P) brought a class action against Teleprompter Manhattan CATV Corp. (Teleprompter) (D), contending its placement of its cable television installation equipment constituted trespass and that the statute allowed for a taking of her property without just compensation. The trial court granted summary judgment for Teleprompter (D), upholding the constitutionality of the statute. The appellate court affirmed, and Loretto (P) appealed to the U.S. Supreme Court.

ISSUE: Is any permanent physical occupation of an owner's property which is authorized by the government a taking of property which requires the payment of just compensation?

HOLDING AND DECISION: (Marshall, J.) Yes. Any permanent physical occupation of an owner's property which is authorized by the government constitutes a taking of property which requires a payment of just compensation. Any occupation, no matter how slight, impacts on the owner's right to exclusive possession of his property. In this case, the equipment occupied a very small area of the property. Yet its presence constituted a physical occupation and thus necessarily must be classified as a taking of property within the meaning of the Fifth Amendment. Therefore, just compensation must be paid. Reversed and remanded.

DISSENT: (Blackmun, J.) The Court goes against established precedent by recognizing a per se "taking" rule. It has previously been held on many occasions that each taking case must be considered on its peculiar facts. A rigid per se rule finding a taking in every physical encroachment will require compensation in situations not justified under previous interpretations of the taking clause.

ANALYSIS

The Court recognizes the fundamental inconsistency with the elements of private ownership presented by any physical invasion of the property by a stranger. When such an invasion is authorized by the government, a compensable taking occurs. The amount of money necessary to constitute just compensation will vary with the case. The Court declined to rule on whether the $1 per unit payment was sufficient in this case.

Quicknotes

CLASS ACTION A suit commenced by a representative on behalf of an ascertainable group that is too large to appear in court, who shares a commonality of interests and who will benefit from a successful result.

JUST COMPENSATION The right guaranteed by the Fifth Amendment to the United States Constitution of a person, when his property is taken for public use by the state, to receive adequate compensation in order to restore him to the position he enjoyed prior to the appropriation.

SUMMARY JUDGMENT Judgment rendered by a court in response to a motion by one of the parties, claiming that the lack of a question of material fact in respect to an issue warrants disposition of the issue without consideration by the jury.

TAKING A governmental action that substantially deprives an owner of the use and enjoyment of his or her property, requiring compensation.

TRESPASS Unlawful interference with, or damage to, the real or personal property of another.

Hadacheck v. Sebastian

Brick yard owner (P) v. Chief of police (D)

239 U.S. 394 (1915).

NATURE OF CASE: Appeal from decision upholding the validity of condemnation proceedings.

FACT SUMMARY: Hadacheck (P) was convicted of violating a municipal ordinance prohibiting the operation of a brick yard or brick kiln.

RULE OF LAW

A municipality may regulate business operations to prevent harm to the public.

FACTS: Hadacheck (P) was convicted of a misdemeanor for the violation of a Los Angeles city ordinance making it unlawful for any person to establish or operate a brick yard or brick kiln within the city limits. Hadacheck (P), whose business was established before the ordinance was enacted, asserted that his business was not a nuisance as defined under state statutes. The enforcement of the ordinance, according to Hadacheck (P), amounted to a taking of property without compensation, violating guarantees of due process. The California Supreme Court upheld the ordinance as a valid, nondiscriminatory regulatory measure.

ISSUE: May a municipality regulate business operations in order to prevent harm to the public?

HOLDING AND DECISION: (McKenna, J.) Yes. The imperative necessity of the police power precludes any limitation on its use when it is not exerted arbitrarily. There must be progress, and if in its march private interests are in the way they must yield to the good of the community. Even granting that Hadacheck's (P) business was not a nuisance per se, the municipality found that fumes and dust from Hadacheck's (P) brick-making plant had occasionally caused sickness and serious discomfort to those living in the vicinity. It may be that brick yards in other localities within the city where the same conditions exist are not regulated or prohibited, but it does not follow that they will not be. That Hadacheck's (P) business was first in time to be prohibited does not make its prohibition unlawful. Affirmed.

ANALYSIS

The doctrines of eminent domain and police power are distinct and separate powers of the government. In eminent domain proceedings, land is taken by the state because it will thereby be of more use to the public. Under the police power, private property rights are impaired by the state not because they have become necessary or useful to the public, but because their free exercise is believed to be harmful to important public interests.

Quicknotes

CONDEMNATION The taking of private property for public use so long as just compensation is paid therefor.

DUE PROCESS CLAUSE Clauses found in the Fifth and Fourteenth Amendments to the United States Constitution providing that no person shall be deprived of "life, liberty, or property, without due process of law."

EMINENT DOMAIN The governmental power to take private property for public use so long as just compensation is paid therefor.

JUST COMPENSATION The right guaranteed by the Fifth Amendment to the United States Constitution of a person, when his property is taken for public use by the state, to receive adequate compensation in order to restore him to the position he enjoyed prior to the appropriation.

NUISANCE PER SE An action, occupation or building that is a nuisance at any time and under any condition.

POLICE POWER The power of a government to impose restrictions on the rights of private persons, as long as those restrictions are reasonably related to the promotion and protection of public health, safety, morals, and the general welfare.

PUBLIC INTEREST Something in which the public has either a monetary or legal interest.

TAKING A governmental action that substantially deprives an owner of the use and enjoyment of his or her property, requiring compensation.

Pennsylvania Coal Co. v. Mahon

Surface rights owner (P) v. Coal company (D)

260 U.S. 393 (1922).

NATURE OF CASE: Appeal from the granting of an injunction.

FACT SUMMARY: Mahon (P) desired to prevent the exercise of the mineral rights which the Pennsylvania Coal Co. (Coal Co.) (D) reserved in a deed transferring certain surface property to Mahon (P).

RULE OF LAW

Private property may be regulated pursuant to the police power of the state to protect public health, safety, or morals; but if such regulation goes so far as to destroy or appropriate a property right, it becomes a "taking" under the Fifth and Fourteenth Amendments, requiring just compensation therefor.

FACTS: In 1878, Coal Co. (D) transfered certain real property to Mahon (P) by a deed in which Coal Co. (D) reserved the mineral rights on the property and Mahon (P) waived all rights to object to or receive damages for the removal of such minerals. In 1921, the Pennsylvania legislature enacted the "Kohler Act," which forbade the mining of coal in such a way as to cause the subsidence of any human habitation. When Coal Co. (D) decided to exercise its mineral rights pursuant to the deed, Mahon (P) instituted an action for an injunction on the grounds that the mining would violate the Kohler Act by causing the subsidence of his home. From a decree granting the injunction, Coal Co. (D) appealed, contending that such an application of the statute would constitute a taking without compensation contrary to due process.

ISSUE: Will an exercise of the police power be upheld if it, in effect, provides for the destruction or appropriation of a private property right?

HOLDING AND DECISION: (Holmes, J.) No. Private property may be regulated pursuant to the police power of the state to protect public health, safety, or morals; but if such regulation goes so far as to destroy or appropriate a property right, it becomes a "taking" under the Fifth and Fourteenth Amendments, requiring just compensation therefor. It is well established, of course, that some property rights must yield to the public interest and the police power. Here, however, the limited public interest in protecting Mahon's (P) surface rights does not justify the total destruction of the mineral rights which Coal Co. (D) reserved in its deed to Mahon (P). As such, the Kohler Act is unconstitutional insofar as it fails to provide for compensation for the taking of Coal Co.'s (D) property rights. The decree which was based upon it is accordingly reversed.

DISSENT: (Brandeis, J.) No taking occurred here. Rather, the state merely exercised the police power to prevent a noxious use of property. The property remains in the possession of the owners.

ANALYSIS

This case illustrates the minority rule. Generally, when a landowner conveys to someone else a right to take minerals underneath the surface of his land, the grantee owes the grantor-landowner the duty to support the surface in its natural state (i.e., without any buildings). Furthermore, generally, ownership of land carries with it the right to have the land supported in its natural state by adjoining land (i.e., the right to have the support of the land undisturbed by excavation on adjoining land). Under this general rule, if an adjoining landowner excavates in such a manner as to cause subsidence on one's own land, he is "absolutely liable" for such subsidence. If, however, there is a structure on the land which subsides "and the land would not have subsided but for such structure," the adjoining landowner is not liable as a matter of law (i.e., he is not "absolutely liable"), but he may be liable for negligent excavation.

Quicknotes

FIFTH AMENDMENT Provides that no person shall be compelled to serve as a witness against himself, or be subject to trial for the same offense twice, or be deprived of life, liberty, or property without due process of law.

FOURTEENTH AMENDMENT 42 U.S.C. § 1983 Defamation by state officials in connection with a discharge implies a violation of a liberty interest protected by the due process requirements of the U.S. Constitution.

INJUNCTION A court order requiring a person to do or prohibiting that person from doing a specific act.

KOHLER ACT Legislation passed in 1921 that prohibited the mining of coal that would cause the caving in, collapse, or subsidence of a number of specific structures or public facilities.

POLICE POWER The power of a government to impose restrictions on the rights of private persons, as long as those restrictions are reasonably related to the promotion and protection of public health, safety, morals, and the general welfare.

Penn Central Transportation Company v. City of New York

Railroad (P) v. City (D)

438 U.S. 104 (1978).

NATURE OF CASE: Appeal from denial of compensatory relief.

FACT SUMMARY: Penn Central Transportation Company (Penn Central) (P) contended that New York (D) had taken its property without just compensation when it declared its station a historical landmark.

RULE OF LAW

A city may place restrictions on the development of individual historic landmarks without effecting a taking requiring just compensation.

FACTS: In 1965, New York City (D) adopted the Landmarks Preservation Law, which was enacted to identify and preserve historic and scenic landmarks. Under the law, the Landmarks Preservation Commission would identify properties and areas to be designated as landmarks. The owner of the property in question had the right to appeal the decision at several levels, including judicial review. The law also allowed such property owners to transfer development rights to other parcels of land. On January 22, 1968, Penn Central (P) entered into a contract with UGP Properties, Inc. to construct a multistory office building above the Grand Central Terminal, which had previously been designated a landmark. After the Commission rejected its application, Penn Central (P) filed suit, alleging that the application of the law had taken its property without just compensation in violation of the Fifth and Fourteenth Amendments. The New York Court of Appeals found no denial of due process, and Penn Central (P) appealed.

ISSUE: May a city place restrictions on the development of individual historic landmarks without effecting a taking requiring just compensation?

HOLDING AND DECISION: (Brennan, J.) Yes. In deciding whether a particular governmental action has effected a taking, the focus is both on the character of the action and on the nature and extent of the interference with rights in the parcel as a whole. It is true that the Landmarks Law has a more severe impact on some landowners than on others, but that in itself does not mean that the law effects a taking. Legislation designed to promote the general welfare commonly burdens some more than others. The Landmarks Law's effect is simply to prohibit Penn Central (P) or anyone else from occupying portions of the air space above the Terminal, while permitting Penn Central (P) to use the remainder of the parcel in a gainful fashion. The New York City (D) law is not rendered invalid by its failure to provide just compensation whenever a landmark owner is restricted in the exploitation of property interests, such as air rights, to a greater extent than provided for under applicable zoning laws. The restrictions imposed are substantially related to the promotion of the general welfare and not only permit reasonable beneficial use of the landmark site but also affords Penn Central (P) opportunities further to enhance not only the Terminal site, but also other properties. Affirmed.

DISSENT: (Rehnquist, J.) The City of New York (D) has imposed a substantial cost on less than one one-tenth of one percent of the buildings in New York City for the general benefit of all its people. It is exactly this imposition of general costs on a few individuals at which the taking protection is directed.

ANALYSIS

One commentary on this case, states: "The majority implied that esthetics is no less a compelling governmental interest than public health and that the relative sizes of the groups benefited and burdened are, at best, of minor importance. With the tests upon which many courts have come to rely no longer controlling, the protection of private property from governmental interference will depend more than ever on each court's subjective interpretation of 'fairness and justice.' " "The Supreme Court, 1977 Term," 92 *Harv. L. Rev.* 57, 228-232 (1978).

Quicknotes

DUE PROCESS The constitutional mandate requiring the courts to protect and enforce individuals' rights and liberties consistent with prevailing principles of fairness and justice and prohibiting the federal and state governments from such activities that deprive its citizens of life, liberty, or property interest.

TAKINGS CLAUSE Provision of the Fifth Amendment to the United States Constitution prohibiting the government from taking private property for public use without providing just compensation therefor.

Lucas v. South Carolina Coastal Council

Beachfront property owner (P) v. State (D)

505 U.S. 1003 (1992).

NATURE OF CASE: Appeal from reversal of award of damages in action for compensation under the Takings Clause.

FACT SUMMARY: After Lucas (P) invested $975,000 in two beachfront lots, South Carolina (D) enacted a statute prohibiting construction on the barrier islands where the lots were located, entitling him, he contended, to compensation under the Takings Clause.

RULE OF LAW

The state must compensate a landowner when a regulatory action denies an owner economically viable use of his land, unless the prohibited use of the land constitutes a nuisance under state common law.

FACTS: Lucas (P) purchased two residential lots for $975,000 on the Isle of Palms, a barrier island off the coast of South Carolina, on which he planned to build single-family homes. The Isle of Palms development, of which Lucas (P) was a co-owner, was located on highly unstable ground, prone to flooding and erosion. At the time of purchase, the state, county and town had not imposed any restrictions on residential use of the property. However, two years after Lucas's (P) purchase, but before he began construction, South Carolina (D) enacted the Beachfront Management Act, in an attempt to counteract the critical erosion of South Carolina beaches. The Act prohibited, without exception, the construction of any habitable improvements seaward of a baseline connecting historical points of erosion on the Isle of Palms. Lucas's (P) lots were located within the restricted area. He filed suit against South Carolina (D), contending that the Act's ban on construction amounted to a taking of his property without just compensation. He conceded that the Act was a lawful exercise of South Carolina's (D) police power but claimed that the Act rendered his property valueless, entitling him to compensation. The trial court agreed and ordered South Carolina (D) to pay $1,232,387. The Supreme Court of South Carolina reversed, ruling that when an otherwise valid regulation respecting the use of property is designed to prevent public harm, as this Act was, no compensation was owed. Lucas (P) appealed, and the Supreme Court granted certiorari.

ISSUE: Must the state compensate a landowner when a regulatory action denies an owner economically viable use of his land?

HOLDING AND DECISION: (Scalia, J.) Yes. The state must compensate a landowner when a regulatory action denies an owner economically valuable use of his land, unless the prohibited use of the land constitutes a nuisance under state common law. Traditionally, compensation has been required for two separate categories of regulatory actions: (1) those that cause a physical invasion of private property and (2) those that deprive a landowner of all economically beneficial or productive use of land. However, there is also a long line of cases denying compensation to owners whose property is regulated to prevent a public harm, the seminal case being *Mugler v. Kansas*, 123 U.S. 623 (1887), in which a law prohibiting the manufacture of alcoholic beverages was sustained against a taking claim brought by a brewery owner. Under this line of cases, regulation of "harmful or noxious uses" of property was allowed to affect property values without obligating the government to pay compensation. This early focus on noxious uses later evolved into the Court's contemporary analysis that finds no taking if a land-use regulation substantially advances a legitimate state interest. Whether the regulation prevents a harmful use can no longer be the basis for an exception from the rule that total regulatory taking must be compensated; if it were, no compensation would ever be necessary, since most regulations may be described as mitigating some harm, depending on the observer's point of view. Instead, a better test is that confiscatory regulations, i.e., those that prohibit all economically beneficial use of land, may not be enacted without compensation, unless the regulation serves to prohibit a purpose that was already unlawful under existing nuisance and property law. In this case, the Act rendered Lucas's (P) lots valueless by requiring that they remain in their natural state. Therefore, South Carolina (D) must either identify the relevant common law principles of nuisance and property that would prohibit construction on Lucas's (P) beachfront property or compensate him for the value of his property. Reversed and remanded.

DISSENT: (Blackmun, J.) This Court has consistently upheld regulations that prohibit an owner from using his property in a way that is harmful to the public. Lucas (P) never challenged the legislature's findings that a building ban was necessary to protect property and life and, therefore, the lower court correctly found no taking. Now, with this case, the majority has created a new rule and an exception, based on the trial court's finding that the property had lost all economic value. Furthermore, the majority alters the traditional rule that the plaintiff challenge the constitutionality of an ordinance, by requiring the state to convince the courts that its legislative judgments are correct. Finally, the majority decides that it will permit a state

Continued on next page.

to regulate all economic value only if the state prohibits uses that would not be permitted under state common law, notwithstanding that the Court has previously and explicitly rejected any consideration of a nuisance when evaluating a taking. There is no reason to believe the majority's claim that new interpretation of old common law nuisance doctrine will be any more objective or value-free than reliance on legislative judgments of what constitutes harm.

DISSENT: (Stevens, J.) The majority's categorical rule that total regulatory takings must be compensated is an unsound and unwise addition to the law, unsupported by prior decisions, and its exception to that rule is too rigid and too narrow. Because the majority's new rule only applies to total regulatory takings, it arbitrarily awards compensation to a landowner whose property is diminished by 100 percent, while denying compensation to one who suffers a 95 percent diminishment. Furthermore, the Court's holding effectively freezes a state's traditional common law, making it immune to legislative revision.

ANALYSIS

Note that the central debate in *Lucas* is, actually over, who should have the authority to allocate loss. *Lucas* allocates the authority to decide which regulations will require compensation to the state judiciary, rather than to the state legislature. *Lucas* implies that the state's ability to completely extinguish the value of a parcel of land gives it too much power and potential for excessive legislative regulation, necessitating an independent judicial determination of what constitutes a nuisance. Although *Lucas* was the most closely watched land-use case of 1991 (over 50 amicus briefs were filed), its impact may turn out to be relatively slight since its fact pattern is relatively rare.

Quicknotes

CERTIORARI A discretionary writ issued by a superior court to an inferior court in order to review the lower court's decisions; the Supreme Court's writ ordering such review.

JUST COMPENSATION The right guaranteed by the Fifth Amendment to the United States Constitution of a person, when his property is taken for public use by the state, to receive adequate compensation in order to restore him to the position he enjoyed prior to the appropriation.

NUISANCE An unlawful use of property that interferes with the lawful use of another's property.

REGULATORY TAKING A governmental action that substantially deprives an owner of the use and enjoyment of his property, whereby the application of a law or regulation deprives the owner of economically viable use of his property, requiring compensation.

TAKINGS CLAUSE Provision of the Fifth Amendment to the United States Constitution prohibiting the government from taking private property for public use without providing just compensation therefor.

Palazzolo v. Rhode Island

Developer (P) v. State (D)

533 U.S. 606 (2001).

NATURE OF CASE: Inverse condemnation action.

FACT SUMMARY: Palazzolo (P) brought an inverse condemnation suit against Rhode Island (D) after his development proposals for a parcel of waterfront property were rejected.

RULE OF LAW

A purchaser or successive title holder is not barred from bringing a takings claim by the mere fact that the title was acquired after the effective date of the state regulation.

FACTS: Palazzolo (P) owned a waterfront parcel of land, almost all of which was designated as coastal wetlands. After his development proposals were rejected he filed suit in state court claiming the State's (D) application of its wetlands regulations constituted a taking in violation of the Fifth Amendment. The state supreme court rejected the claim that Palazzolo (P) was denied all economically beneficial use of the property since the regulation predated his ownership of the property. Palazzolo (P) appealed.

ISSUE: Is a purchaser or successive title holder barred from bringing a takings claim by the mere fact that the title was acquired after the effective date of the state regulation?

HOLDING AND DECISION: (Kennedy, J.) No. A purchaser or successive title holder is not barred from bringing a takings claim by the mere fact that the title was acquired after the effective date of the state regulation. We agree with the court's decision that all economically viable use of the property was not deprived since the uplands portion of the property could still be developed. Reversed in part, affirmed in part, and remanded.

ANALYSIS

The Court here did away with the prior rule under *Lucas* and *Penn Central* that a purchaser or successive title holder was deemed to have notice of an earlier-enacted restriction and was barred from bringing a takings claim. The Court also held that a state does not avoid the duty to compensate based on a "token interest." So long as a landowner is permitted to build a substantial residence on the parcel, then it is not deemed to constitute a deprivation of all economic value.

Quicknotes

FIFTH AMENDMENT Provides that no person shall be compelled to serve as a witness against himself, or be subject to trial for the same offense twice, or be deprived of life, liberty, or property without due process of law.

INVERSE CONDEMNATION the taking of private property for public use so as to impair or decrease the value of property near or adjacent to, but not a part of, the property taken.

NOTICE Communication of information to a person by an authorized person or an otherwise proper source.

TAKING A governmental action that substantially deprives an owner of the use and enjoyment of his or her property, requiring compensation.

Tahoe-Sierra Preservation Council, Inc. v. Tahoe Regional Planning Agency

Landowners (P) v. Regional planning agency (D)

535 U.S. 302 (2002).

NATURE OF CASE: Appeal from reversal of judgment finding a per se taking of property.

FACT SUMMARY: Tahoe Regional Planning Agency (TRPA) (D) imposed two moratoria, totaling 32 months, on development in the Lake Tahoe Basin while formulating a comprehensive land-use plan for the area. Landowners (P) affected by the moratoria filed suit, claiming that TRPA's (D) actions constituted a taking of their property without just compensation in violation of the Takings Clause.

RULE OF LAW

A moratorium on development imposed during the process of devising a comprehensive land-use plan does not constitute a per se taking of property requiring compensation under the Takings Clause.

FACTS: TRPA (D) imposed two moratoria, one, from 1981 to 1983, and a more restrictive one, from 1983 to 1984, totaling 32 months, on development in the Lake Tahoe region while formulating a comprehensive land-use plan of environmentally sound growth for the area. During the moratoria, virtually all development was prohibited. Landowners (P) affected by the moratoria filed suit, claiming that TRPA's (D) actions constituted a taking of their property without just compensation in violation of the Takings Clause. The district court found a taking, but the court of appeals reversed. The U.S. Supreme Court granted review.

ISSUE: Does a moratorium on development imposed during the process of devising a comprehensive land-use plan constitute a per se taking of property requiring compensation under the Takings Clause?

HOLDING AND DECISION: (Stevens, J.) No. A moratorium on development imposed during the process of devising a comprehensive land-use plan does not constitute a per se taking of property requiring compensation under the Takings Clause. The attack on the moratoria is only facial. The landowners contend that the mere enactment of a temporary regulation that, while in effect, denies a property owner of all viable economic use of the property gives rise to an unqualified constitutional obligation to compensate for the value of the property's use during that period. The landowners want a categorical rule, but the Court's cases do not support such a rule. The answer to any given case depends on the particular circumstances of the case, and the circumstances in this case are best analyzed within the framework of *Penn Central Transp. Co. v. New York*, 438 U.S. 104 (1978). The long-standing distinction between physical and regulatory takings makes it inappropriate to treat precedent from one as controlling on the other. The landowners (P) in this case rely on *First English Evangelical Lutheran Church of Glendale v. County of Los Angeles*, 482 U.S. 304 (1987) and *Lucas v. South Carolina Coastal Council*, 505 U.S. 1003 (1992)—both regulatory takings cases—to argue for a categorical rule that whenever the government imposes a deprivation of all economically viable use of property, no matter how brief, it effects a taking. In *First English*, the Court addressed the separate remedial question of how compensation is measured once a regulatory taking is established, but not the different and prior question whether the temporary regulation was in fact a taking. Nor is *Lucas* dispositive of the question presented. Its categorical rule—requiring compensation when a regulation permanently deprives an owner of "all economically beneficial uses" of his land—does not answer the question whether a regulation prohibiting any economic use of land for 32 months must be compensated. The landowners (P) attempt to bring this case under the rule in *Lucas* by focusing exclusively on the property during the moratoria is unavailing. This Court has consistently rejected such an approach to the "denominator" question. To sever a 32-month segment from the remainder of each fee simple estate and then ask whether that segment has been taken in its entirety would ignore *Penn Central's* admonition to focus on "the parcel as a whole." Both dimensions of a real property interest—the metes and bounds describing its geographic dimensions and the term of years describing its temporal aspect—must be considered when viewing the interest in its entirety. A permanent deprivation of all use is a taking of the parcel as a whole, but a temporary restriction causing a diminution in value is not, for the property will recover value when the prohibition is lifted. *Lucas* was carved out for the "extraordinary case" in which a regulation permanently deprives property of all use; the default rule remains that a fact specific inquiry is required in the regulatory taking context. Nevertheless, the Court will consider the landowners' (P) argument that the interest in protecting property owners from bearing public burdens "which, in all fairness and justice, should be borne by the public as a whole," justifies creating a new categorical rule. "Fairness and justice" will not be better served by a categorical rule that any deprivation of all economic use, no matter how brief, constitutes a compensable taking. That rule would apply to numerous

Continued on next page.

normal delays—in obtaining building permits, variances, zoning changes, etc.—and would require changes in practices that have long been considered permissible exercises of the police power. Such an important change in the law should be the product of legislative rulemaking, not adjudication. More importantly, the better approach to a temporary regulatory taking claim requires careful examination and weighing of all the relevant circumstances—only one of which is the length of the delay. A narrower rule excluding normal delays in processing permits, or covering only delays of more than a year, would have a less severe impact on prevailing practices, but would still impose serious constraints on the planning process. Moratoria are an essential tool of successful development. The interest in informed decision-making counsels against adopting a per se rule that would treat such interim measures as takings—regardless of the planners' good faith, the landowners' reasonable expectations, or the moratorium's actual impact on property values. The financial constraints of compensating property owners during a moratorium may force officials to rush through the planning process or abandon the practice altogether. And the interest in protecting the decisional process is even stronger when an agency is developing a regional plan than when it is considering a permit for a single parcel. Here, TRPA obtained the benefit of comments and criticisms from interested parties during its deliberations, but a categorical rule tied to the deliberations' length would likely create added pressure on decision makers to quickly resolve land-use questions, disadvantaging landowners and interest groups less organized or familiar with the planning process. Moreover, with a temporary development ban, there is less risk that individual landowners will be singled out to bear a special burden that should be shared by the public as a whole. It may be true that a moratorium lasting more than one year should be viewed with special skepticism, but the district court found that the instant delay was not unreasonable. The restriction's duration is one factor for a court to consider in appraising regulatory takings claims, but with respect to that factor, the temptation to adopt per se rules in either direction must be resisted. Affirmed.

ANALYSIS

With this case, the majority of the Court seems to have adopted the approach recommended by Justice O'Connor's concurring opinion in *Palazzolo v. Rhode Island,* 533 U.S. 606 (2001)—namely, an ad hoc approach that evaluates the circumstances of each case using the *Penn Central* framework—and rejected a categorical rule for all regulatory takings cases. The majority also seemed to resolve the "denominator" issue that had hitherto been unsettled in takings jurisprudence.

Quicknotes

CONDEMNATION The taking of private property for public use so long as just compensation is paid therefor.

LAND-USE PLAN General plan for real estate, including local zoning ordinances or real estate development scheme.

MORATORIUM Suspension of legal remedies or proceedings.

REGULATARY TAKING A governmental action that substantially deprives an owner of the use and enjoyment of his property; where the application of a law or regulation deprives the owner of economically viable use of his property, requiring compensation.

Nollan v. California Coastal Commission

Beachfront property owner (P) v. State (D)

483 U.S. 825 (1987).

NATURE OF CASE: Review of court order upholding conditional land-use permit.

FACT SUMMARY: The California Coastal Commission (D) conditioned a building permit on the owners' granting of a public beach access easement.

RULE OF LAW

A state may not condition a property use permit on an act not addressing the problem caused by the permitted use.

FACTS: The Nollans (P) owned certain beachfront property. They applied for a permit to build a residence upon it. The California Coastal Commission (D), finding that such a use would impede public viewing of the beach, conditioned the permit upon the Nollans' (P) granting of a public easement permitting lateral movement along the Nollans' (P) property to adjacent public beaches. The Nollans (P) challenged this as a deprivation of property rights without due process. The trial court agreed and enjoined the condition. The court of appeal reversed. The U.S. Supreme Court accepted review.

ISSUE: May a state condition a property use permit on an act not addressing the problem caused by the permitted use?

HOLDING AND DECISION: (Scalia, J.) No. A state may not condition a property use permit on an act not addressing the problem caused by the permitted use. A land-use regulation does not effect a taking if it substantially advances legitimate state interests and does not deny an owner economically viable use of his land. Thus, when a state finds a public interest and does not leave the owner with useless property, no taking occurs when a land use is prohibited. However, this constitutional propriety disappears when the condition substituted for outright prohibition fails to further the end advanced as the justification for the prohibition. When this occurs, the prohibition no longer becomes a vehicle for advancing a state interest, but rather a manner of extorting a property right without paying just compensation. Here, the recognized public interest was preventing the blockage of the beach from public view. The condition, providing an easement for lateral public access along the beach, does nothing to alleviate this perceived problem. The conditional use, therefore, fails to advance a state interest and therefore constitutes a taking. Reversed.

ANALYSIS

The Court was far from clear as to what sort of nexus must exist between a condition and the interest advanced by the original prohibition. At one point, the opinion notes that a taking will occur if there is "utterly" no connection, which implies only a slight relationship as being necessary. On the other hand, language in the opinion speaks of a "substantial relationship" as being necessary.

Quicknotes

DUE PROCESS CLAUSE Clauses found in the Fifth and Fourteenth Amendments to the United States Constitution, providing that no person shall be deprived of "life, liberty, or property, without due process of law."

JUST COMPENSATION The right guaranteed by the Fifth Amendment to the United States Constitution of a person, when his property is taken for public use by the state, to receive adequate compensation in order to restore him to the position he enjoyed prior to the appropriation.

LAND-USE PERMIT Permit to utilize or develop property for a particular use described therein.

NEXUS Presence; contact.

PROHIBITION Law or statute that prohibits certain activity.

PROPERTY RIGHTS A legal right in specified personal or real property.

PUBLIC EASEMENT The right to utilize a portion of another's real property for a specific use that is reserved to the public.

PUBLIC INTEREST Something in which the public has either a monetary or legal interest.

TAKING A governmental action that substantially deprives an owner of the use and enjoyment of his or her property, requiring compensation.

Dolan v. City Of Tigard

Beachfront property owner (P) v. City (D)

512 U.S. 374 (1994).

NATURE OF CASE: **Review of order upholding conditions imposed on a building permit.**

FACT SUMMARY: **The City of Tigard (D) conditioned approval of Dolan's (P) application for a building permit on dedication of a part of her property for a floodplain easement and pedestrian/bicycle path.**

RULE OF LAW

A city may condition a land-use permit upon dedication of the land to a public use if such dedication is roughly proportional to the impact upon the community caused by the proposed land use.

FACTS: Dolan (P) operated a retail establishment in Tigard, Oregon (the City) (D). She applied for a building permit that would have approximately doubled the size of the store. The local planning commission conditioned approval of the permit on Dolan (P) dedicating a portion of the property, which fronted a 100-year floodplain, as a public easement for a floodplain and a bikeway. The dedicated portion of her property would have equaled about 15 percent thereof. The stated rationale for the condition imposed by the commission was that the easement would address concerns of increased traffic congestion due to the larger store, and increased flood hazard due to the increase in impermeable surface. After the city council approved the conditions, Dolan (P) challenged the dedication requirement as an uncompensated taking of her property under the Fifth Amendment. The trial court found in favor of the City (D), and the Oregon Supreme Court affirmed. The Supreme Court granted review.

ISSUE: May a city condition a land-use permit upon dedication of the land to public use if such dedication is roughly proportional to the impact upon the community caused by the proposed land use?

HOLDING AND DECISION: (Rehnquist, C.J.) Yes. A city may condition a land-use permit upon dedication of the land to public use if such dedication is roughly proportional to the impact upon the community caused by the proposed land use. The Fifth and Fourteenth Amendments mandate that, if government takes private property, just compensation must be paid. This rule conflicts with the right of local government to properly regulate use of property within its jurisdiction, and litigation on this issue usually deals with where legitimate regulation ends and taking occurs. This Court has held that a land-use permit cannot be conditioned on a giving up of property rights having no relation to the owner's proposed use. What must be answered in this case is the level of relation needed between the proposed owner's development and the city's mandated dedication that will sustain Fifth Amendment scrutiny. Some states require only a generalized statement as to the connection to survive due process concerns, a standard this Court considers too lax. Others require an exacting, particularized nexus between the development and the conditions imposed thereon, which this Court considers too stringent a standard. Rather, this Court believes that the best test to balance the competing interest is one that requires a "rough proportionality" between the burden caused on the community by the development and the condition placed on the owner. Using that standard here, the alleged burdens cited by the commission were (1) increased flooding hazard due to increased impermeable surface, and (2) increased traffic. The condition imposed, dedication of about 15 percent of Dolan's (P) land for a floodplain and bike path, bears little relation to the concerns supposedly being addressed. This being so the condition imposed was in violation of the Fifth and Fourteenth Amendments. Reversed and remanded.

ANALYSIS

For most of the Twentieth Century, federal courts had been extremely deferential to governments when use regulations were challenged. The Takings Clause seemed to be something of a constitutional dead letter. Then, the case *Nollan v. California Coastal Commission*, 483 U.S. 825 (1987), suddenly turned matters around, in that a landowner was able to prevail over a governmental regulatory body. The present case seems to portend a continuation of that trend.

Quicknotes

DEDICATION Conveyance of land to the public by a private owner.

EASEMENT The right to utilize a portion of another's real property for a specific use.

FIFTH AMENDMENT Provides that no person shall be compelled to serve as a witness against himself, or be subject to trial for the same offense twice, or be deprived of life, liberty, or property without due process of law.

JUST COMPENSATION The right guaranteed by the Fifth Amendment to the United States Constitution of a person, when his property is taken for public use by the state, to receive adequate compensation in order to restore him to the position he enjoyed prior to the appropriation.

Continued on next page.

LAND-USE PERMIT Permit to utilize or develop property for a particular use described therein.

PUBLIC USE Basis for governmental taking of property pursuant to its power of eminent domain so that property taken may be utilized for the benefit of the public at large.

TAKING A governmental action that substantially deprives an owner of the use and enjoyment of his or her property, requiring compensation.

Glossary

Common Latin Words and Phrases Encountered in the Law

A FORTIORI: Because one fact exists or has been proven, therefore a second fact that is related to the first fact must also exist.

A PRIORI: From the cause to the effect. A term of logic used to denote that when one generally accepted truth is shown to be a cause, another particular effect must necessarily follow.

AB INITIO: From the beginning; a condition which has existed throughout, as in a marriage which was void ab initio.

ACTUS REUS: The wrongful act; in criminal law, such action sufficient to trigger criminal liability.

AD VALOREM: According to value; an ad valorem tax is imposed upon an item located within the taxing jurisdiction calculated by the value of such item.

AMICUS CURIAE: Friend of the court. Its most common usage takes the form of an amicus curiae brief, filed by a person who is not a party to an action but is nonetheless allowed to offer an argument supporting his legal interests.

ARGUENDO: In arguing. A statement, possibly hypothetical, made for the purpose of argument, is one made arguendo.

BILL QUIA TIMET: A bill to quiet title (establish ownership) to real property.

BONA FIDE: True, honest, or genuine. May refer to a person's legal position based on good faith or lacking notice of fraud (such as a bona fide purchaser for value) or to the authenticity of a particular document (such as a bona fide last will and testament).

CAUSA MORTIS: With approaching death in mind. A gift causa mortis is a gift given by a party who feels certain that death is imminent.

CAVEAT EMPTOR: Let the buyer beware. This maxim is reflected in the rule of law that a buyer purchases at his own risk because it is his responsibility to examine, judge, test, and otherwise inspect what he is buying.

CERTIORARI: A writ of review. Petitions for review of a case by the United States Supreme Court are most often done by means of a writ of certiorari.

CONTRA: On the other hand. Opposite. Contrary to.

CORAM NOBIS: Before us; writs of error directed to the court that originally rendered the judgment.

CORAM VOBIS: Before you; writs of error directed by an appellate court to a lower court to correct a factual error.

CORPUS DELICTI: The body of the crime; the requisite elements of a crime amounting to objective proof that a crime has been committed.

CUM TESTAMENTO ANNEXO, ADMINISTRATOR (ADMINISTRATOR C.T.A.): With will annexed; an administrator c.t.a. settles an estate pursuant to a will in which he is not appointed.

DE BONIS NON, ADMINISTRATOR (ADMINISTRATOR D.B.N.): Of goods not administered; an administrator d.b.n. settles a partially settled estate.

DE FACTO: In fact; in reality; actually. Existing in fact but not officially approved or engendered.

DE JURE: By right; lawful. Describes a condition that is legitimate "as a matter of law," in contrast to the term "de facto," which connotes something existing in fact but not legally sanctioned or authorized. For example, de facto segregation refers to segregation brought about by housing patterns, etc., whereas de jure segregation refers to segregation created by law.

DE MINIMIS: Of minimal importance; insignificant; a trifle; not worth bothering about.

DE NOVO: Anew; a second time; afresh. A trial de novo is a new trial held at the appellate level as if the case originated there and the trial at a lower level had not taken place.

DICTA: Generally used as an abbreviated form of obiter dicta, a term describing those portions of a judicial opinion incidental or not necessary to resolution of the specific question before the court. Such nonessential statements and remarks are not considered to be binding precedent.

DUCES TECUM: Refers to a particular type of writ or subpoena requesting a party or organization to produce certain documents in their possession.

EN BANC: Full bench. Where a court sits with all justices present rather than the usual quorum.

EX PARTE: For one side or one party only. An ex parte proceeding is one undertaken for the benefit of only one party, without notice to, or an appearance by, an adverse party.

EX POST FACTO: After the fact. An ex post facto law is a law that retroactively changes the consequences of a prior act.

EX REL.: Abbreviated form of the term "ex relatione," meaning upon relation or information. When the state brings an action in which it has no interest against an individual at the instigation of one who has a private interest in the matter.

FORUM NON CONVENIENS: Inconvenient forum. Although a court may have jurisdiction over the case, the action should be tried in a more conveniently located court, one to which parties and witnesses may more easily travel, for example.

GUARDIAN AD LITEM: A guardian of an infant as to litigation, appointed to represent the infant and pursue his/her rights.

HABEAS CORPUS: You have the body. The modern writ of habeas corpus is a writ directing that a person (body) being detained (such as a prisoner) be brought before the court so that the legality of his detention can be judicially ascertained.

IN CAMERA: In private, in chambers. When a hearing is held before a judge in his chambers or when all spectators are excluded from the courtroom.

IN FORMA PAUPERIS: In the manner of a pauper. A party who proceeds in forma pauperis because of his poverty is one who is allowed to bring suit without liability for costs.

INFRA: Below, under. A word referring the reader to a later part of a book. (The opposite of supra.)

IN LOCO PARENTIS: In the place of a parent.

IN PARI DELICTO: Equally wrong; a court of equity will not grant requested relief to an applicant who is in pari delicto, or as much at fault in the transactions giving rise to the controversy as is the opponent of the applicant.

IN PARI MATERIA: On like subject matter or upon the same matter. Statutes relating to the same person or things are said to be in pari materia. It is a general rule of statutory construction that such statutes should be construed together, i.e., looked at as if they together constituted one law.

IN PERSONAM: Against the person. Jurisdiction over the person of an individual.

IN RE: In the matter of. Used to designate a proceeding involving an estate or other property.

IN REM: A term that signifies an action against the res, or thing. An action in rem is basically one that is taken directly against property, as distinguished from an action in personam, i.e., against the person.

INTER ALIA: Among other things. Used to show that the whole of a statement, pleading, list, statute, etc., has not been set forth in its entirety.

INTER PARTES: Between the parties. May refer to contracts, conveyances or other transactions having legal significance.

INTER VIVOS: Between the living. An inter vivos gift is a gift made by a living grantor, as distinguished from bequests contained in a will, which pass upon the death of the testator.

IPSO FACTO: By the mere fact itself.

JUS: Law or the entire body of law.

LEX LOCI: The law of the place; the notion that the rights of parties to a legal proceeding are governed by the law of the place where those rights arose.

MALUM IN SE: Evil or wrong in and of itself; inherently wrong. This term describes an act that is wrong by its very nature, as opposed to one which would not be wrong but for the fact that there is a specific legal prohibition against it (malum prohibitum).

MALUM PROHIBITUM: Wrong because prohibited, but not inherently evil. Used to describe something that is wrong because it is expressly forbidden by law but that is not in and of itself evil, e.g., speeding.

MANDAMUS: We command. A writ directing an official to take a certain action.

MENS REA: A guilty mind; a criminal intent. A term used to signify the mental state that accompanies a crime or other prohibited act. Some crimes require only a general mens rea (general intent to do the prohibited act), but others, like assault with intent to murder, require the existence of a specific mens rea.

MODUS OPERANDI: Method of operating; generally refers to the manner or style of a criminal in committing crimes, admissible in appropriate cases as evidence of the identity of a defendant.

NEXUS: A connection to.

NISI PRIUS: A court of first impression. A nisi prius court is one where issues of fact are tried before a judge or jury.

N.O.V. (NON OBSTANTE VEREDICTO): Notwithstanding the verdict. A judgment n.o.v. is a judgment given in favor of one party despite the fact that a verdict was returned in favor of the other party, the justification being that the verdict either had no reasonable support in fact or was contrary to law.

NUNC PRO TUNC: Now for then. This phrase refers to actions that may be taken and will then have full retroactive effect.

PENDENTE LITE: Pending the suit; pending litigation under way.

PER CAPITA: By head; beneficiaries of an estate, if they take in equal shares, take per capita.

PER CURIAM: By the court; signifies an opinion ostensibly written "by the whole court" and with no identified author.

PER SE: By itself, in itself; inherently.

PER STIRPES: By representation. Used primarily in the law of wills to describe the method of distribution where a person, generally because of death, is unable to take that which is left to him by the will of another, and therefore his heirs divide such property between them rather than take under the will individually.

PRIMA FACIE: On its face, at first sight. A prima facie case is one that is sufficient on its face, meaning that the evidence supporting it is adequate to establish the case until contradicted or overcome by other evidence.

PRO TANTO: For so much; as far as it goes. Often used in eminent domain cases when a property owner receives partial payment for his land without prejudice to his right to bring suit for the full amount he claims his land to be worth.

QUANTUM MERUIT: As much as he deserves. Refers to recovery based on the doctrine of unjust enrichment in those cases in which a party has rendered valuable services or furnished materials that were accepted and enjoyed by another under circumstances that would reasonably notify the recipient that the rendering party expected to be paid. In essence, the law implies a contract to pay the reasonable value of the services or materials furnished.

QUASI: Almost like; as if; nearly. This term is essentially used to signify that one subject or thing is almost analogous to another but that material differences between them do exist. For example, a quasi-criminal proceeding is one that is not strictly criminal but shares enough of the same characteristics to require some of the same safeguards (e.g., procedural due process must be followed in a parole hearing).

QUID PRO QUO: Something for something. In contract law, the consideration, something of value, passed between the parties to render the contract binding.

RES GESTAE: Things done; in evidence law, this principle justifies the admission of a statement that would otherwise be hearsay when it is made so closely to the event in question as to be said to be a part of it, or with such spontaneity as not to have the possibility of falsehood.

RES IPSA LOQUITUR: The thing speaks for itself. This doctrine gives rise to a rebuttable presumption of negligence when the instrumentality causing the injury was within the exclusive control of the defendant, and the injury was one that does not normally occur unless a person has been negligent.

RES JUDICATA: A matter adjudged. Doctrine which provides that once a court of competent jurisdiction has rendered a final judgment or decree on the merits, that judgment or decree is conclusive upon the parties to the case and prevents them from engaging in any other litigation on the points and issues determined therein.

RESPONDEAT SUPERIOR: Let the master reply. This doctrine holds the master liable for the wrongful acts of his servant (or the principal for his agent) in those cases in which the servant (or agent) was acting within the scope of his authority at the time of the injury.

STARE DECISIS: To stand by or adhere to that which has been decided. The common law doctrine of stare decisis attempts to give security and certainty to the law by following the policy that once a principle of law as applicable to a certain set of facts has been set forth in a decision, it forms a precedent which will subsequently be followed, even though a different decision might be made were it the first time the question had arisen. Of course, stare decisis is not an inviolable principle and is departed from in instances where there is good cause (e.g., considerations of public policy led the Supreme Court to disregard prior decisions sanctioning segregation).

SUPRA: Above. A word referring a reader to an earlier part of a book.

ULTRA VIRES: Beyond the power. This phrase is most commonly used to refer to actions taken by a corporation that are beyond the power or legal authority of the corporation.

Addendum of French Derivatives

IN PAIS: Not pursuant to legal proceedings.

CHATTEL: Tangible personal property.

CY PRES: Doctrine permitting courts to apply trust funds to purposes not expressed in the trust but necessary to carry out the settlor's intent.

PER AUTRE VIE: For another's life; during another's life. In property law, an estate may be granted that will terminate upon the death of someone other than the grantee.

PROFIT A PRENDRE: A license to remove minerals or other produce from land.

VOIR DIRE: Process of questioning jurors as to their predispositions about the case or parties to a proceeding in order to identify those jurors displaying bias or prejudice.

Casenote Legal Briefs

Administrative Law .... Breyer, Stewart, Sunstein & Vermeule
Administrative Law .... Cass, Diver & Beermann
Administrative Law .... Funk, Shapiro & Weaver
Administrative Law .... Mashaw, Merrill & Shane
Administrative Law .... Strauss, Rakoff & Farina (Gellhorn & Byse)
Agency & Partnership .... Hynes & Loewenstein
Antitrust .... Pitofsky, Goldschmid & Wood
Antitrust .... Sullivan & Hovenkamp
Bankruptcy .... Warren & Bussel
Business Organizations .... Allen, Kraakman & Subramanian
Business Organizations .... Bauman, Weiss & Palmiter
Business Organizations .... Hamilton & Macey
Business Organizations .... Klein, Ramseyer & Bainbridge
Business Organizations .... O'Kelley & Thompson
Business Organizations .... Soderquist, Smiddy & Cunningham
Civil Procedure .... Field, Kaplan & Clermont
Civil Procedure .... Freer & Perdue
Civil Procedure .... Friedenthal, Miller, Sexton & Hershkoff
Civil Procedure .... Hazard, Tait, Fletcher & Bundy
Civil Procedure .... Marcus, Redish, Sherman & Pfander
Civil Procedure .... Subrin, Minow, Brodin & Main
Civil Procedure .... Yeazell
Commercial Law .... LoPucki, Warren, Keating & Mann
Commercial Law .... Warren & Walt
Commercial Law .... Whaley
Community Property .... Bird
Community Property .... Blumberg
Conflicts .... Brilmayer & Goldsmith
Conflicts .... Currie, Kay, Kramer & Roosevelt
Constitutional Law .... Brest, Levinson, Balkin & Amar
Constitutional Law .... Chemerinsky
Constitutional Law .... Choper, Fallon, Kamisar & Shiffrin (Lockhart)
Constitutional Law .... Cohen, Varat & Amar
Constitutional Law .... Farber, Eskridge & Frickey
Constitutional Law .... Rotunda
Constitutional Law .... Sullivan & Gunther
Constitutional Law .... Stone, Seidman, Sunstein, Tushnet & Karlan
Contracts .... Ayres & Speidel
Contracts .... Barnett
Contracts .... Burton
Contracts .... Calamari, Perillo & Bender
Contracts .... Crandall & Whaley
Contracts .... Dawson, Harvey, Henderson & Baird
Contracts .... Farnsworth, Young, Sanger, Cohen & Brooks
Contracts .... Fuller & Eisenberg
Contracts .... Knapp, Crystal & Prince
Copyright .... Cohen, Loren, Okediji & O'Rourke
Copyright .... Goldstein & Reese
Criminal Law .... Bonnie, Coughlin, Jeffries & Low
Criminal Law .... Boyce, Dripps & Perkins
Criminal Law .... Dressler
Criminal Law .... Johnson & Cloud
Criminal Law .... Kadish, Schulhofer & Steiker
Criminal Law .... Kaplan, Weisberg & Binder
Criminal Procedure .... Allen, Hoffmann, Livingston & Stuntz
Criminal Procedure .... Dressler & Thomas
Criminal Procedure .... Haddad, Marsh, Zagel, Meyer, Starkman & Bauer
Criminal Procedure .... Kamisar, LaFave, Israel, King & Kerr
Criminal Procedure .... Saltzburg & Capra
Debtors and Creditors .... Warren & Westbrook
Employment Discrimination .... Friedman
Employment Discrimination .... Zimmer, Sullivan & White
Employment Law .... Rothstein & Liebman
Environmental Law .... Menell & Stewart
Environmental Law .... Percival, Schroeder, Miller & Leape
Environmental Law .... Plater, Abrams, Goldfarb, Graham, Heinzerling & Wirth
Evidence .... Broun, Mosteller & Giannelli
Evidence .... Fisher
Evidence .... Mueller & Kirkpatrick
Evidence .... Sklansky
Evidence .... Waltz, Park & Friedman
Family Law .... Areen & Regan
Family Law .... Ellman, Kurtz & Scott
Family Law .... Harris, Carbone & Teitelbaum
Family Law .... Wadlington & O'Brien
Family Law .... Weisberg & Appleton
Federal Courts .... Fallon, Meltzer & Shapiro (Hart & Wechsler)
Federal Courts .... Low & Jeffries
Health Law .... Furrow, Greaney, Johnson, Jost & Schwartz
Immigration Law .... Aleinikoff, Martin & Motomura
Immigration Law .... Legomsky
Insurance Law .... Abraham
Intellectual Property .... Merges, Menell & Lemley
International Business Transactions .... Folsom, Gordon, Spanogle & Fitzgerald
International Law .... Blakesley, Firmage, Scott & Williams
International Law .... Carter, Trimble & Weiner
International Law .... Damrosch, Henkin, Murphy & Smit
International Law .... Dunoff, Ratner & Wippman
Labor Law .... Cox, Bok, Gorman & Finkin
Land Use .... Callies, Freilich & Roberts
Legislation .... Eskridge, Frickey & Garrett
Oil & Gas .... Lowe, Anderson, Smith & Pierce
Patent Law .... Adelman, Radner, Thomas & Wegner
Products Liability .... Owen, Montgomery & Davis
Professional Responsibility .... Gillers
Professional Responsibility .... Hazard, Koniak, Cramton & Cohen
Property .... Casner, Leach, French, Korngold & VanderVelde
Property .... Cribbet, Johnson, Findley & Smith
Property .... Donahue, Kauper & Martin
Property .... Dukeminier, Krier, Alexander & Schill
Property .... Haar & Liebman
Property .... Kurtz & Hovenkamp
Property .... Nelson, Stoebuck & Whitman
Property .... Rabin, Kwall & Kwall
Property .... Singer
Real Estate .... Korngold & Goldstein
Real Estate Transactions .... Nelson & Whitman
Remedies .... Laycock
Remedies .... Shoben, Tabb & Janutis
Securities Regulation .... Coffee, Seligman & Sale
Securities Regulation .... Cox, Hillman & Langevoort
Sports Law .... Weiler & Roberts
Taxation (Corporate) .... Lind, Schwartz, Lathrope & Rosenberg
Taxation (Individual) .... Burke & Friel
Taxation (Individual) .... Freeland, Lathrope, Lind & Stephens
Taxation (Individual) .... Klein, Bankman, Shaviro & Stak
Torts .... Dobbs, Hayden & Bublick
Torts .... Epstein
Torts .... Franklin & Rabin
Torts .... Henderson, Pearson, Kysar & Siliciano
Torts .... Schwartz, Kelly & Partlett (Prosser)
Wills, Trusts & Estates .... Dukeminier, Sitkoff & Lindgren
Wills, Trusts & Estates .... Dobris, Sterk & Leslie
Wills, Trusts & Estates .... Scoles, Halbach, Roberts & Begleiter